Luxembourg

Liechtenstein

Seborga

San Marino

Mount Athos

Malta

LITTLE IS THE LIGHT

Other books by Vitali Vitaliev:

Special Correspondent
Dateline Freedom
Vitali's Australia
The Third Trinity

LITTLE IS THE LIGHT

Nostalgic travels in the mini-states of Europe

VITALI VITALIEV

Touchstone Books
London . New York . Singapore . Tokyo . Toronto . Sydney

First published in Great Britain by Touchstone, 1995
An imprint of Simon & Schuster Ltd

Simon & Schuster Ltd
West Garden Place
Kendal Street
London W2 2AQ

Simon & Schuster of Australia Pty Ltd
Sydney

A CIP catalogue record for this book is available from the British Library

ISBN 0 671 71925 4

Typeset in 12/13^1/$_2$ Brighton Light by
The Word Shop, Bury, Lancashire

Printed in Great Britain by
The Bath Press, Avon

FOR MY BELOVED SON MITYA
my travel companion for life

We travel not for trafficking alone:
By hotter winds our fiery hearts are fanned:
For lust of knowing what should not be known
We make the Golden Journey to Samarkand.

James Elroy Flecker

A good traveller is one who does not know where he is going to, and a perfect traveller does not know where he came from.

Lin Yutang, Chinese writer

CONTENTS

From the Author   xi

Introduction: Confessions of a Dromomaniac   1

1.   Liechtenstein   11

2.   San Marino   57

3.   Mount Athos   83

4.   Isle of Man   119

5.   Luxembourg   149

6.   FAROESE FLASHES
     (The Faroe Islands)   187

7.   GIBANMAMORGA
     (Gibraltar, Andorra, Malta, Monaco, Seborga)   217

Appendix: A Phrase or Two on Phrase Books   329

From the Author

This book was a pleasure to write and fun to research.

Before starting my literary journey to eleven mini-states of Europe, I'd like to say a word of thanks to those whose support has made this book possible.

First and foremost, they are my colleagues and friends from the *European* newspaper – Michael Maclay, former assistant editor of the *European*, now Special Advisor to the British Foreign Secretary; Charles Garside, the editor: Herbert Pearson, James Fergusson, Henry Sutton, Roman Rollnick and Ronnie Payne.

I want to thank Kurt Gmeiner of Globus Tours for re-introducing me to Europe in August 1992.

I am grateful to the Danish Tourist Board for organising my visit to the Faroe Islands and to Doug Goodman Public Relations for taking me to Mount Athos.

My special gratitude goes to Judy Cohen for her help and advice, and to my mother Rimma for looking after me while I was writing.

Little is the Light

I am indebted to my numerous contacts in eleven mini-states of Europe, and to many engaging characters I was lucky to encounter in the course of my journeys. You will meet some of them in this book. Others will know who they are.

Happy journey!
Vitali Vitaliev
November 1994, London

Introduction

Confessions of a Dromomaniac

Vast is my beloved country!
It has many a forest, a field and a stream.
I don't know any other land,
where a man can breathe so freely!

A popular Soviet song

I loathe megalomaniacs. There is nothing worse than a little fellow pretending he is a giant. There is nothing more pathetic than a worm trying to look and bite like a snake.

Life in the former Soviet Union was characterised by a severe case of megalomania on a national scale. Starting from kindergarten we were led to believe that our country was the greatest, the freest and the largest in the world (the latter was true, by the way). At school we were taught that Russia always conducted only just wars; that everything – from the wheel to the electric bulb – had been invented by the Russians; that all Russian writers (except for those who were banned or shot, of course) were great and cared for the 'common people'. 'A poet in Russia is more than a poet!' Yevgeny Yevtushenko once wrote. '*More*? Or *less*?' I couldn't help wondering.

The first powered aircraft, of course, was plagiarised by Wilbur and Orville Wright from the Russian scientist Zhukovsky. Wireless telegraph was discovered not by Guglielmo Marconi, but by Alexander Popov. The steam-engine was a creation of Ivan Polzunov's genius, and James Watt simply nicked his idea. And so on and so forth. By the age of twelve, a Soviet child could be forgiven for thinking that there was no real life west of Kaliningrad and east of Khabarovsk. I must confess that even at a fairly mature age, I used to experience serious doubts as to whether the Western world existed at all and was not just another KGB invention to keep the Soviet people on the alert.

As I have just said, there was one little grain of truth in this otherwise mendacious flow of indoctrination. With an area of 22,402,202 square kilometres, the USSR was by far the world's largest country, and that was a popular excuse for food shortages and inefficiency. 'You see, our land is so vast that we simply cannot provide for all hungry mouths, like they do in Switzerland, ha-ha.' Switzerland, for some reason, was a common butt of jokes and unfavourable (to Switzerland, of course) comparisons (luckily they seemed to be unaware of Liechtenstein or Andorra). Maybe it was because Switzerland was 543 times smaller than the Soviet Union. And 543 times more prosperous and efficient.

The very vastness of the USSR was the system's first, last and only real argument in its favour. Statistics might have been blown out of all proportion; 'elections', even with only one candidate to choose from, might have been rigged, but one thing was indisputable: it *was* the largest country in the world. This added an aura of trustworthiness to heaps and heaps of meaningless propaganda.

A popular semi-official rebuff to growing pro-independence movements in the Soviet Union's smaller dominions (Estonia, Moldavia, Lithuania etc) was: 'How can you possibly exist without us, being so small? You simply won't survive on your own!' A typical Big Brother attitude. The fact that countries like Belgium, Iceland or Luxembourg not only survive, but even prosper was either forgotten or ignored (or both) as if none of them actually existed.

But we were not easily fooled. Every force breeds counterforce, as proved by one great Russian physicist and later repeated by Sir Isaac Newton. Very few were prepared to believe seriously in any 'final truth' the system was trying to impose on its seemingly submissive subjects. In fact, the harder it tried, the less we believed. Totalitarian ideology never fails to achieve results which are poles apart from what it pretends to have achieved. The Soviet system pretended to have built the planet's only classless paradise, while in actual fact ours was the most stratified society in the world, with the eternal handful of senile rulers enjoying their tiny internal heaven, and all the rest immersed in infernal reality. It was falling over itself to make us all rabidly patriotic and anti-Western, but instead created a totally rootless breed of *homo soveticus*, more pro-Western than Westerners themselves and ready to embrace everything coming from the forbidden capitalist world. It wanted to crush dissent, but instead turned almost the whole Soviet population into dissidents. The most widely read writers were those who were the most violently attacked. There was no better publicity for a book or a film than a devastating review in *Pravda*. The system wanted to turn us all into hooray-patriots and megalomaniacs, but instead infected us with its own deeply in-rooted inferiority complex.

'Big is beautiful!' it kept insisting, but we refused to believe. The recent fragmentation of the Soviet empire is a triumph of Small over Big.

I can't remember exactly where I came across the wonderful English proverb: *'Little is the light will be seen far in a murky night'*. Perhaps it was not English and not even a proverb but an invention of Comrades Kuzmin and Shadrin, who compiled the *Russian-English Dictionary of*

Proverbs and Sayings (published in Moscow in 1989), in which they succeeded in converting the gems of Russian and English folk wisdom into rhyming doggerels. This is how they poeticised some other English proverbs: 'You say you are a mushroom, so – into a basket you go!' (In for a penny – in for a pound); 'A word warmly said gives comfort even to a cat' (Soft fire makes sweet malt).

Wherever it was that I saw it, I liked this unsophisticated rhyme, with its nicely sounding sonorant alliteration: 'little – light – night.' It was exactly this little light of freedom that kept us alive and warm in the murky totalitarian night. A light doesn't have to be big, if it's bright (sorry for the unintended rhyme – the style of Comrades Kuzmin and Shadrin must be contagious). A light, even if small, means hope, and little hope is better than no hope at all.

All my life in the Soviet Union I had been secretly preoccupied with little things. One winter day, when I was six, I saw a tiny yellow toy truck in a shop window on the way from the kindergarten, and froze in my step. My mother, who was holding me by the hand, froze too, which was not difficult since it was freezing anyway. With my nose flattened against the window, I stood there for a good half-hour, tearfully begging my mother to cough up. She didn't feel like coughing, despite the cold weather. I had lots of toys at home, and a whole fleet of almost life-size toy trucks among them. But this one was special: the size of a matchbox, it was all bright and gleaming, like a clot of condensed sunlight. I managed to persuade my mother eventually (I usually did), and triumphantly went home, clutching my (or rather my mother's) little purchase in my little hand, clad in a little *varezhka* – a Russian woollen glove with thumb but no fingers. The fact that the truck had two pairs of miniscule rotating wheels and could actually move added to my childish delight.

The sheer magic of motion. I didn't know then it was called travelling.

I would play with this toy for hours, until I got bored with it finally, and the beautiful mini-truck ended up in the pile of discarded toys in a big cardboard crate under my bed – its first and last garage.

4

As I grew up, my fascination with little things grew accordingly. Looking back now, I can see that this was most likely just a spontaneous, and often subconscious, protest against the officially cultivated gigantomania. As a boy I was addicted to midget tin soldiers, micro steam-engines and tiny 'one-tooth' lollies. My favourite book was Jonathan Swift's *Gulliver's Travels*, where the protagonist alternately travels among the Lilliputians or turns into a Lilliputian himself (in the land of giants). As a youngster I was keen on microscopes and the life of African pigmies. As a mature man (still far from a giant) I am attracted to small screen, short stories and (let's face it) diminutive (petite) women.

Having never suffered from illusions of grandeur, I nevertheless failed to avoid another mental disease – *dromomania*. Don't hurry to put me away in a psychiatric asylum: among all manias, phobias and brain disorders, dromomania is probably the most innocent. It is a *medical condition characterised by an irrepressible itch to travel*.

Journalists and writers are passionate travellers (read *dromomaniacs*) as a rule, and I am no exception.

I contracted dromomania at an early age, shortly after acquiring the miniature yellow truck, or so I guess. 'If you have the doubtful happiness of being born, you must at least see the world' – these words from Konstantin Paustovsky's romantic novel *The Black Sea* kept echoing in my soul. It was easy for Paustovsky to say . . . I suspect he was a dromomaniac, too.

I was gradually going mad (I didn't know that my madness had a medical name then). I collected maps and train schedules. I treasured a tarred wooden chip that I covertly peeled off a cargo car at a railway station. My parents didn't mind, only shrugged. I kept the chip in a special box which I would open and sniff from time to time: it smelled of journeys and adventures.

At school they would tease me for carrying this fancy snuff-box with me and nicknamed me Engine Driver. I was secretly proud of this nickname.

In the evenings, before falling asleep on my old-fashioned narrow bed, I would knock its nickel-plated leg gently (not to wake up my parents) with my knuckles: Ta-ta, ta-ta; ta-ta, ta-ta; ta-ta, ta-ta — to imitate the rattling of train wheels. I was falling asleep to the sweet music of the railroad.

Trains were so special to me simply because I travelled seldom. Forbidden fruit. I had no idea what freedom of movement was. Without knowing it, by the age of fourteen I had turned into a typical armchair buccaneer, a vicarious traveller with no prospect of ever seeing the world.

The city where I lived could not boast any architectural masterpieces or historic monuments, apart from a regulation statue of Lenin with his outstretched hand pointing either to the bright future or, as local wits assured, to the nearest vodka shop. The only monument it could take some fiendish pride in was a huge railway terminal — an ugly, pompously decorated building, dominating the cityscape. Inside, on the walls and even on the ceiling, were frescoes in the best traditions of socialist realism: heroic workers and peasant women with bulging eyes clutching red banners in their sinewy muscular hands. This particular style of architecture and interior design was privately (in whispers) called 'Stalin Gothic'.

Indeed, the station building had something to do with Stalin. When, in 1951, 'The great leader and teacher' was travelling by rail to one of his dachas in the south and was passing through our city (there were usually three identical trains in the procession, and no one, not even Stalin himself perhaps, knew exactly which of them carried the paranoid dictator), he allegedly peeped out of the window and saw the old decrepit building of the terminal. 'What a disgrace to have a station like this in our socialist country! I don't want to see it again!' he remarked angrily to one of his aides in his broken Russian aggravated by a heavy Georgian accent.

A month later, when Stalin was returning to Moscow, the new grandiose station building was already there. The builders in their ardour (or rather fear) must have broken all time records to construct the architectural monster which was destined to stand for ages as an impressive monument to totalitarianism.

Big was not always beautiful as I was coming to understand.

Despite its ugliness and intimidating proportions, the railway station attracted me like an oversized magnet. Playing truant, I used to go there with my best friend and a fellow-dromomaniac, Sasha Kasjanov. We would stand on a wooden footbridge hanging above the tracks and gape at the moving trains below for hours on end, until our heads started spinning and we had the illusion that it was we who were moving, floating in the air above immobile trains.

It was from there that we ventured on our first real journey one day. 'Real' meant that we travelled on our own, without parents or any other adults to keep an eye on us. Of course, the whole venture was planned and undertaken in utter secrecy, under cover of a normal school day. It was just a forty-minute journey by a shuttle train, but to us it was no less dangerous and revealing than the first round-the-world voyage of Magellan. In line with the forced and all-permeating patriotic ardour, almost all whistle-stops on our way had the word *'krasniy'* (red) in their names: Red Village, Red Field, Red Corner, Red Excavator, even Red Whitewash, as far as I can recall. We got off the train in the sleepy suburban town of Liubotin, bought a couple of elderly, wrinkled meat-pies at the station and headed back. It was an unforgettable feeling – looking through the window of the moving (or rather crawling) train, chewing meat-pies and being on our own.

I can still feel the oily smack of these cheap (and not very fresh) meat-pies on my lips.

Our small and guilty Earth, in the form of a tattered old globe, stood on the bookshelf in my room. It might just as well have been the Atlas of the Moon. We had to be happy with what we had. Travelling, especially outside the country, was reserved for party functionaries and big shots – not little boys. In the well-oiled mechanism of privilege, the main moving force behind the system, this was one of the main gears. The corruptive value of a trip abroad was on a par with an out-of-town dacha or a personal Volga sedan.

We were all encaged. True, ours was the biggest cage in the world, occupying one sixth of the planet's territory, but it didn't make much of a difference to those who were inside it.

Much later, when already a journalist in Moscow, I was able to travel all over the Soviet Union. I would board a plane in Moscow and fly for ten hours non-stop, with my knees stuck in the back of the seat in front and someone else's sharp knees stuck into my back from behind ('prop my back and I'll prop yours' could be Aeroflot's official logo), only to disembark in precisely the same country, in an almost identical city somewhere in the Soviet Far East, with exactly the same buildings; the same newspapers, full of the same inflated lies; the same never-ending queues; the same downtrodden people with bleak expressionless eyes. It was mind-boggling.

It was then, with the image of this huge country-size cage under the plane wing, the cage from which there was no escape, that I started hating things that were excessively, inhumanely big. And not just the countries. I hate international trusts, cartels and monopolies, grown out of all proportion and entangling the world with their sticky tentacles, octopus-like. I hate press empires that are run very much like totalitarian states, through dictate and fear, with no concern for the individual. I hate throngs of fanatics (even football fans), obsessed with one and the same fervour. I hate 'broad masses' and 'collective mentality' that can never be right.

I am lucky, at least luckier than most of my compatriots. Luckier than my father, who died prematurely twelve years ago without ever getting a glimpse of the outside world. Luckier than Leonid Prudnikov, my omni-scient University professor of English, fluent in eighteen languages, who also died young having never been abroad. Wherever I go, I am looking at the world with their eyes too. Wherever I travel, they travel with me.

Yes. I am lucky: in my five years in the West not only have I travelled the world, I have even managed to buy a second-hand Volga sedan. Its colour is bright-yellow, like the toy-truck of my childhood. Yet I feel more like a vagabond than a traveller. The difference? A traveller has a place to come back to, a vagabond hasn't. Having visited dozens of countries on four continents of the globe and having lived in several, I have failed so far to find the place where I would feel happy and hence choose to settle. Maybe I never will. But I must keep looking. I must keep travelling.

This was how the idea of this book was born. Why not try to unite under one cover my two great passions – love for travelling and fascination with things little? It occurred to me that these two ideas can be reduced to one – travelling in small countries. What could be more different from my native Soviet Union than a Ruritanian state that was not just tiny and free, but also worked?

A European by birth and by soul (I realised this with clarity after two and a half years in Australia), I decided to go to several mini-states of Europe. None of them is more than a tiny spot on the map – a drop of fruit juice spilt on the green tablecloth of our continent. None has more than 400,000 inhabitants, the population of Babush-kinsky district, where I used to live, one of the thirty-six districts of Moscow. But each of them is interesting in its own way, each of them is proud and each is a model of this or that larger state, in a way. Each of them works.

Some of these mini-states (like Andorra, San Marino and Luxembourg, say) are frequented by hordes of tourists, others (like Mount Athos or Seborga) are pretty obscure. Some are thriving little tax havens and mini industrial giants (Liechtenstein), others are like tiny boats tossed up and down in the stormy ocean of the world economy (Malta, Isle of Man, the Faroe Islands). Some are as old as the hills that surround them (Gibraltar), others are more recent creations (Monaco).

After all, it is not really important where you travel. It is what you discover. Remember Henry Longfellow:

> In vain we look, in vain uplift
> Our eyes to Heaven, if we are blind.
> We see only what we have the gift
> Of seeing. What we bring – we find.

And I don't think that to make discoveries one must necessarily travel to the end of the earth. Travelling is like poetry, for which, if we believe Boris Pasternak, you don't have to look high up in the mountains, since there is plenty of it scattered in the grass under your feet; you only have to go to the trouble of bending down and picking it up.

This book is subtitled 'Nostalgic travels'. Why? Despite the tremendous importance of the right to choose in any democratic society, there are certain things which are not open to option. We don't choose our parents, we don't choose our motherland. The choice is made for us. Nostalgia – a longing for the place where you were born – is one of the most creative human emotions. Since I was forced to emigrate in 1990, I have had a chance to go back to my native city and to see the house of my youth lying in ruins. I don't want to travel there again, and I am no longer nostalgic for the place. But wherever I go in this world, I keep subconsciously looking for the country of my childhood – impoverished and chaotic, cruel, hungry and unimpressive – but dear. I spent many years of my life there, I know its ways like the back of my hand, I can see it clearly – with all its warts – from any distance.

The truth is that this country does not exist any longer.

You can replace the wallpaper and rearrange the furniture in the house of your past, but you cannot change the view from its window.

1.   Liechtenstein

Preparing for a journey can be as exciting as the journey itself, often more so. As an armchair buccaneer of many years sitting, I am in the habit of getting the nitty-gritty on the place I am about to visit: books, maps, flight schedules, etc. With Liechtenstein though, I faced an almost complete information blackout, except for a couple of paragraphs in guidebooks. The problem with maps was that to find Liechtenstein (twenty-five kilometres long and fifteen kilometres wide) on them, one needed a powerful magnifying glass.

The only work of fiction I could find which featured Liechtenstein was *Midnight Plus One*, a fast-moving and witty thriller by Gavin Lyall, which was not so much on Liechtenstein itself, but rather on getting there. The journey involved plenty of shooting, fist-fights, car-crashes, police ambushes, and a budding romance, of course. Having turned the last page of *Midnight Plus One* in the Eurolounge of Heathrow airport, I braced myself for a hard and eventful trip. I wasn't seriously looking forward to being shot at or punched in the face on my way, but I didn't want to exclude altogether the possibility of a little (and quick) romance – something that most travellers secretly hope for.

The romance started earlier than I expected – on the Swissair flight London–Zurich, when I fell head-over-heels in love with beautiful Swiss . . . yogurt, which they served for breakfast. Never before (or after) have I eaten a dairy product so delicious. Savouring it in a semi-recumbent position was an almost orgiastic delight.

At this point, you might ask why I was flying to Zurich at all. The fact is that Liechtenstein, due to its miniature size, has neither airports nor railways. There is a tiny extension of an Austrian railway line passing through the town of Schaan, next to Vaduz, Liechtenstein's capital, but trains there are almost as rare as snowstorms in the Sahara desert. Guidebooks unanimously agree that the only practical way to get to Leichtenstein is to take a train from Zurich to the Swiss town of Sargans and change for a Liechtenstein post bus there.

The bliss of my yogurt-dominated flight was consummated with a smooth cab ride from Zurich airport to the railway station. The taxi was a long black limo with carpets on the floor and enough leg-room for Michael Jordan.

A young, neatly dressed railway clerk at the ticket window started respecting me the moment I demanded a single ticket to Vaduz. 'First class, sir?' he enquired enthusiastically. His oomph (and respect) evaporated as soon as I replied: 'Second, please!' He must have thought initially that I was a millionaire going to Liechtenstein to say hello to my money: who esle would want a single ticket to Vaduz on a Thursday morning?

'Are you from Yugoslavia?' he asked squeamishly, holding my second-class ticket with the tips of his fingers as if it was a wriggling grass-snake.

'No. I am a Ukrainian-born Russian with an Australian passport living in Britain.' I replied honestly.

From the look on his face it was clear that I had had my little revenge.

My train had a romantic name, *Maria Theresia*. Indeed, it was sliding, almost flying, along the track with feminine grace. Having comfortably installed myself at the window of a spotlessly clean second-class compartment, I gazed at the Zurich lake, framed by the snow-capped Alps on the horizon. White swans were crisscrossing the lake's flat surface like floating question marks on a blank page of my yet unwritten travel book. Robust and self-important locals in colourful, stylish parkas were unhurriedly walking their no-less-self-important dogs along the shores.

A smiling conductor peeped into the compartment, switched on the lamp and retired. We were in broad daylight, and I was about to protest at the intrusion, when the train rattled into a tunnel. As soon as we emerged back into the sunshine, a woman with a trolley sagging under food and drinks knocked at the door. She insisted on pouring some beer into my glass and left a stack of snow-white serviettes on the table.

Why can't British railways be as efficient as that? I thought. There seem to be four major factors behind BR's proverbial inefficiency: winter, spring, summer and autumn. And they never fail to find an excuse. In winter they struggle with snow, in spring – with floods, in autumn – with 'leaves slippage', in summer – with God knows what. One morning my London colleague was two hours late to the office. Her train was delayed by a dead dog on the track in Catford. Or maybe it was a dead cat in Dogford, I can't remember.

Are the leaves in Switzerland less slippery than in Britain? And why is it that Swiss cats and dogs never play Anna Karenina?

I think I know the answer. It's no use struggling for cleanliness, it's much better just to sweep the floor, as one Russian writer put it. In Switzerland they don't struggle or look for excuses, they simply do their job, and that's what makes it tick like a brand-new Omega clock.

* * *

Looking at ornate ivy-covered chalets behind the window, it was hard to believe that each of them was likely to be stuffed with ammunition. Yes, military service is compulsory in Switzerland, and every male gets drafted for several weeks once a year until he reaches a fairly mature age. In-between the call-ups, he is supposed to store his arms and military equipment at home, so it wouldn't be too far-fetched to assume that you can find a couple of mortars and machine-guns, to say nothing of bullets and grenades, under every Swiss bed. Can there be a connection here with Switzerland's constantly declining birth rate?

Obviously, the perennial peace of the country, where you can go to prison for making noise after eleven p.m., has to be protected. From whom? That's an entirely different question.

The more I looked through the window, the more I had the feeling of having seen this placid pastoral landscape before. But where? Then I remembered: in Tasmania! This beautiful island off the Australian coast has a sizeable community of Swiss migrants. There is even a showcase Swiss village, built by an eccentric Dutch millionaire, Rolf Voss. In a gesture of homesickness, the Jenni family, who migrated from Switzerland to Hobart (Tasmania's capital) many years ago, constructed a 350-metre-long model railway recreating the views of the Swiss Alps in minute detail. They demonstrate this papier-mâché Switzerland to tourists in their Hobart home.

Meanwhile, the real, not papier mâché Alps were running towards me at break-neck speed, growing in size by the minute. Soon they were dominating the landscape and blocking the sunlight. When their presence became almost totalitarian, the train came to a smooth stop. We were in Sargans.

I was the only passenger to get off the train. Walking along the platform with my suitcase, I saw two middle-aged Swiss soldiers waiting for the train. They were both in their late forties and wearing glasses. Despite their grey helmets, green khaki uniforms and military knapsacks behind their backs, they looked like two peaceful bank clerks (which they probably were between annual drafts) dressed up as soldiers for an office Christmas party.

Looking around for a bus to Vaduz, I was expecting to find a tattered jalopy of a post van, smelling of sealing wax, where I would ride among boxes and parcels in the best traditions of wild-west movies. Instead, an oblong and spacious bright-yellow bus, with postal horns painted on both sides, was waiting behind the station building. It was probably waiting for me, since the moment I got inside, it started off.

The fare to Vaduz was just two Swiss francs — unbelievably cheap. A black mail-bag (not a *blackmail* bag, mind you: no tax-dodging or money-smuggling connotations here — not yet) was tucked under the dashboard, next to the driver. A special rack for bulkier items was in the back of the bus.

This was one of the fleet of Liechtenstein's famous *post autos*. It was, in a way, exterritorial. Once inside, I was already in Liechtenstein.

Yellow post buses were to become my best friends for the whole of my stay in Liechtenstein. They were ubiquitous and always on time. If the timetable said that the bus from Vaduz to Schellenberg was to arrive at Vaduz post office at 10.37, it meant that it would be there neither at 10.38, nor at 10.36, but at 10.37 on the dot. You could bet on the bus and never lose. The drivers were invariably helpful and friendly (they knew most passengers by name), and the fares, as I have already said, were incredibly low. A ride up to thirteen kilometres cost two Swiss francs (less than one pound); a journey over thirteen kilometres, three francs. A monthly ticket was fifteen Swiss francs only, and an annual one went for just sixty. Children, students and senior citizens were entitled to fifty per cent discounts. And for 120 francs you could buy a family annual ticket that, irrespective of your family size, enabled each of your family members to unlimited travel during the whole year. Luckily, the average size of a Liechtenstein family is much smaller than, say, in India, and they don't allow polygamy, like in some Arabic countries. Otherwise, the yellow buses would have long ago gone bust, despite the generous state subsidies they receive.

It was these family passes, with 'Furstentum Liechtenstein' (principality of Liechtenstein) in bold letters across them, that the in-coming passengers were showing to the driver. They were the first Liechtensteiners I'd ever seen. Normal people: housewives with shopping bags, schoolkids in holey jeans. I examined their faces for traces of an inferiority complex: after all, they were citizens of one of the world's tiniest countries. There were none. They all looked no less self-important and proud than the Swiss on the shores on the Zurich lake, and, indeed, they had plenty of things to be proud of. Liechtenstein boasts one of the world's highest living standards and life expectancies. 'Small' must be conducive to wealth and long life. The number of privately owned cars is almost equal to the overall population figure, and the number of telephones exceeds it.

Unlike their Swiss neighbours, the Liechtensteiners are spared military draft, except at the time of national emergency (probably meaning an all-out strike of yellow bus drivers or the Prince catching the flu). The principality has no army, and its last military engagement was in 1866, when Prussia declared war on Austria. All eighty Liechtenstein soldiers were deployed on the frontier between Tyrol and Italy for one week, during which they witnessed a blizzard (in August!), but never set eyes on the enemy. They returned to Liechtenstein safe and sound (in fact, there were eighty-one of them to return: they made a new recruit on the way back), were welcomed by a band, given refreshments at Vaduz castle and then sent home. The Prince paid for the whole campaign out of his pocket.

Liechtenstein's last soldier died in 1939.

Apart from fifty-five sleepy and slow-moving policemen, you won't see a uniformed person in Liechtenstein. There was an incident in October 1992, when a group of Swiss recruits tried by mistake to set up an observation post in the Liechtenstein village of Triesenberg on the Swiss border. A local woman, who had never seen a soldier before and was obviously unnerved by their rifles and gas-masks, simply shooed them away across the frontier. Switzerland had to apologise officially for the incident.

Yes, my travel companions on the Liechtenstein post bus were a proud lot. Theirs was a quiet sort of pride, very different from the militant xenophobic conceit they tried to infect us with in the Soviet Union: 'We, the Soviets, have a pride of our own that enables us to look down on capitalists,' (a popular Soviet rhyme). The passengers were not looking down on anyone (nor did they seem to care much about anyone who might want to look down on them), they were looking straight ahead, at the approaching bridge across the Rhine with a blue and red flag in the middle. This was the official border of Liechtenstein, the country whose very name sounds somewhat domesticated, like that of a friendly Jewish dentist, Dr Liechtenstein. I think we had one in the city where I was born . . .

The first thing I saw in Liechtenstein was the Bahnhof Chinese restaurant in the town of Balzers right across the border.

Chinese restaurants have become ubiquitous. I find them in the most unlikely places: a tiny Essex village, the Australian miners' town of Kalgoorlie in the middle of the Nullarbor Plain, in the Finnish town of Rovaniemi on the Arctic Circle.

Looking for the house where Beethoven was born in Bonn, I eventually discovered that it was fully occupied by a Chinese restaurant. Had Beethoven been alive, he would have had to write a Yum Cha sonata.

In less than twenty minutes we were in Vaduz. Walking to my hotel from the bus stop, I looked up to admire a flock of sky-gliders hovering bravely above the town under their bright-red parachutes, and saw an old medieval castle (complete with a moat, a drawbridge and embrasures) sitting pretty and high on top of a hill. This was the residence of the country's ruling monarch — His Serene Highness Prince Hans Adam II von and zu Liechtenstein — whom I was hoping to meet shortly. Looking at the view of the castle on top of the mountain, the words 'Serene Highness' became full of concrete meaning.

The window of my room in Hotel Real overlooked the Alps, which was not a big advantage in Vaduz, where every window of every room overlooked the Alps too. But there were two obvious disadvantages about my room. One was that all electric appliances in it were connected to one carefully hidden switch which I managed to locate only after twenty minutes of intense search. The KGB bugging devices in the new American Embassy in Moscow must have been easier to find. The second disadvantage manifested itself at night. Trying to fall asleep, I realised that my room, facing, apart from the Alps, the town's main (and only) thoroughfare, possessed a rare acoustic quality which allowed it not just to accumulate but also to amplify every sound coming from the street. It was like a room-size radio receiver with me inside.

Soon it was plain that all the 20,000 private cars in Liechtenstein had colluded to pass under my window one by one, and that each of the 5,000 residents of Vaduz had vowed to keep me awake with every imaginable noise a throat (and all other parts of the human body) could emit.

Lying wide awake on my bed, I had nothing much left to do but remember the worst hotels I have stayed at. It is amazing what you can sometimes find in your own hotel room. I don't mean just a tuft of someone else's hair or a used soap bar in the bathroom. One late evening, having returned to my room in Yubileini Hotel in Archangel, Northern Russia, I discovered an elderly floor-lady sleeping in my bed. Floor-ladies in the Soviet Union were hotel employees whose main task was to guard the inmates' morals by keeping their visitors at bay. When I woke her up, she got very angry: 'I thought you were not coming back tonight and decided to take a nap here. Why the hell did you return so late?' She didn't even bother to change the sheets after she left.

On the door of my room in Ala-Too hotel in Alma Ata, Kazakhstan, there was an emergency notice – 'In case of fire, open the window and scream for help!' Luckily, I never had a chance to check whether it worked or not.

In the Intourist hotel in Baku, Azerbaijan, the bathroom was in the corridor. It had a large window with a wonderful view of the city and of the monument to Lenin in the park. One evening I was taking a leisurely shower and simultaneously admiring the city lights. People were walking in the park and pointing their fingers at me. It took me some time to realise they also had a view! I don't remember how I found myself back in my room, but there was little privacy even there. The hotel was a voyeur's paradise: in the doors of all rooms were square windows through which guests could watch people in the corridor, and similarly they could be clearly seen from outside. I found out later that the building was a hastily reconstructed prison, and the door windows were former peep-holes.

I would be at a loss if asked to name the best hotel I have stayed in. One in Cairns with a spare TV set in every bathroom could qualify, were it not for geckos (little tropical lizards) swarming on the ceilings. But I know only too well where the world's worst hotel is. It is in Turkmenistan, in the town of Mari, bordering on Afghanistan. I arrived there as a guest of the local Russian language newspaper with the surprisingly ingenious name *Mari Pravda*. That's why I was in for a special treatment.

In the hotel's lobby, an old bearded Turkmen woman solemnly gave me the key to the hotel's only 'luxury suite'. The room was full of flies and smelt like a mortuary. There was an air-conditioner in the wall (it was forty-two degrees), but it didn't work. The shower didn't work either. The biggest surprise, though, was that I was supposed to share my room and the only medium-size bed with a male Communist Party official from Ashkhabad. He was snoring and fidgeting on his side of the bed all night, and when I finally managed to nod off, I dreamt of an earthquake.

To add apples to oranges, I got severely poisoned at the hotel's restaurant (it only had eggs and cucumbers on offer, but this proved to be enough) and nearly died.

If fate throws you to Mari, stay away from the local hotel (there's only one in town), if you want to stay alive.

This is all a far cry from the standard of service at the Metechi Palace

Hotel in Tbilisi, Georgia, where a colleague of mine received an extremely polite letter from the management:

> On behalf of the management of the Metechi Palace Hotel we would like to inform you that as from today the Diplomatic Police will ensure the security of the hotel and help us to realise our goal *to keep the interior of the hotel arms free.*
> Wishing you a pleasant stay with us.
> Thank you,
>
> > Tamriko Vardiashvili,
> > Public Relations Manager

Having somewhat pacified myself with these sweet recollections, I didn't notice how I fell asleep in the noise . . .

The first thing I did next morning was move to a room in the opposite wing of the building. Strangely enough, it was facing the Alps too . . .

Next morning I realised why the receptionist at my hotel had only reluctantly agreed to make a wake-up call to my room the night before: sleeping seems to be the Liechtensteiners' favourite pastime outside money-making hours, hence alarm clocks and wake-up calls are not exactly popular there.

It was a public holiday, and Vaduz was as empty as an artillery range one minute before shelling practice is due to commence. I failed to establish exactly what sort of a holiday it was. The ever-helpful hotel receptionist told me in her peculiar English ('You've got a dialect,' she said to me, meaning I had an accent, of course) that it was St Joseph's Day, but the answering machine at the British Consulate assured me it was a Bank Holiday. St Joseph's Day made more sense to me, since Joseph was the second name of the late Prince Franz Joseph II who ruled Liechtenstein for forty-five years – from 1938 to 1983 – which made his reign the world's second longest after that of the Japanese emperor Hirohito. Franz Joseph's full name, by the way, was Prince

Franz Josef II Maria Alois Alfred Karl Johann Heinrich Michael Georg Ignatius Benediktus Gerhardus Majella, the Twelfth Ruling Prince of Liechtenstein, Duke of Jagerndorf, Count of Reitberg, and Knight of the Golden Fleece. If they had one holiday for each of his names, there wouldn't be many working days left in Liechtenstein . . .

The bell-chimes of the local parish church were sweeping through the town and echoing in the mountains. On the door of the church there was a sign in broken English:

DIVINE SERVICE. NO VISIT

Not a living soul was in sight.

'F * * * the school!' ran an English graffito on the fence around the government building. The very fact that the sign was in a foreign language and without spelling mistakes demonstrated that, whether the pupils liked it or not, the local school was somehow coping with its unrewarding task . . .

I stood in the middle of the deserted Aulestrasse, studying the window of a closed souvenir shop full of panda bears, porcelain clocks, red-nosed clowns, wooden Easter eggs and fridge magnets that could be on sale anywhere in the world — from Jamaica to Japan. On a special stand there was a set of gift cigarette lighters with names like Hubert, Beatrix, Beate, Horst, Hans, and Kirstin on them. I didn't fancy buying any of them as a present, mainly because I didn't know anyone called Hubert, Horst or Beate. As to Beatrix, I was once on a cross-Channel ferry named after the Dutch Queen Beatrix, but I wasn't sure whether she was a smoker (I mean the Queen of course, the ferry certainly smoked). I looked for a Vitali lighter in vain — there were none.

I did like one of the souvenirs though: a bed-pillow in the shape of a heart with 'I love Liechtenstein' embroidered on it. It did reflect the soporiphic atmosphere of the country.

After half-an-hour of window shopping, I decided to find the famous

Postage Stamps Museum, in case, by some crazy twist of fate, it was open. I needed directions. 'Your tongue can lead you as far as Kiev,' an old Russian proverb goes. I didn't want to go to Kiev, I was born not far from it. I needed the Postage Stamps Museum. But Russian folk wisdom was hardly applicable to Liechtenstein on a public holiday; there was no one about I could practice my tongue upon.

And suddenly I saw HIM. I should have guessd he was a tourist. Who else would be hanging around Vaduz on a morning like that? From his red baseball cap I also should have guessed he was an American. But I was so happy to spot a fellow human that I rushed towards him and barked into his face: 'Do you speak English?' 'Yeah, that's all I speak,' he replied readily. He spoke with an unmistakable American slur, as if he had a small Capitol building in his mouth. I felt myself in the shoes of the hapless London-based Soviet diplomat who, when introduced to the Queen at a reception, inadvertently asked her: 'Do you speak English?' He was recalled to Moscow shortly afterwards . . .

From our further verbal exchange I learned that he had been in 'this damned town for three damned days, but had no damned idea where the damned Postage Stamps Museum was.'

We were standing in front of it, by the way . . .

Apart from a flood or an earthquake, the biggest trap awaiting a reckless European tourist nowadays is travelling in the company of Americans. I fell into this trap myself some time ago when, while living in Australia, I decided to have a quick coach tour of several European countries.

As soon as I boarded our bus in London, I discovered that I was one of three non-Americans on the tour. The other two were Kurt — a middle-aged polyglot Austrian, our guide and tour director, and Antonio — our young Italian driver, blond and taciturn which made him the most unlikely Italian on earth. The Americans were of all ages and skin-colours but looked like twins nevertheless. Their boisterous speech enveloped me from the start like a rough US Army blanket.

The first turmoil on the bus occured several minutes later, when Kurt introduced himself in his perfect English. The Americans began turning in their chairs and asking each other: 'What's his name? Is it Court or Kurd?' Finally they reached a consensus and started calling him 'Card'.

The second confusion happened when Kurt exchanged several sentences in Italian with Antonio. 'What language do they speak?' a retired nurse from Milwaukee sitting next to me shouted in my ear. 'Is it French or German?' She was a knowledge-hungry person, my neighbour, but her curiosity, like that of a child, was usually ignited by the most unexpected things. 'Are there many Japanese in Europe?' she would ask me one day. 'Do all the dogs in Europe wear leashes?' she would inquire vociferously on another occasion.

A typical tour day. We are riding through Burgundy (or Tuscany, or Provence). 'Look at this castle at your left!' Kurt pleads from time to time. In vain. The Americans are busy reading paperbacks. They have heaps of them, and never let them out of their hands. Their titles vary between *Death at Dawn* and *Love Me Forever*. Where do they get them from? From some American 'Pulp, Etc' booksellers? After Kurt's repeated pleas, they reluctantly look up from their books, throw a furtive look at the castle, say in chorus 'Wow!' (without much enthusiasm) and return to their reading. 'This castle was built in the fifteenth century!' Kurt proceeds with renewed energy, encouraged by their fleeting interest. The best reaction he can hope for in this case is a half-hearted 'Really?' (sounding very much like 'Rally?') and the frantic rustle of turning pages.

There were very few things which were able to excite my travel companions. As if on command, they all burst into applause at the sight of the Eiffel Tower, as if expecting this elaborate creation of Gustave Eiffel to curtsey in response. They got agitated when Kurt told them that the average per capita income in Switzerland was $2,500 a month; having ferreted micro-calculators out of their pockets, they started counting this figure's weekly, quarterly and yearly expressions.

They were not impressed by museums and churches, though made sure they visited each one on the list. Whether it was St Peter's in

Rome, Notre Dame in Paris ('The Empire State Building is taller!') or St Mark's basilica in Venice, for them it was all 'ABC' — another bloody church, as they would put it. But it was enough for Kurt to suggest that they could skip this or that sight on the itinerary, and they would go berserk and heroically trudge through yet 'another bloody church' (was it the Sistine Chapel this time?), looking at their feet with deadpan expressions on their faces.

As a group they were a curious sight — all dressed in shorts and sandals, all with the regulation plastic bottles of mineral water pressed to their T-shirted chests. They were dead sure that one could not drink water from the tap anywhere in the world, apart from the US, of course. They had a strong sense of collectivism and seemed to move invariably in a crowd. If every Englishman, as George Mikes once observed, forms a queue on his own, every American is a one-person crowd.

In the evenings they never went out to gape at the cities where we were staying, but sat at stuffy hotel bars, exchanging views on American politics and forthcoming elections. They were spending fortunes in these bars. One would have thought they had been to Paris or Venice dozens of times before, but no: for most of them it was their first (and last, as they would never miss a chance to say) visit to Europe. You couldn't help wondering why they had bothered to come to Europe at all. Was it just for the sake of being able to mutter one day at a party: 'Venice? Yeah . . . I've been there. A lousy place. It's just too damned old. And not a single baseball field!'?

After a while I started noticing that, instead of feasting my eyes upon the beauties of Europe, I was watching my travel companions. By the end of the tour I realised with horror that I had myself acquired a touch of an American accent and was addressing Kurt as 'Card'. I got so used to them that, believe it or not, when it was time to part I felt 'rally' sad. Why? Simply because, apart from being noisy, poorly educated and uninquisitive, these American nurses, workers, accountants and pensioners were all warm and amiable people, quickly forging friend-ships and always ready to help. I suddenly realised that, irrespective of their age, they were all youngsters in spirit. Teenagers of our civilisation. Cultural adolescents. As it was written by George Santayana, 'the American seems to bear lightly the sorrowful burden of human knowledge. In a word, he is young.'

The Postage Stamps Museum, which was indeed open, proved to be a disappointment: it was just one room full of stands with Liechtenstein stamps under glass. Most of the stamps featured smiling Princes and Princesses. It was curious to discover that all of them (the stamps, not the Princes) were actually printed in Austria. In the corner of the room there stood a wooden bureau, behind which a woman was nodding with a round seal in her hand. For a couple of Swiss francs she offered to stamp our passports with a special souvenir postmark. The American volunteered, but on contact with his solid USA passport the delicate Liechtenstein seal broke, leaving a Tasmania-shaped ink blot on the page. This little incident upset the American so much that he stormed out of the museum and went to look for the nearest open bar. He must be still looking for it, as I haven't seen him since.

The Liechtenstein State Art Collection was displayed in the same building (maybe it was even in the same room, I was not sure). The leaflet, given to me by the seal of a woman, said that 'a visit to the Liechtenstein State Art Collection can always make a sojourn in Liechtenstein and Vaduz a memorable aesthetic experience' and added that 'the visitor can contemplate important works of European art in appropriately intimate surroundings.' I desperately needed some 'aesthetic experience' and the surroundings could not be more intimate. I was expecting to find some of the paintings from the Prince's collection, considered to be the second largest private collection in the world (the first belongs to the Queen of England), but all of it was probably kept in the castle, and I had to be satisfied with several avant-garde paintings by modern Liechtenstein artists.

A large red square on an otherwise virgin-white canvas by Peter Brand was called *Magic Square*. It reminded me of the Red Square in Moscow, and I lost interest. Another picture was called *Coloured Paper*

25

Image XXI and consisted of five vertical stripes — orange, blue, black, green and brown, whereas *Coloured Paper Image III* was nothing but ten horizontal stripes on white paper. Well, you can call me a retrograde, but I was not particularly impressed by these works of modern art: whatever the hidden meaning, to paint five strips is much easier than to create a *Mona Lisa* or *The Return of the Prodigal Son*.

Having despaired of gaining 'aesthetic experience' out of paintings, I decided to look for it elsewhere, namely in the restaurant of my hotel. My omniscient guidebook assured that it was run by one of the world's most celebrated chefs, Felix Real. Coming down the stairs in the morning I couldn't help noticing that the walls of the hotel's corridors were covered not in wallpaper but in countless diplomas and certificates of merit, celebrating the unparalleled cooking skills of Felix Real and his numerous sons and brothers — all renowned chefs, wine-makers and hoteliers. Among the exquisite titles awarded to Felix Real there were CHEVALIER DU TASTENIR, LE CONSEILLER CULINAIRE DU BAILLAGE NATIONAL DU LIECHTENSTEIN. COMMANDEUR DE LA COMMANDERIE DES CORDONS BLEUS and even L'AM-BASSADEUR DES VINS VAUDOIS which in plain English meant THE AMBASSADOR OF VADUZIAN WINES, no less. A couple of diplomas were signed by LE GRAND MAITRE DE L'ORDRE which, ignoring the inescapable masonic order connotations, sounded to me pretty much like THE GREAT MASTER OF ALL RESTAURANT ORDERS.

I decided I wanted to meet Felix Real, the only real ambassador (even if only of wines) in Liechtenstein, which boasts consulates of Costa Rica, Lesotho, Luxembourg, Monaco, Peru, Rwanda, Senegal, Togo, Hungary and Britain (The Honorary British Consul Bryan Jeeves), but not a single embassy.

Felix Real was a pleasant elderly man, with lively youthful eyes and slightly elongated features. He moved around the hotel with the grace of a retired ballet dancer.

'To be a good cook, you must love life!' he said with his inimitable German (or was it Liechtensteiner?) accent, introducing his son Martin, who now owned Hotel Real and his wife Theresia who acted as a family PR person and kindly provided me with a typewritten copy of her husband's short biography in English:

'Felix Real was born in Vaduz in 1919 as son of the innkeeper family. He discovered his interest already during the early years of his apprenticeship and began to apply himself to the mastery of the culinary art . . .'

The biography went on to cover his time as 'commis de cuisine in the first-class establishments in Switzerland' and as a chef at Maxim's in Paris. The highlights of his career included heading the team of cooks for the marriage of the Hereditary Prince of Liechtenstein in 1967; 'assuming gastronomic leadership' at the celebrations of the 2,500th anniversary of the Persian Imperial House in 1971; being guest chef at the famous Harmonie Club in New York and Club de Gents in Paris (chefs, like actors, go on tours and give guest perform-ances); for which he was decorated with the Prince of Liechtenstein Order of Merit. IIIn number of awards, he could easily compete with Leonid Brezhnev who, as a Soviet joke went, had to undergo a special chest-enlarging operation to accommodate all his medals and orders.

'What makes me different?' Felix Real paused before replying. 'We take things easy!'

All this was more than enough to make me start salivating, and I could hardly wait for the next evening, when I was invited to have dinner at Felix Real's restaurant.

To tell you the truth, I've never been a gourmet. It was hard to be one in the former Soviet Union, where there was never the problem of what to eat. You ate anything you could get hold of. You certainly couldn't eat something that you didn't manage to get. That was it. It was like wearing an old worn jacket which you don't throw out because you've got nothing else to put on. We ate for the sake of living, whereas in the West it is often the other way round: living for the sake of eating. At least, that's what I thought during my first months in Austrailia.

The newspaper where I worked had a sixteen-page weekly supplement on food, called *The Epicure*. I discovered there existed a special sort of journalist called food writers, who wrote exclusively about food. For some reason, they were all thin and nervous. I used to promise to myself that under no circumstances was I going to contribute to this particular section of the newspaper.

It was not long before I changed my mind. By that time I already had half a dozen favourite restaurants in Melbourne and was finding that food was one of the most exciting things in Australian life. I started contributing to *The Epicure* from time to time. I began putting on weight too.

The only thing I found hard to cope with was wine. In the Soviet Union we used to drink with only one aim in mind – to get drunk as quickly (and as cheaply) as possible, in order to forget about the gloomy reality, at least for a short while. That's why we didn't care much about what we drank: but solely for the aftereffect, and vodka was certainly ideal for this purpose: it brought you to the desired state of mind with the speed and comfort of a Qantas jet. Whereas drinking wine could be compared with a long and bumpy Aeroflot flight: you are not exactly sure when you are going to reach your destination, or whether you are going to reach it at all. It was hard for me to understand how someone could sip alcohol rather than gulp it down the throat and wait for it to hit you from inside. And since I had no particular desire to strive for oblivion in the West (simply because the reality was so much nicer), I eventually decided to give up drinking altogether.

So, during my dinner, to Felix Real's great regret, I had to refuse the offer of Vaduse Rosé and Cuvee Felix Real from his cellars. 'But it is so good, so good – um-m-m . . . ' he kept saying, kissing his own fingers as proof. The old man was so upset by my refusal that I started becoming seriously worried about his health, and even his life. 'If you don't try this cake, the chef will commit suicide.' This threat from some obscure Russian film was ringing in my head.

Finally, the grief-stricken Felix Real stumbled out of the restaurant to continue his suffering in the privacy of his house, or so I thought. I was left in the hands of three buxom blonde waitresses who immediately brought me a menu the size of the Gutenberg Bible. The names of the dishes sounded like a French prayer – 'Homard, langoustines et coquille St Jacques grillés à l'estragon'. Amen!

I think that all these long names are deliberately construed to confuse the customer. It was much easier in the restaurant of the world's worst hotel in Mari (see above) where the choice was of just three dishes: fried eggs, cucumber salad and swarms of greasy Turkmenistan flies as a free dressing to go with both.

As soon as I had coped with the starter of wonderfully delicate smoked eel, the waitress brought a set of six knives and forks (plus a special little spoon for the sauce) and threateningly placed them on a wooden board on my table. I started frantically counting my money . . .

My main course (I think it was some sort of lamb fillet) was brought on a gleaming trolley, which resembled a gun-carriage carrying the body of Brezhnev, Andropov or Chernenko to be buried near the Kremlin Wall. The procession stopped next to my table, the waitresses synchronistically lifted stainless steel lids from the plates to reveal the garnish of beans and potatoes and a huge piece of meat. The lids looked exactly like brass cymbals, and I could almost hear the sounds of Chopin's Funeral March. Armed with two large-toothed knives, they started chopping at my lamb, shredding it into pieces, of which one – thin and almost transparent – slice, just big enough to feed an ant, ended up on my plate. The trolley was then solemnly driven back to its kitchen stable. Like an obnoxious stallion, it didn't want to go and was kicking the waitresses with its wheels.

Mesmerised by the ceremony, I didn't notice how I swallowed my tiny slice of meat, which was delicious indeed, and started watching other customers – giggling local women in sparkling evening dresses, bearded Slivowitz-tossing men in suits. One striking feature about them was that all seemed to have extremely healthy snow-white teeth. This is hardly surprising though, when you remember that Liechtenstein is the world's main exporter of false teeth and sausage skins. One needs good quality teeth to be able to bite through good quality sausage skin, no doubt.

After I finished eating, the waitress swept away the crumbs from my table (there weren't many left) with a special brush. 'How was it?' she asked, and without waiting for my reply said: 'Very good!'

I decided to be naughty, asked for the list of desserts and ordered *Crêpes au fromage blanc* but without *glace de vanille* as it was on the menu. The waitress was somewhat puzzled, but I could see that she started to respect me more. The desserts menu had waiting times indicated under each item. In my case it was fifteen minutes. Exactly fifteen minutes later my crêpes arrived with the precision of a yellow post bus.

At this point Felix Real reappeared in the restaurant. He had obviously overcome his distress and offered me an apéritif. I explained that I had just finished my meal, so he invited me to see his holy of holies – the kitchen.

The kitchen was so spotlessly clean you could safely eat from its floor. In the middle there was an electronic (or maybe electric) stove which could bring a pan of water to the boil in fifteen seconds. In a separate room two young cooks in starched white gowns were preparing sauces. 'My sauces are the best in the world!' boasted Mr Real, before plunging into reverie: 'The Prince sometimes phones me from his castle and asks whether there's a table for him in my restaurant. If I say yes, he just comes down with his wife. One night he brought Princess Diana with him. I was told she wouldn't eat anything but, to my relief, she said: 'Bring me everything you have got!' (She must have been in a bulimic mood.)

I admired this frail old gentleman who had spent all his life catering for others. He made me realise again that there was much more to eating than just stuffing your belly with food.

One Australian travel writer advised in his book that it is best to stay away from floating, rotating or hotel-based restaurants (he also said that one of the signs of a good restaurant was a pepper-grinder on your table). He was wrong: Felix Real's Aux Premier restaurant at the Real Hotel in Vaduz was excellent.

After dinner I went to consult the timetable of buses to the Alpine village of Malbun: next morning I wanted to explore the highlands of Liechtenstein. The bus stop was near the main post office, across the road from my hotel. I was breathing crisp mountain air. The shop windows were glowing in the darkness. Two local young women drifted by in a cloud of exquisite perfume. The brightly lit Prince's castle sat firmly on top of the rock. A lonely police car cruised by. Here I was in the centre of Europe, in the tiny state of Liechtenstein, after a hearty dinner, free to do whatever I wanted. Life was wonderful, and it was hard to believe that the war-ridden former Yugoslavia was nearby, just across the Alps.

It takes only fifteen minutes by bus to get from Vaduz to the highlands, and the fare is the standard two francs. The yellow post bus, loaded with skis and skiers, climbed up the mountain road, and in no time spring gave way to winter: the trees became few and far between and patches of snow could be seen here and there. Suddenly the Prince's castle no longer dominated the landscape. In fact, I was able to look down upon it. His Royal Highness became His Royal Lowness. On both sides of the winding road there were chalets the size of chateaux, and chateaux as cosy as chalets.

Soon snow was lying everywhere and we arrived at the village of Malbun, where I got off the bus and, together with several dozen cheerful skiers, boarded a chairlift to the mountain top. The chair trembled and shook treacherously. I beat the air with my legs and admired the striking panorama of the Alps, with black dots of skiers sliding along ski-slopes like ants hurrying down their anthills. It was twenty degrees Centigrade in Vaduz, but here the temperature was close to zero, and I was shivering for all my light summer jacket was

31

worth. Fierce gusts of piercing cold wind came close to blowing me off the chair into the abyss.

A tiny flat landing on the mountain peak was big enough to accommodate a café and a shop selling, among other things, a variety of porno magazines. It was hard to imagine a pervert (or a sex maniac) who would bother to climb that high to buy a dirty magazine and then take a chairlift back to the valley. Perhaps it was just an attempt to uplift the magazines' standards?

On the open terrace of the café (there were no seats inside) with the tongue-tieing and mysterious name Selbstbedienungs, I sipped hot coffee which was quickly turning into ice in my cup. Even here, above the clouds, it was served as everywhere else in Liechtenstein – with two tiny chocolates on a plate. The wind nonchalantly blew their foil wrappings away and down the precipice.

The place was full of skiers, mostly Germans. All of them, including kids and octogenarians, wore skis as naturally as if they were born with them on their feet. When, in a futile attempt to warm myself up, I stumbled into the graceful Alpine church of St Joseph near the bus station, I half expected to find a painting of Madonna in a skiing outfit and the baby Christ with little skis on his tiny pink feet. In fact, I was the only human being in Malbun who was not on skis – I was wearing a pair of disgraceful Turkish cross-country shoes, bought in Moscow five years before after several hours of queueing.

On the way back to Vaduz, I stopped at the big mountain village of Triesenberg, the home of the unique Walser community. The village has 600 houses and 2,380 people, most of whom work for Ivoclar, the false teeth company and Liechtenstein's main employer. The Walser people settled here in the thirteenth century. They have managed to preserve their own language, costumes and dances (including the good old waltz). In the centre of the village I visited a well-stocked Walser museum, where, among other exhibits, I saw a curious tool called a *Butterstempel*, or butterstamp, for stamping a farmer's name on a piece of butter, and then settled down for an unhurried lunch on the terrace of the Hotel Kulm restaurant. It couldn't be quieter: the terrace overlooked the Alps, and the only movement around me was that of air-bubbles in my mineral water glass. It was much warmer here than in Malbun.

While still in the Soviet Union, I learnt about the mysterious and indecently rich Baron Edward von Falz-Fein, a Russian émigré aristocrat and patron of the arts living in Liechtenstein and donating paintings from his private collection of Russian art to Soviet museums every now and then. The Baron's family had resided in Russia since the time of Catherine the Great. Herself a German, the Empress encouraged members of the German gentry to settle throughout the vast Russian Empire. One of the Baron's ancestors founded Askania-Nova, a natural reserve of a million acres and the world's largest open-air zoo, in Ukraine. In the beginning of the twentieth century the ill-fated Tsar Nicholas II visited Askania-Nova and raised the whole family to nobility. After the revolution, the Baron, still a young child, had to flee Russia with his mother and, like many other political refugees, found shelter in Liechtenstein, where the Prince immediately gave them citizenship. Later, Baron Falz-Fein became the founder of the principality's tourist industry and played an active role in promoting the tiny country's culture and sport. He was entrusted with carrying the flag of Liechtenstein during the opening ceremonies of several Olympic Games. He was also closely involved in the search for the 'Amber Room', the priceless treasure, stolen by the Germans from one of the Tsar's palaces near Leningrad during the Second World War. The room has not been found so far, and its whereabouts remain one of this century's biggest mysteries.

I had to try to meet the legendary Baron. It proved to be easier than I thought. 'You should ask for him at a Quick souvenir shop,' a government official in Vaduz advised me.

'Of course, we know the Baron very well!' a shop assistant told me and added: 'He owns all Quick shops in Liechtenstein.' He then volunteered to make a phone call to the Baron on my behalf. As he spoke, I could hear his interlocutor's loud screams in German from the telephone. 'The Baron would be delighted to see you at any moment,' the shop assistant announced and offered to give me a lift up the hill to the Baron's villa.

The villa was situated half-way between the centre of Vaduz and the Prince's castle. 'Villa Askania-Nova' ran the brass plate on the gate. I pressed the intercom button and the Baron's youngish voice shouted in Russian: 'What a shame! Why didn't you come to see me earlier? Come straight in!' His voice sounded energetic and cheerful for his age: I calculated that the Baron must be in his mid-eighties now.

The gates opened with a buzz and the Baron was already running out to meet me. He had a slim youthful figure and the lively aristocratic face of an elderly playboy. 'Shame, shame upon your head!' he was thundering. 'You call yourself a Russian, and you are not in a hurry to come and see the old Baron! What a disgrace!'

'Welcome, welcome!' he yelled, leading me across the vegetable garden to the house. 'I've been planting radishes since morning, you see . . . And now I am having coffee . . . '

His house was like the St Petersburg's State Russian Museum in miniature. Paintings by the best Russian artists of the nineteenth and twentieth centuries were hanging on all the walls – Repin, Levitan and Kuindzhi among them. A ceremonial portrait of Emperor Alexander I was displayed in the corridor next to a number of landscape drawings depicting Russian winter. Sculptures, bronze figurines, pieces of fine porcelain, the Baron's sportive trophies and old, dog-eared copies of *The Herald of the Russian Nobility* were everywhere, which made the house look like an oversized antiques shop. Packets of Marlboro were scattered all over the lounge, despite the fact that, as I found out later, the Baron was a non-smoker.

'To my dear Edward in memory of the unforgettable Prince Narishkin,' was written in Russian across one of the paintings. The Narishkins were something like Russia's Tudors.

In one corner there was a TV set with the largest screen I've ever seen. 'I am the only person in Liechtenstein who can receive Moscow television. Even the Prince cannot do this!' the Baron said proudly, switching on his TV set. The familiar face of a Russian news reader with a deadpan expression, as if she had just buried her own mother, appeared on the screen. 'You must excuse me now,' the Baron said with sudden curtness. 'I have to finish my coffee . . .'

He was a true aristocrat, this Baron. Hospitable or not, commoners are not supposed to share noblemen's meals.

When he returned, we lowered ourselves into big leather armchairs. Mine was so deep and soft that it made my self-esteem plummet. The Baron burst into an uninterrupted three-hour-long monologue. He told me about his genealogical tree, Askania-Nova, the Amber Room and Liechtenstein, for which he seemed to have a real affection. He recalled how about thirty years ago he decided to organise a conference of the Little Four countries (Andorra, Monaco, Liechtenstein and San Marino) as opposed to the Big Four, but, for some reason, the conference never took place.

There was one point in this monologue though, where I became all eyes and ears. The story of 500 Russian soldiers who found refuge in Liechtenstein at the end of World War II sounded incredible, and later in the week I had to spend a couple of days in *Landesbibliotek* to make sure it was all true. I also had a meeting with Henning von Vogelsang, the editor-in-chief of *Liechtensteiner Vaterland* (one of the two daily newspapers in Vaduz), who wrote a book (or rather a small brochure) on this little-known episode of the Second World War, which helped to change my whole perception of Liechtenstein.

THE STORY OF 500 RUSSIAN SOLDIERS IN LIECHTENSTEIN AS RECOUNTED BY EDWARD VON FALZ-FEIN, CONFIRMED BY HENNING VON VOGELSANG AND FURTHER RESEARCHED BY VITALI VON VITALIEV

To say Liechtenstein was spared foreign invasions for all 250 years of its history is not entirely true. On the night of 2 May 1945, 500 fully armed Russian soldiers, under the command of Major General Holmston-Smyslovsky, crossed the Austrian frontier into Liechtenstein near the village of Schellenberg. This 'invasion', one of the most moving and obscure chapters of the Second World War, was peaceful and bloodless.

The Russians, remnants of the First Russian Army of the German Wehrmacht, had entered Liechtenstein in search of political asylum. Unlike two and a half million other Russian soldiers and Cossacks, who fought on the German side and were captured by the Allies only to be handed over to Stalin for execution under the ignominious Yalta agreement, they were not extradited and were allowed to stay.

The tiny Ruritarian principality was firmly committed to its status of neutrality during the last war. Near Malbun there is a church built in 1950 'to thank God for sparing Liechtenstein the terrors of the Second World War'. In actual fact, it was thanks not to God but to the political prowess of Prince Franz Joseph II (ironically, he was the nephew of Archduke Franz Ferdinand, whose assassination in Sarajevo precipitated the 1914-1918 war), who bravely paid a surprise visit to Berlin in May 1939.

As the Prince himself later recalled, Hitler 'was visibly ill at ease and didn't make any impression at all' during their ninety-minute meeting in the Reich Chancellery, but since his visit 'flattered Hitler's ego' (as a typical 'commoner' he probably felt a good deal of trepidation in the face of one of Europe's most famous noblemen), the Nazis decided to leave Liechtenstein alone.

Having come back from Germany, the Prince ordered Liechtenstein's two political parties, the Reds (the Patriotic Union) and the Blacks (the Progressive Citizens' Party), to form a coalition and join forces to protect Liechtenstein's independence.

The First Russian Army of the Wehrmacht was made of Russian émigrés and freedom-fighters, most of whom were not even Soviet citizens. Its main objective was not to contribute to Russia's occupation, but rather to help it to get rid of Bolshevism, which was seen as the greater of two evils. Hitler never fully trusted the Army, and even had Holmston-Smyslowsky, a former Russian count, imprisoned and his unit disbanded for a couple of years. The army didn't commit any atrocities and its involvement in combat action was minimal.

As soon as the news reached Vaduz of the 500 Russians in German uniforms, with all their arms and equipment, crossing the border, the Prince sent his representatives to Schellenberg. Baron Falz-Fein was asked to act as a translator.

The negotiations with Holmston-Smyslowsky took place in the Zum Lowen Inn on the border. 'It was a curious sight for our peaceful Liechtenstein,' the Baron recalled. 'Hundreds of heavily armed men, with their horses and vehicles, camping on the lawn behind the inn. Later we built barracks for them at the town of Ruggel.'

Asylum was granted to all the men, but shortly afterwards the Prince found himself under considerable pressure from the Soviets. Unlike his British, French and American counterparts, the ruler of the tiny Liechtenstein firmly resisted all attempts to have the asylum-seekers extradited. 'Despite strong pressure, and in contrast to the bad example set by other countries, these unfortunate refugees were not handed over to the executioners,' the valiant Prince Franz Joseph II wrote in 1980.

The only thing the Prince had to agree to was to allow a Soviet delegation to come to Liechtenstein and interview the asylum-seekers. By stick and carrot, Stalin's emissaries managed to dupe 300 into returning to the USSR. Despite generous guarantees of safety, each of them was executed on arrival.

Most of the remaining 200, including Holmston-Smyslowsky, stayed for two years before moving on, most of them to the safety of Argentina. One soldier, named Sokhin, married a local girl and lived a happy life in Liechtenstein until his death in the early nineties.

'Moscow would have had many opportunities to make matters very awkward for little Liechtenstein,' said Henning von Vogelsang. 'Why these opportunities were not taken is inexplicable. Perhaps, with all the troubles and upheavals at that time, Russia had other problems . . . '

My point of view is somewhat different, though. The huge, victorious totalitarian giant had to retreat when confronted with the tiny state's unadulterated courage, pride and integrity, something that the Stalinist Soviet Union was lacking completely. It was like a flock of knife-brandishing bullies beating up a woman in the street suddenly being told off by a little old lady with shopping bags in her hands, while scores of younger and stronger pedestrians quietly pass by. Courage breeds respect even among the cruelest of criminals, whereas cowardice (*pace* France, Britain and the USA) breeds contempt only.

'Liechtenstein is a happy country because it is small,' Prince Franz Joseph II, who died in 1989 after fifty-one years at the principality's helm, used to say. The 1945 episode in Schellenberg, to my mind, turned Liechtenstein from just a happy country into a proud one.

With an area of only 160 square kilometres and a population of only 30,000, Liechtenstein might be small indeed, but it has much to teach the world.

At the end of his story the Baron told me how he raised the money to build a monument to the 500 Russian soldiers in Schellenberg. 'This modest stone obelisk is still there, and the locals call it simply the Russian Monument,' he concluded.

Naturally, after hearing his story I wanted to see the monument with my own eyes, and decided to undertake a trip to Schellenberg next morning. 'It is very easy to find,' the Baron reassured me. 'Just take a bus to Schellenberg and ask the locals for directions there. They all know it.'

The Baron was in a hurry: he was to take a group of Russian tourists along the trail of Suvorov, the famous eighteenth-century Russian military commander who crossed the Alps with his army in the Liechtenstein area in 1799. I didn't realise I was in for an unwilling repetition of Suvorov's ordeal.

It sounds stupid to confess to having got lost in Liechtenstein, a country so minuscule that, when asked for directions, a local would sometimes say: 'Go to the next corner, turn right into Switzerland, cross the road back to Liechtenstein and at the next traffic lights, just opposite the Austrian border, there will be the post office you are looking for.' For the second time in just a few days, however, I had to make this confession. After three hours of hiking through the Alps in search of the Russian Monument, I got irretrievably lost in the Alpine forest, somewhere near the Austrian border. The Baron was wrong. The residents of Schellenberg had no idea where the Russian Monument was. In fact, none of them had ever heard about it. A curt 'Nein!' was all they could say. The last person whom I asked for directions was the local priest, standing outside a modern glass-and-concrete parish church. He pointed his finger somewhere up the mountain, and there was nothing left for me to do but start climbing it under his gaze.

The village of Schellenberg spiralled around the hill. Ornate chalets with ubiquitous satellite dishes on their roofs gradually gave way to forest. After the picturesque ruins of the New Schellenberg castle (I couldn't imagine what the old castle would look like, the new one was in such a deplorable state) with the Liechtenstein tricolour on top, there were no more houses in sight. By this time, my head was spinning and my sense of direction (if any) had been completely lost.

And then I saw a small road sign with one word 'Borscht' on it. For those of my readers who do not know what *borscht* is, I have to explain that it is a Russian, Polish or Ukrainian beetroot soup, one of the wonders of East European cuisine. There are dozens (if not hundreds) of recipes for hot or cold *borscht*: with dumplings, meat, potatoes or pure lard – but whatever its ingredients or temperature it is always delicious. The sight of this yummy word in the middle of the Alpine forest, apart from making me salivate (I was already quite hungry after hours of hiking), conjured up images of bearded Russian soldiers teaching the locals the secrets of Russian cuisine which, who knows? might even constitute the topographic reason for calling a tiny Liechtenstein hamlet (I was sure it was a hamlet) Borscht. Journalistic inquisitiveness and writer's imagination prevailed over common sense. The titillating smell of freshly cooked *borscht* was teasing my nostrils, and I followed the narrow forest path into the thicket.

It was April, and the forest was still light and barren, like a freshly built house ready to receive the tenants: the rooms are still empty of furniture, and every sound you make echoes from the walls, but soon the tenants will move in, and the house will be full of fuss and laughter.

I love the European forest, and during my several years in Australia I missed its smells and sounds terribly. The gum-trees in the Australian bush, with their stiff glossy leaves, make a low buzzing sound like the wings of a dragonfly, whereas in the European forest the trees rustle soothingly above your head as if whispering something to you. In fact, it was in a small polluted forest near Gatwick airport, where I found myself after a small flying accident, that my decision to return to live in Europe was made.

The path soon ended with no sign (or smell) of *borscht*. I started walking back and lost my track completely. The awful truth was that looking for *borscht* I found myself in the soup. The sounds of church bells and the muffled screams of roosters reached me from the distance, and I started trudging desperately through the thicket in the direction of these sounds. It was a no-man's-forest-land and, despite occasional red paint marks on the trees, probably selected for logging, I was sure that I was the first human ever to set foot in this god-forsaken forest.

When I was about to throw myself on the ground and weep, I saw . . . a rubbish-bin. A neat plastic rubbish-bin one is likely to find in the streets of Vaduz or (much less likely) of London. I gave a triumphant scream, like a savage who has found an empty beer can. Rubbish-bin meant civilisation. And rubbish-bin in the forest meant Germanic civilisation at that! So I was still in Liechtenstein. Or in Switzerland? Or in Austria? Or, who knows, may be, even in Germany? . . . In any case, as long as it was not Russia, I was safe.

Ten metres away from the rubbish-bin, I stumbled across a short concrete post with two letters, 'FL', on it, and next to the post there was a large German sign, where the only familiar word was '*verboten*' – 'forbidden'. Staring at this forbidding sign I felt very much like a wandering knight from a Russian fairy tale who once came upon a heavy moss-covered boulder lying at the cross-section of three forest roads. 'Go right – lose your horse; go left – lose your life; go straight – lose both,' was carved on the stone. Of course, after some hesitation, the brave knight went for the last, and the least promising option, only to bump into a three-headed, flame-spitting dragon round the corner. I made a similar choice, not out of bravery though, but simply guided by the old Russian custom – to go where your eyes look. No longer hoping to find the Russian Monument or even *borscht*, I went forward nevertheless.

The re-emerged path soon brought me to the edge of a cliff. I looked down: a tiny caterpillar of a train was chugging away across the valley towards a town with lots of high-rise apartment blocks and smoking factory chimneys. Once again, I was reminded of the model Alpine railway I saw in Tasmania. What town could this be? It was too large for Schellenberg and even for Vaduz . . .

I started heading down into the valley where a country pub, Gasthaus Auf der Egg, nestled. I was dying for a drink.

It was Sunday afternoon and the pub was full of patrons, mainly families, all drinking beer and eating . . . Wait . . . No, this couldn't be true . . . They were all eating enormous *Wiener schnitzels* that were larger than plates, in fact, the area of some of them was almost equal to that of Liechtenstein! I froze and choked on my beer: *Wiener schnitzels* of this size could be found only in one country, and that country was not Liechtenstein!

I looked up from my glass and saw the portrait of Federal Chancellor Franz Vranitzky on the wall. The barman was pouring cider into thick tall glasses . . . Yes, there was no doubt about that: trudging through the forest, without realising it, I had *illegally* crossed the border into Austria! Letters 'FL' on the post in the forest stood for 'Furstentum Liechtenstein' (principality of Liechtenstein).

Awesome visions from my Soviet past came rushing at me. Ominous words like 'extradition', 'deportation' and '*persona non grata*' started echoing in my brain. With alarm I remembered that I had left my brand-new Australian passport in my hotel in Vaduz. And it didn't have an Austrian visa anyway . . .

* * *

Like any former Soviet citizen, I had a deep-rooted fear of borders. The very word *zagranitsa* (abroad) had a sinister connotation in the USSR. 'Abroad' was that mysterious part of the world where devious whisky-drinking and golf-playing capitalists were constantly plotting something against the Soviet Union – pok-pok . . . plot-plot . . . It was a decadent and pornography-ridden place from where spies would try to infiltrate our glorious country, only to be stopped and arrested by our vigilant heroic frontier guards with their equally heroic dogs.

We were fed with such stories at school.

Trips abroad were taboo for ordinary people, the privilege of the most ideologically sound bureaucrats and foreign correspondents with their unchanging mantra: 'The sun is shining above London (New York, Rome), but the mood of ordinary Londoners (New-Yorkers, Romans) is gloomy.'

I shall never forget my first border crossing, the moment our train rattled across the bridge over the Yuzhniy Bug River, with carefree stateless ducks floating on its gleaming surface.

Nor shall I forget my first encounter with the Berlin Wall, the Mother of All Borders, if we use Saddam Hussein's terminology. Pimpled East German frontier guards with ladders, screw-drivers and snarling dogs on leashes boarded our train at Berlin Friedrichstrasse and started unscrewing everything which could be unscrewed in our coach. They were staring at our faces, comparing them with our passport photos with such cold mistrust that I started having serious doubts as to whether it was indeed me fidgeting nervously under the border guard's unblinking stare . . .

Or how can I ever forget my first return trip from the West, when in Brest a Soviet customs officer asked: 'Are you bringing back Bibles and pornography?'

Even now, with a 'normal' Western passport in my pocket, I find it hard to get used to being waved through immigration in Western airports. I am scared that they might forget to put some important stamp in my passport and this will mean trouble. I cannot help lingering in front of an immigration officer with a sycophantic look on my face.

Old habits die hard. Old fears die even harder.

In prehistoric times, people lived happily without borders. The first frontier was probably triggered by jealousy and greed, by sheer reluctance to share a bit of fertile land or game-rich hunting ground with a neighbour. Stone hedges appeared. Doors, fences and concrete walls followed. Today the world is entangled with barbed wire, crisscrossed with patches of ploughed 'neutral' land and no-go areas. True, some have come down, but many more have been erected inside the former Communist bloc countries.

Nothing can stop a human being in his quest for freedom. The little memorial cemetery near the Brandenburg Gate in Berlin, next to the now-defunct Berlin Wall, is the best proof. Eleven-year-old Brigitte Frauendorf and eighty-year-old Olga Stegler are among those who were killed by the East German border guards simply because they wanted to live in a free world. 'Here the free world ends, and the domination of the Kremlin starts', this bitter inscription on the house near Checkpoint Charlie in Berlin never failed to send shivers down my spine.

People seeking freedom are desperate, ingenious and foolhardy. They cross roaring oceans in flimsy boats, they climb fences and swim across rivers under the crossfire of machine-guns, they ram walls with trucks or fly over them in home-made balloons.

In Australia I looked into the amazing feat of Yuri Beigman, the former Soviet Army captain who, cornered by the KGB, had to flee the Soviet Union illegally in October 1990. In eleven months he made it to Australia via a dozen countries – without one visa or valid passport. I am far from glorifying him, but he had no choice. This shows how irrelevant and conventional all borders and walls are. Force breeds counterforce; the more barriers on the way to freedom, the harder people try to negotiate them. Forbidden fruit is always the most coveted.

I am still hopeful that the day will come when all borders are scrapped, and the world will immediately become a much happier place to live . . .

* * *

Immersed in reverie, I didn't immediately realise that the man sitting next to me at the table had been talking to me for a while in English, starting and ending his every sentence with 'sir'. He was a tall, stoopy Austrian with a sunburnt face and the rough hands of a peasant, and he was drunk. Burping and blowing his nose amicably every now and then, he was telling me about his stint as a fisherman in Alaska. 'Sir, if you look over there, you will see a postcard of Alaska above the bar, sir . . .' His wife was sitting next to him, sipping cider, with a little girl on her lap. Plastic hearing aids stuck out of the child's ears. 'Sir, this is my granddaughter, she has a problem, sir,' the fisherman said, pointing at her ears. At this point, his wife started crying.

I felt almost at home sitting there, under an old-fashioned red lampshade (just like the one at my grandparents' flat in Kharkov many years ago), surrounded by these nice and modest people with their own joys and tragedies.

'Sir, good-bye, sir!' The fisherman stood up unsteadily and slowly stumbled out of the pub. His wife and his deaf granddaughter followed him.

And I remembered the precariousness of my situation: here I was, illegally sitting in an Austrian pub having illegally crossed the Liechtenstein border . . . Without finishing my beer, I hastily paid my bill (luckily they accepted Swiss Francs as well as Austrian Schillings) and, having asked for the shortest way to the border (in a whisper, so as not to arouse suspicion), I started along the highway towards Liechtenstein. The border, according to the constantly blushing barmaid in a checked apron, who was very pleased to practise her English with a whispering foreigner, was just a mile away.

The road went up the hill, and I could almost hear the pounding steps of angry Austrian policemen behind my back. In the distance, I could see the tiny hut of a border post and was bracing myself for a painful showdown with the frontier guards.

A huge lock hung on the door of the empty border post. I looked inside, but was able to discern only a radio, a reading lamp and a poster with the photographs of *TERRORISTEN* on the wall. I made sure my photograph was not yet among them (just to be on the safe side, you know), and only then noticed a sign above the locked door:

The frontier post is open daily from 8 a.m. to 8 p.m. except for holidays and weekends

Remembering it was Sunday, I gave a deep sigh of relief and briskly walked across the border into Liechtenstein.

No one was there to stop me.

I stumbled upon the Russian Monument back in Schellenberg. It was hidden behind the still functioning Zum Lowen Inn, where I feasted upon wonderful *kas-knopeli* (cheese dumplings). Exactly as the Baron said, it was a simple stone obelisk with a long inscription in German. As to Borscht, it turned out to be a thoroughly unimpressive small 'reservoir' near the old Schellenberg pump station. Its name might have indeed been jokingly prompted by the Russians.

While in Liechtenstein, I kept pondering over the ongoing mystery of Robert Maxwell's trusts. Due to its status as one of the world's safest tax havens, Liechtenstein is a very lucrative place to register a company, or just to keep money in.

About 90,000 'letterbox companies' (that is, companies existing on paper only) are registered in Liechtenstein — three companies for each resident. Despite high registration fees (one of Liechtenstein's main sources of income), foreign-owned companies registered in Leichtenstein pay only 0.1 per cent tax on their assets.

The banks in Vaduz look deceptively small, quiet and inconspicuous from the outside, and only God (and, maybe Maxwell) knows how many secrets are hidden in their dark, air-conditioned vaults. With only one diplomatic representation in Switzerland, Liechtenstein is practically immune from the pressure of foreign fiscal authorities, and any breach of professional discretion in financial and tax matters is punishable there.

Each letterbox company is required to have a Liechtenstein citizen on its board, but the real owners' names remain in the dark. If the police want to find out who the owner of this or that company is, they have to make an official request to the High Court and prove that it is in the public interest that they be given this information. It takes months and sometimes years for the High Court to make a decision on whether to reveal the names or not. In the case of Ferdinand Marcos, the former President of the Phillipines, it took the High Court five years to authorise the disclosure of his name. Maxwell (as well as Marcos) had dozens of companies registered in Liechtenstein. Now you can understand why his millions are so hard, if not impossible, to trace.

After Captain Bob went for his record-breaking dive from the deck of his yacht, there was a lot of speculation about what exactly happened: was it suicide, murder or an accident? I've got my own version of the event.

Robert Maxwell was the largest single investor in Liechtenstein. When Prince Hans Adam II was visiting Britain in spring 1990, he went to see Maxwell at Maxwell House, his London headquarters, to thank him for his contributions to the principality's well-being. In fact, many of his bank accounts in Liechtenstein were opened on behalf of the KGB and the Soviet Communist Party. 'Robert Maxwell set up Liechtenstein bank accounts for Soviet KGB and Communist Party officials throughout the 1980s, taking a commission for himself,' reported the *Guardian* on 18 June, 1992.

Maxwell had a longstanding love affair with the Soviet officialdom. A multi-millionaire and a press baron, he was a champagne socialist who fraternised with all Soviet leaders, from Brezhnev to Gorbachev. He was also friendly with the head of the KGB, Yuri Andropov, and his greatest publishing success, Pergamon Press, specialising in scientific books and Soviet leaders' memoirs, was used to launder the KGB money. In his book *The Unknown Maxwell*, Nicholas Davies, one of Captain Bob's closes confidants, argues that Maxwell was not a KGB spy, but rather a KGB 'banker'.

Significantly, Maxwell died several weeks before the Soviet Union ceased to exist. The KGB suddenly needed all their money to try to keep themselves afloat. They must have contacted Maxwell demanding access to his (or rather their) accounts in Liechtenstein, and Maxwell. who was virtually broke by that time, must have denied it to them. The KGB were running out of time. They tried to reason with Maxwell, to cajole him (he had lots of suspiciously secretive meetings with strange people shortly before his death), then they started threatening. And there were no better masters of threats in the whole world (I know this from first-hand experience). They must have promised Maxwell such exquisite torture and suffering, if he didn't cough up, that drowning seemed bliss in comparison. This, and only this, I am sure, could persuade this robust, boisterous and life-loving character to jump overboard, after having a couple of stiff drinks 'for courage'.

My closest 'encounter' with Maxwell was in 1990, when I was sitting in Maxwell House in the City of London, discussing a book idea with an editor of one of Maxwell's publishing companies. Suddenly, from behind the window we heard a whirring sound, which was getting louder and louder and soon grew into a thunderous rattle. 'The boss,' the editor commented. I looked out and saw a helicopter landing on the roof of the building, straight above our heads. 'He is certainly a high-flier,' I thought then.

Well, no matter how high Maxwell used to fly, his final landing was nothing more than a big splash . . .

Not an admirer of Maxwell's dodgy personality, I was nevertheless interested to try and find out what had happened to his Liechtenstein funds, still unaccounted for. My contact at the principality's government office suggested I should see Rainer Kindle, an officer in the money frauds department of the Liechtenstein *Landespolizei* (police) who had investigated the Maxwell affair and might have some clues.

The country's only police station in the centre of Vaduz was a modern stone-and-concrete structure with a small prison wing, surrounded by a neat stone wall without a trace of barbed wire. Rainer

Kindle turned out to be a cheerful round-faced man in civilian clothes. Alone in the large police station that early Tuesday afternoon, he kept laughing throughout our conversation. Whenever he was not laughing, he was giggling or cackling. Before answering my questions about Maxwell, he offered me a tour of the building.

'Where are the rest of the policemen?' I asked him as we were going from one empty room to another.

'They are having a coffee break!' he laughed. 'There is not much for them to do here, you see. We are a landscape place, not like New York or London. The policeman's main duty in Liechtenstein is to make sure the shops observe their opening and closing hours, ha-ha . . .'

'What was the last crime committed this year in Liechtenstein?'

On hearing this question, Mr Kindle burst into such a long paroxysm of laughter that I started to have worries about his sanity.

'Ha-ha-ha! Ho-ho-ho! The year is still very young!'

In the short intervals between gusts of laughter, he informed me that the last murder in Liechtenstein was committed in 1989, and that the victim was . . . the ex-chief of the local police CID, who was on the trail of some German extortionists (telling me this story, Mr Kindle was rocking with laughter – just like my son when watching *The Adventures of Mr Bean*).

'And last year there was a bank robbery in Balzers,' he went on proudly.

'Did you catch the robber?'

'Not yet, ha-ha-ha!'

The police station was as stuffed with electronic equipment as Hamley's is with toys. Blank computer screens blinked at us from empty desks.

'Each police officer has his own computer,' boasted Mr Kindle.

We passed through a wonderfully equipped (and empty) forensic laboratory and found ourselves in a thirty metre-long computerised shooting gallery.

'Here we practise shooting robbers,' said my guide and pointed at countless bullet holes on the ceiling. This time his laughter, echoing in the gallery walls, was so loud that a couple of flat plywood targets fell down under its impact, as if bullet-ridden (which they weren't).

I thought I knew what the world's best sinecure was: to be one of the fifty-five Liechtenstein policemen (don't hurry to accuse me of political incorrectness: women are not accepted into the country's police corps). But I was wrong.

To get to the prison, we had to pass through a control room, where a duty officer was sitting among dozens of computers, watching a cycling race on television, oblivious of the world around him. I was sure that if a tank rolled into the room, he wouldn't stir an eyelid. Everything was in place at the Liechtenstein police headquarters. There were only a couple of little things missing: criminals and policemen.

The prison block was a set of bright, sun-lit rooms with breathtaking views of the Alps from the windows. Instead of iron bars, the windows were supplied with neat electric curtains that could be drawn at the push of a button. There were paintings on the walls. 'According to our government regulations, we have to spend one per cent of the prison budget on works of art,' explained Mr Kindle.

The women's block, painted red, was totally empty. Tame and law-abiding, the Liechtenstein women, who were the last in Europe to get their right to vote (narrowly approved by the all-male referendum in 1984), were unlikely law-breakers. The same could probably be said about the men: among thirteen inmates of the male block there was not a single Liecthensteiner. The prisoners were all illegal entrants from Albania and former Yugoslavia. They were all well-dressed and almost as cheerful as Mr Kindle. No wonder: their meals were delivered to them thrice a day from the restaurant of the nearby Liechtenstein Hotel, by a van with the words 'Gourmet Service' on its sides! On top of all this, the prisoners were getting paid for each day of their detention.

Now I know for sure what the world's biggest sinecure is: being a prisoner in Liechtenstein. When I am old and unable to hold a pen any longer, I'll come to Liechtenstein, steal a seal from the woman at the Postage Stamps Museum (or something else) and spend the rest of my days eating gourmet food and admiring the Alps from the comfort of my Liechtenstein prison cell.

I was stunned when Mr Kindle told me with a cackle that three inmates tried to escape from this penitentiary heaven a couple of years ago. What could I say? There are lots of lunatics around, even in Liechtenstein . . .

The smile vanished from Mr Kindle's jovial face the moment I asked him about Maxwell's millions.

'I have nothing to say. I have sent all the documents to London,' he said sternly. 'To start with, Maxwell's money never came to Liechtenstein. From reading some British newspapers, you'd think that we provide cover-up for fraudsters. Nothing could be further from reality. In fact, it is harder to launder money here than in Britain, but it is always easier to blame a small country than to look at your own doorstep.'

He sounded defensive, despite the fact that I personally hadn't accused him of anything. One thing I realised from his angry diatribe was that my modest attempt to uncover the secret of Maxwell's millions in Liechtenstein was bound to fail.

As we parted Mr Kindle, back to his normal facetious self, presented me with the pamphlet: 'Establishment and Management of Companies in the Principality of Liechtenstein' – a gripping title. Maybe this ever-smiling policeman was hoping that one day I would establish the 90,0001st letterbox company in Liechtenstein and then commit a fraud that he would be assigned to investigate.

Perhaps I will . . . Only let me earn my first million honestly . . .

Liechtenstein is often called 'a mini-industrial giant'. Its 1,600 industrial enterprises specialise in precision engineering, metal finishing, textile and ceramic industries. The country's main employer is Ivoclar, the world's biggest manufacturer of false teeth. The headquarters of the company are in Schaan, Liechtenstein's largest 'metropolis' of 5,000 people, about ten minutes walk from Vaduz. I wanted to visit Ivoclar, since dentistry had always been a sore point with me, as with most of my 290 million former compatriots.

To start with, I haven't got many teeth left. One London dentist fainted after a quick glimpse of my mouth cavity, which resembles a railway junction – plenty of gaping tunnels, cavities and iron bridges crisscrossing at different levels (the dentist referred to them as 'Lenin bridges' when he regained his senses). The reason for this is simple: the most popular method of dental treatment in the Soviet Union was tooth extraction. My extracted teeth are scattered all over the former Soviet Empire, since, as we all know, teeth have a nasty habit of causing you pain as soon as you hit the road. I had them extracted with pliers (with no anaesthetic), knocked out with a hammer and a chisel and pulled out with bare (and not very clean) hands.

I remember waking up in excrutiating pain at my small summer dacha outside Moscow one night. The only way to bear that pain was to keep my mouth full of ice-cold water from the well. When the water warmed up a bit, the pain would return, and I had to have a thermos handy to keep replenishing my mouth water supplies.

With water in my mouth and a thermos in my hand, I took the last shuttle train to Moscow in the middle of the night. I was heading for Moscow's only emergency dental clinic, open twenty-four hours a day.

Several hundred of my fellow-sufferers, with swollen cheeks and doomed expressions on their distorted faces, were queueing and moaning outside – a fine illustration of the old Russian proverb: 'Until thunder strikes, a Russian peasant won't cross himself.' The surgeons, all bulky grinning men, looked like market butchers at the end of a long trading day: their gowns were heavily splashed with blood, and countless removed teeth, scattered on the floor, crunched under their feet. It was Dante's, sorry dentists, ninth circle of hell reincarnated.

I am sure the surgeons were some kind of dental perverts and sadists, since they thoroughly enjoyed torturing you. They were getting kicks from it, I can tell you. When my turn came, one of the butchers, without any hesitation, shoved a pair of dirty, saliva-covered forceps into my mouth and pulled for all he was worth. A bright lightning of pain, starting somewhere in the depths of my brain, shattered my whole body. 'Here we go!' the surgeon mumbled with almost orgiastic delight. He was holding my former tooth in his forceps.

On the train back to my dacha, I felt somewhat better: the surgeon took pity on me and did use a bit of hard-to-get anaesthetic. Knackered after the sleepless night, I started nodding off. Soon pain returned, and I was climbing the walls again, only there was no more cold water left. It turned out that the surgeon had pulled out a wrong (and perfectly healthy) tooth by mistake . . .

Michael Both, the public relations manager of Ivoclar, did not look like a butcher. He was wearing a smart Italian suit and an impeccably white shirt, without a single spot of blood or even saliva on it. He showed me around the company building which was modern, bright and sterilized. In the corridors, false teeth of all imaginable shapes and sizes – from tiny baby's milk-teeth to Dracula's fangs – were displayed in special glass containers.

'Each year we produce forty million high-quality aesthetic teeth which we export to more than a hundred countries worldwide,' Mr Both was saying. 'The teeth come in sixteen different colours . . .'

'Sixteen colours?' I repeated in disbelief.

'Yes!' smiled Mr Both, revealing a set of perfect (Ivoclar-made?) teeth. 'You see, human teeth are not necessarily snow-white ('Mine are definitely not,' I thought). It's only Americans who like snow-white teeth these days. Most people prefer diffent shades of colour . . .' (Like light-brown, dark-brown and pitch-black, in my case, I wanted to say, but thought better of it: I was ashamed of my teeth, these little fragments of the rotten Soviet empire I carry in my mouth, and I didn't feel like exposing them by opening my mouth too often.)

He went on to explain that Ivoclar employed 720 people, half of whom lived in neighbouring Austria and Switzerland, and had branches in many countries of the world, including Australia. I tried to visualise all those millions of people around the globe who carry little ceramic pieces of Liechtenstein in their mouths.

Unfortunately, I was not one of them.

'Goodbye!' I said to Mr Both through my remaining clenched teeth.

On my last day in Liechtenstein I managed to get an appointment with Prince Hans Adam II, the ruling monarch.

It took me one hour to walk up the hill to the Vaduz castle where the Prince lives and works. I was climbing from grass-roots level to the peak of power. Soon I was puffing and blowing in my suit and tie, and had to stop every now and then to regain my breath. This gave me time to read the signposts with information on Liechtenstein and the royal family, which were stuck all over the mountain path, probably aimed at inexperienced climbers like myself. From them I learnt that Prince Hans Adam II was born in 1945; educated in Vienna, London and Switzerland; that he was married to Countess Mary Kinsky von Wchinitz und Tettau; that he had four children, the youngest of whom, Princess Tatjana, was born in 1973.

I already knew that Liechtenstein was Europe's last fully functioning constitutional monarchy. In plain words, this meant that the Prince and people were supposed to rule the country together.

The Prince in Liechtenstein is at the top of the state pyramid. He represents the state and sanctions all the laws. His consent is necessary before any law can be implemented, although so far there have been very few cases when he actually refused to give it. The Prince can pardon and issue decrees in an emergency. He appoints the members of the government and judges and convenes the Diet (parliament) consisting of twenty-five deputies and representing two main political parties – the Reds and the Blacks. So, as you see, the expression 'to be on a diet' can be totally devoid of culinary connotation in Liechtenstein. The two political parties, in coalition since 1938, despite differences in colour, share the common motto 'Faith in God, Prince and Fatherland'.

Decisions on many matters in Liechtenstein are taken with the help of referendums, announced by the Prince. In the 1992 referendum, the majority of Liechtensteiners voted in favour of joining the European

Economic Area (EEA), although neighbouring Switzerland, with which the principality is closely associated, voted against — a sign of real political integrity.

A piece of advice to those wishing to get Liechtenstein citizenship: don't bother, it is a cumbersome procedure. First of all, a referendum must be held in the village (or town) where the applicant lives. If the decision is positive, the matter is taken up for vote by the Diet, and then (again, if the Diet says yes) it has to be confirmed by the Prince. Unsurprisingly thirty-six per cent of the country's population are foreign passport holders.

In September 1993, in an extraordinary demonstration of the monarch's power, Hans Adam II flexed his muscle and made headlines worldwide by peremptorily dissolving the parliament, declaring general elections and rejecting the no-confidence vote against the Prime Minister Markus Buchel — an event normally associated with the seventeeth century, not the late twentieth. Such was the person I was about to meet.

At the government information office, the day before, I was solemnly informed that the correct form of address for the Prince was 'Your Serene Highness'. I was not on very good terms with protocol, or with royalty in general, I have to confess.

Once, in Australia, I was covering the visit of the British royal couple for my newspaper. Before being introduced to the Queen and the Duke of Edinburgh at the press reception, I spent several hours studying *Debrett's Book of Etiquette* in my Sydney hotel room.

'If the royal hand is extended, take it lightly and briefly, at the same time executing a brief bob with the weight on the front foot, or a bow from the neck (not from the waist).' Standing in front of a mirror and looking at the book out of the corner of my eye, I tried to follow it to the letter — shaking an imaginary hand and simultaneously executing a bob. The immediate result was that I dropped the book and collapsed on to the floor.

I also learnt that I had to be careful to address the Queen as 'Your Majesty' in the first instance and as 'ma'am' ('pronouced like am, not arm' – thanks, Debrett) on subsequent occasions (if any), and the Duke as 'Your Royal Highness' and 'sir'. I was slightly puzzled, though, as to how to address other listed members of the royal party, such as the Queen's lady-in-waiting, private secretary to the Queen, to say nothing of lady clerk to the private secretary to the Queen. And how on earth should I address the Queen's hairdresser? Your Royal Hairness?

Naturally, I did it wrong. After hours of bruising rehearsals, I ended up addressing the Queen as 'Your Royal Highness' (at least it was not 'hairness', thank God) and her husband as 'Your Majesty'. To my great relief, the royal couple themselves didn't seem to mind, or more likely they simply didn't notice my awful blunder. They must have had other, more pressing, things to worry about.

Since then I have had several other chances to meet the Queen and the Duke and even to have short off-the-record conversations with them, but I could never fully overcome my initial awkwardness.

Ranks, titles of nobility and other matters of protocol were largely ignored during my hour-long audience with Prince Hans Adam II. His office inside the castle was unexpectedly modest and totally unguarded. A beautiful wooden and leather lectern stood in a corner.

A sprightly smiling man strode in. We shook hands, and I immediately felt at ease. The Prince had a warm disarming smile. On his wrist he was wearing a simple electronic watch.

'Our country is indeed a happy one,' he said in impeccable English with a slight German accent. 'We've got hundred per cent literacy, high living standards and practically no crime. There are problems, of course. In the last couple of years unemployment has grown from 0.1 per cent to 0.7 per cent.'

I made some hasty calculations on a piece of paper: 0.1 per cent of Liechtenstein's population is thirty people.

'Our world has become much smaller of late, and we all live in a global village, where people are keen to find their roots, their own community,' continued the Prince. 'On the other hand, the world has become more vulnerable: a major conflict in any part of the planet now means war in your own backyard. Small countries these days can flourish only in an atmosphere of peace and trade. That's why membership of the EEA is so important for us: we haven't got a domestic market. The influence of the state on business in Liechtenstein is very small. We strongly believe in free enterprise. We also work very hard, having the longest working week in Europe. The working day here, and my working day too, starts at eight a.m. There is no lunchbreak culture . . .'

Having spent several years as a London banker in his youth, the Prince certainly knew what he was talking about. Indeed, it is not unusual in Liechtenstein to fix business appointments for one or two p.m. – a sacrilege by British standards.

'What else makes Liechtenstein tick? We have strong democracy, where people can really influence their own future. Taxes are low. Even after the war, when the state had little revenue, we preferred to lower taxes instead of increasing them, to let our businesses survive. The more you increase taxes – the less people buy. So, I think, we have found quite a good balance for our mini-state. Our slogan is "stability through monarchy", and the fact that we are so small makes us nearer to the people.

'Our monarchy works because it has much to do with the family. We try to promote family values and live a normal family life without getting too much into the public eye. I try to keep my family out of the press, although we are not inaccessible. All my children went to an ordinary school in Vaduz, and I walk around the town unguarded.'

Early in the morning one can see a tall sinewy man jogging alone in the mountains near Vaduz castle. 'It's hard to find bodyguards who would be fit enough to accompany me,' joked Prince Hans Adam II. As the most hard-working man in this tiny hard-working country, he has to keep fit.

2.   San Marino

The middle-aged orator was vigorous and vociferous. From a small podium next to a stationary Toyota van, with a red hammer-and-sickle flag on the roof, he was spurting out a passionate diatribe about the imminent triumph of Communism over the planet. His audience consisted of a couple of self-important sleepy cats on the porch of a nearby house and myself looking down at the scene from a hotel balcony.

It was late afternoon in May 1692 in the republic of San Marino.

Don't worry: I haven't gone crazy. And the date is not a misprint. In San Marino the calendar officially begins in 301AD, the year of the country's foundation.

It was the eve of the general elections, and the orator spoke for the Rifondazione Communista Sammarinese, the organisation with the not too original a motto: 'Fatherland, Labour, Communism' (I would add one more word, 'Tyranny'). There was a considerable historical irony in the fact that Communists were now trying to recruit supporters in one of the world's tiniest states above the clouds and, even so, there was no one who would listen to them (apart from the cats, who always struck me as fairly apolitical creatures).

My trip to San Marino, Europe's smallest and oldest republic, started in Venice, where I had to attend the General Assembly of the International Press Institute (IPI), of which I am a member. IPI, uniting leading editors and journalists from more than one hundred countries of the world, is a human rights organisation, yet its annual gatherings are rather reminiscent of a gourmet society meeting: every single night we had to attend plush receptions at different Venetian palaces — complete with exquisite food, local dignitaries and live baroque music. The walls of the palaces were eaten by rot that seemed to affect everything in Venice. Everything but our appetites . . .

It is banal to fall in love with Venice. It's even more banal *not* to fall in love with it. For me Venice is an ageing but still graceful woman suffering from insomnia and dragging restlessly around the house in her loose-fitting slippers in the night — soft splashes of water against the stones are like the shuffle of slippers against the floor.

Yes, Venice is geriatric and slowly dying. This 800-year-old town-sized toy was never intended to last so long. The spice-trading Venetian merchants lived by the principle 'after us — the deluge', and succeeded in translating it into reality (or rather into unreality, since Venice is a thoroughly unreal place). They built this baroque equivalent of Disneyland for their own delight, without giving much thought to the future. Its underwater supports, made of Siberian cedar, are no longer able to withstand the pressure of time. The walls of the palaces on the banks of the Grand Canal are covered with cracks and moss. Priceless paintings inside are being slowly but surely destroyed by moisture. Fastidious American tourists are right: Venice smells. Who wouldn't after 800 years?

And yet Venice is like no other place in the world. At sunset, when the water gleams with a magic translucent light of its own, as if slowly, almost reluctantly, discharging the sunlight it has accumulated during the day; when blinds fall like thick black eyelids on the gaping eye-sockets of tired old houses; when the gentle tolling of distant church bells mingles with the soft sound of lovers' kisses – there suddenly comes a whiff of a fresh sea breeze, a reminder of the days when Venice signified ships and trade routes to be explored.

The walls of Venice are also being eaten by the eyes of tourists, mainly couples, who have come here in search of romance. Venice is romance guaranteed. No one knows how many families have been ruined and how many love affairs moulded by this tender sea breeze, full of lust and libido. To come to Venice as a loner is a torture. The place is so overwhelmingly romantic that you feel an irresistible urge to share it with the one you love.

What is happening behind these tightly shut blinds, which make Venetian houses look lifeless and aloof after dark? Everyday life in Venice is an agony, and some 20,000 to 30,000 native Venetians leave their city every year in search of a more mundane existence. The city's sewage system is in a deplorable state. Antediluvian rubbish-collecting boats cannot cope with the tons of waste which floats in the canals like tiny archipelagoes of empty Coke cans, potato peelings, shreds of paper and other refuse of our slovenly civilisation.

One of the main reasons for the exodus is that in Venice one can't own a car. A carless Italian is like a beerless German, a micro-computerless American, or a Nikonless Japanese. True, some young Venetian males do try to impress their dark-eyed girlfriends by tearing along the canals in their motorboats at breakneck speed, with a roaring ghetto blaster astern. But even this popular sort of local courting is growing more and more difficult with the tightening of water-traffic regulations. After a careless tourist drowned in the Grand Canal a couple of years ago when her gondola was overturned by a wave raised by a passing motorboat, the Venetian police clamped down on reckless drivers, or rather, sailors. Speed limits were introduced. Special parking harbours were established. The first boat parking tickets were issued. Life is tough – that's why the Venetians are leaving. And no town, not even Venice, can survive without locals.

Venice has its morning and afternoon rush-hours, with flotillas of boats chugging up and down the Grand Canal: taxi boats, fruit-and-vegetable boats, fire boats, bread delivery boats, even funeral boats. One rainy Venetian morning, after several days of intensive IPI partying, I found myself with my suitcase on board an elderly *vaporetto* (commuter steam-boat) on the way to the *ferrovia* (railway station). The surface of the Grand Canal was covered with traces of raindrops and looked like a heavily pock-marked face.

I was to take a train to the Italian sea resort of Rimini, then a bus to San Marino.

The train was full of noisy, chain-smoking Italians. Unlike the English train with its stiff upper berth, this one was a rolling chatterbox and felt like an ongoing party on wheels.

The journey took almost four hours, and I had plenty of time to study my flamboyant travel companions. To be frank, I was mainly gaping at the women, who were all stunning. And those who were not stunning were beautiful. An ugly, or even a plain-looking Italian female is a rarity, a paradox, a four-angled triangle. They look at you as if they give you a rouble, as an old Russian saying goes. With hyperinflation rife in Russia, though, one should paraphrase this saying into 'they look at you as if they give you 4,100 roubles, or one US dollar, according to the existing exchange rate.' After half an hour of gaping, I felt like a rouble millionaire.

Reluctantly, I tore my gaze from the female passengers and started looking through my notes – the result of painstaking, yet not very fruitful, research in the libraries of London, which seemed to have much more stuff on the obscure East Carribean nation of Saint Vincent and the Grenadines or on the no-less-obscure African country of São Tomé e Príncipe than on the European mini-state of San Marino.

San Marino, this pocket handkerchief of a European republic with an area of sixty-two square kilometres and a population of 23,000, was founded in the year 301 by a stonecutter from Dalmatia named Marinus, who was later canonised and gave his name to the country. Marinus ended up in the Appenines fleeing the wrath of the Roman Emperor Diocletian and his no-nonsense legions.

Another, and more colourful, hypothesis has it that Marinus was driven up the hills by the persistence of an exalted and devil-possessed 'evil woman', who wanted the sinewy hard-working stonecutter to marry her. As a future saint, Marinus certainly couldn't get married so he escaped to Mount Titano, where he led a holy life, overcoming every temptation the devil put in his way. One year later, shepherds discovered his hiding place and spread the news. The tireless 'evil woman', whose name history hasn't preserved, found him soon afterwards. As the ancient chronicle puts it, 'at the sight of her, Marino, who was working in his small kitchen garden, shut himself in a cave on his cliff. After six days of prayer and fasting he finally came out and exorcised the evil spirit which possessed the woman. She then returned to Rimini where she endeavoured to extol the Saint's virtues and glory.'

Whether this medieval fatal attraction story was true or not, in May 1993 the republic of San Marino was enjoying its 1,692nd year of independent existence. For all these long years it had been occupied only twice, and for just a few months at a time: in 1503 by Caesar Borgia, and in 1739 by Cardinal Guilio Alberoni. Even the jingoistic Emperor Napoleon Bonaparte, rather than invading San Marino like any other country, for some unknown reason offered it 'gifts and friendship' and declared: 'We must preserve San Marino as an example of Liberty.'

In 1849 Giuseppe Garibaldi, surrounded by three enemy armies after the fall of the Roman republic, found safety here with the remnants of his legion and his pregnant girlfriend and deputy commander, Anita, who – scandalously – wore trousers. (Women always seemed to play an important role in Italian history – no wonder, being so beautiful . . .) General Garibaldi was so much taken with the peaceful atmosphere of San Marino that he decided to lay down his arms and disband his legion there.

It was then that the Papal Government in Rome urged the Duke of Tuscany to invade this 'den of liberals', but the clever Duke thought better of it.

During the Second World War, the republic opened its borders to more than 100,000 refugees from the Nazi-occupied countries. For that it was duly rewarded by the Allies who dropped 243 heavy bombs on San Marino, killing sixty-three and wounding over a hundred innocent people on 26 June, 1944. This bombing was totally unjustified, since there were neither German troops nor arms depots on San Marino's territory, and its borders had been marked with huge white crosses, clearly visible from the sky. The Allies probably hurried to write the incident off as an example of 'collateral damage' or 'friendly fire', but for the peaceful people of San Marino, where the last recorded incident of violence occurred in the eighteenth century when a border patrolman shot himself in the foot when frightened by a chicken, this was the greatest disaster in their whole history.

I was somewhat puzzled to discover that, in a striking contrast to Liechtenstein, modern San Marino, this haven of peace and liberty, had three separate voluntary armies – the Territorial Army, the Fortification Guards and the Noble Guards, not to mention its traditional Crossbowmen Corps. Spared the never-ending turmoil of neighbouring Italy, San Marino, with its zero crime rate and one prison of just four cells (from where the last and only prisoner escaped in 1986), nevertheless boasted of two police forces – the *gendarmerie* and the civil police.

The republic's ruling hierarchy, modestly calling itself 'Serenissima' (Most Serene), seems cumbersome to the point of madness. It is made up of six bodies: the Arengo, the Grand and General Council (another modest name), the Captains Regent, the Council of the Twelve, the Sindaci (high officials) and the State Congress.

The Arengo, or the assembly of the heads of families, used to be the country's parliament. Nowadays it has only one (and pretty vague) function – the right of petition, whatever that means. The sixty-seat-strong Grand and General Council, San Marino's highest legislative body, nominates two Captains Regent who jointly rule for six months and then get re-elected (what if they disagree on a certain matter, I wonder). Executive power is wielded by the State Congress, composed of three secretaries and seven ministers, among them the minister for culture and universities, even though there is not a single university in the country.

The Council of Twelve's main role is 'to authorise the sale and transfer of dowry possessions by the wife' – a very important matter. As to the mysterious Sindaci, it is just the body of government inspectors representing the state.

There is also the Castle Board, presided over by the Captain of the Castles and comprising delegates of San Marino's nine districts (castles). The structure of the judiciary system is no less complicated. And all this for just 23,000 people!

It became clear to me why twenty-five per cent of San Marino's workforce were employed in 'public administration', and I realised suddenly that I was heading for Europe's smallest pimple of a state that has developed into the world's largest boil of a bureaucratic power. The reason for that was simple: Communists and pro-Communist 'socialists' had been in power in San Marino throughout most of the post-war period. Communism and bureaucracy go together like two legs of one and the same pair of trousers. Bureacracy in its turn implies lack of efficiency. And plain stupidity too.

I felt it on my very first contact with San Marino. The leaflet, published by the Sanmarinese State Tourist office, that I picked up at Rimini station while waiting for a bus (which was late), helpfully listed winter, summer, spring and autumn under the headline 'Suitable times of the year for holidays and excursions in San Marino'. It also had a separate section 'Frontier Formalities' with only one sentence in it: 'There are no frontier formalities.' Nice and simple!

When, finally, I boarded the long-awaited bus, bound for La Citta de San Marino, and handed my ticket over to a gregarious young driver, he collected it and gave me . . . another ticket. Having hardly started

63

my journey, I had already wasted two pieces of paper. Welcome to San Marino!

The bus itself was a far cry from a Liechtenstein yellow post bus: it was as battered and dishevelled as an old dog-eared paperback. The passengers and the driver seemed to know each other well. They laughed, screamed and chattered in exalted high-pitched voices. They were like relatives trying to settle some age-long family dispute, with the driver acting as arbiter: passengers were appealing to him for judgement, which he was always ready to provide, keeping one hand on the wheel and vividly gesticulating with the other.

My basic Italian, consisting mostly of culinary terms, was not enough to understand all the intricacies of their heated conversation (moreover, as I found out later, they were speaking the peculiar Sanmarinese dialect), but it sounded to me something like this:

Driver (turning his head towards the salon): No, uncle Giacomo, I think you were not quite right to hit Auntie Gina on the head with a pizza pan. You must apologise.

Uncle Giacomo: Yes, Dino, but don't forget, it was she who hurled a bowl of spaghetti at me first and poured shampoo into my martini.

Driver (craning his neck even further): Is this true, Auntie Gina?

Auntie Gina: Yes, Dino, but prior to that he stuck a dead mouse into my lasagna . . .

Driver: In this case, Uncle Giacomo, you must apologise to the mouse too . . .

And so on.

The driver was hardly looking in front of himself, and I was getting nervous, since the road, twisting around the three-peaked Mount Titano, was getting narrower and narrower.

To make things worse, there was a succession of beautiful young girls standing next to the driver and flirting with him. One *ragazza* would get off the bus, and another, even more attractive, would get in and take her place.

Yes, he was a respected man, this driver of the Rimini–San Marino bus, who, like his ancestor Julius Caesar, was capable of doing several things at the same time: driving the bus up the steep mountain road, solving his countrymen's problems and chatting up girls.

Looking through the window, I played hide-and-seek with the sun: the moment I put my sunglasses on, the sun would disappear behind the cloud, as soon as I took them off my nose, it would peep out and blind me again. Murphy's Law . . .

'Welcome to the ancient land of liberty!' announced the road sign as we crossed into San Marino. The leaflet was right: there were no frontier formalities. There was no frontier, to begin with . . .

The entrance to the City of San Marino under the very top of Mount Titano was guarded by two policemen (or soldiers) in blue uniforms with bright-yellow gloves. I wondered which of the two police forces (or three armies) they belonged to. Here, foreign soldiers were required to hand over their arms: since time immemorial there has been a strict punishment for bringing arms into the town. An old stone by the fourteenth-century Porta San Francesco, the city gate, warning travellers about it, is still there.

Yet the city itself is no longer arms-free. The first shop I spotted as I made my way from the bus station to the Titano Hotel, dragging my suitcase up a steep lane, its wheels rattling against the old cobblestones like the caterpillars of a heavy tank platoon at a military parade, was a weapons shop. It was brimming with pistols, muskets, shotguns, flick knives and knuckle-dusters. The inconspicuous window sign in broken English: 'For fun only. Not intend using as real weapons' – did not sound very convincing, each of the weapons looked real enough to scare you shitless. I was pleased not to have handed over my little penknife at the city gate.

It was Friday afternoon and I was hoping I would still be in time to make some official contacts. My long experience of travelling on journalistic assignments taught me to try to do as much as possible on my first day in a new country, no matter how tired I was. A fruitful first day was a great time-saver for the rest of the trip. A good beginning was half the battle, or half the story, in my peaceful case. So, having dropped my suitcase at the hotel, I hurried down the hill, past innumerable souvenir shops and administrative buildings, to the Foreign Ministry.

The colourfully uniformed guard at the Ministry's reception could not understand my broken pizza-and-lasagna Italian. For some reason, he thought I wanted to buy postage stamps from him. He said that he would try to find the only English-speaking person at the Ministry. 'Her English is *perfetto!*' he assured me.

After many loud phone calls he did manage to get hold of the English speaker. She was a young and extremely shy woman who blushed at my every word. Natural shyness was not the only reason for her blushing since, as it turned out, she could not speak (or understand) a word of English. '*Francese . . .*' she mumbled with a timid smile. The woman was obviously a polyglot. '*C'est magnifique!*' excalimed I. My French was much better than my Italian.

A second later, though, it transpired that she could not speak French either. In gestures, supplemented by some Italian words (even her native Italian sounded somewhat uncertain) she explained that there was a woman at the neighbouring Ministry of Culture who could speak some English, but now it was already four o'clock in the afternoon on Friday, and she was likely to have gone home, so I'd better come back on Monday morning. I decided to check and, indeed, the massive wooden doors of the Ministry of Culture and Universities were firmly locked for the weekend.

Well, I knew there were no universities in San Marino. Now I started having serious doubts about culture, too. I cursed the State Tourist Office leaflet which, among other things, shamelessly asserted that 'the ordinary man in the street can usually speak at least one foreign language'.

I trudged back to my hotel, trying to face the prospect of spending the weekend on top of a mountain without any contacts, or even anyone to talk to. 'Ordinary men in the streets' did seem able to speak 'one foreign language', only it was foreign to me, not to them. I looked around; the streets were lined with countless souvenir shops. There were many more of them than people, and all were full of junk: playing cards decorated with naked women; San Marino-by-night pitch-black postcards, lighters in the shape of bottles and bottles in the shape of lighters; key-holders with hearts; plastic cats and piglets; dolls with bulging eyes; porcelain clocks and Mickey Mouses. Compared to these, souvenir stalls in Liechtenstein started looking like purveyors of refined taste, like Harrods compared to an Oxfam store. Shop-owners-turned-touts hung around on street corners, grabbing tourists by the sleeve and attempting to drag them inside.

There were lots of shops specialising in booze, too. 'Bottoms up! Come and try the San Marino special wines and spirits!' the English poster in front of one of them read. Inside the shop, among batteries of wines, cognacs and liqueurs, I saw a neat arrangement of vodka bottles. It was neither Smirnoff nor Stolichnaya, but 'Vodka Imperial. Blue Label. Made in San Marino'. As soon as I saw this label, I knew I had a companion for the evening.

I was still a drinker at that time — not a dipsomaniac, yet no teetotaller either. I am still of the opinion that spirits are one of the great inventions of mankind, comparable to the creation of gunpowder. Just like powder, they can be explosive if mishandled or abused.

I am equally convinced that Russian vodka is the best drink in the world, and not just because we are of the same origin — vodka and myself, I mean. Want me to prove it? Here I go:

The first distilleries in Russia appeared in the twelfth century. Distilling is the most important stage of vodka-making, together with filtering. A good vodka (like Stolichnaya or Moskovskaya, say) is filtered four times before being bottled and is practically devoid of fusel oils and suspensions. That's why, if you drink it correctly, it will never give you a hangover. It is removed from your blood within twenty-four hours whereas beer and wine stay there for many days.

What do I mean by correct vodka-drinking? People in the West are fond of mixing their drinks and are always ready to add tonic, juice, ice or even milk (*pace* the English) to their spirits. Vodka, being the purest beverage on earth, doesn't require any additives — it must be drunk straight, on its own. And it should never be sipped, because despite its good qualities, it has an unpleasant taste, or rather no taste at all.

Vodka is drunk not for taste, but solely for aftereffect — that's why it should be gulped quickly without sniffing. Also, if you add something to it, you automatically reduce its strength: the experience of many generations of vodka-makers shows that it must be forty per cent proof — not forty-one, not thirty-nine, but forty. This figure has been maintained for centuries, so the many experiments with different levels of alcohol in vodka usually bring adverse results. Minus forty outside and plus forty inside — that's what we Russians call symmetry.

Another common mistake is that the Westerners like to keep vodka bottles in the freezer. Being a spirit it won't freeze there, but will become oily and lose some of its best qualities. Ice-cold vodka is almost as bad as warm vodka. So where is the golden mean? It is in the fridge, but not in the freezer. It would be ideal, of course, to put a bottle out in the snow for several minutes, but in some countries (like Australia, Italy or even Britain) it is hardly feasible. Conclusion: drink vodka cool, not cold.

It is no less important how you breathe when you drink vodka. Before gulping a glass you should breathe out and inhale only after the shot is safely down in your stomach, with some food and/or a soft drink on top of it. Then you will feel a ball of warmth being formed inside you and spreading a wave of soothing 'central heating' all over your body. Vodka (if not abused, of course) doesn't affect your brain, but makes your body warm and supple. It gives you an easy floating feeling and removes stress. Again, only if you stick to it during the evening without having wine or beer — before or after it. Vodka is like a Russian peasant woman — faithful, but also jealous. If while drinking vodka you start playing around with other drinks, you are likely to experience a family scandal in your stomach.

For centuries vodka in Russia was also used as a medicine (it started as a warming-up medicine, by the way). When you feel you may be beginning to catch a cold, the best thing to do is to have a glass of heavily peppered vodka and go to bed quickly. Next morning you will feel as fit as a fiddle. I have tried it myself more than once, although some of my Western friends, to whom I've recommended the cure, complain that they feel they are about to catch a cold every five minutes now. Also, when you are having stomach trouble (nothing like cancer, God forbid, but just minor indigestion), there's nothing like a shot of vodka with a spoonful of salt. Don't believe those Russian 'experts' who tell you that vodka's healing effects begin after the third bottle only.

An acquaintance of mine, who was on the Soviet Olympic volley-ball team when it won the gold medal in Tokyo in 1964, told me how after the competition the coach gave each player a glass of vodka to remove stress. Vodka is an excellent stress-remover. Mind you: they had vodka *after* the Games, not before or during them.

Vodka (again, in moderation) is not just a drink – it's a companion and an equaliser. It destroys barriers between people and provides for good conversation. How can I forget those Moscow kitchen sessions with my friends, with a bottle of vodka in the middle of the table and the telephone covered with a cushion to give us the illusion of privacy: we believed naively that a cushion could somehow neutralise the KGB's bugging devices.

I am no longer a practising drinker – just a theoretician (stomach ulcer, you know). I hate to sound like a vodka propagandist. Drinking is evil in itself, but it exists. So why not choose the lesser of the evils? Remember: drinks are innocent. It is people who turn them into hazards.

The San Marino-made vodka did help me to while away the evening. After dinner, having puffed my way to the very top of Mount Titano, I suddenly understood why no medieval warrior in his right mind would bother to invade San Marino: it simply was not worth climbing that high with all his heavy armour and ammunition to conquer this pocket handkerchief of a state. There were lots of souvenir shops with the same choice of junk on top of the mountain, luckily all closed at that late hour. The dim lights of Rimini were blinking in the distance and the sweet aroma of blooming chestnut trees was strong in the air.

The Sanmarinese, just like the Italians, start their day by screaming at each other. Next morning I was woken by thunderous multiple '*Buon Giorno!*'s behind my window. I already knew that when Italians yelled at each other, it meant they were in a good mood. When they start whispering though, it means danger.

On that Saturday morning the city of San Marino was teeming with shoppers and tourists from all over the world. There were flocks of unsmiling, Nikon-clicking Japanese, groups of detached Brits and taciturn Scandinavians, herds of hissing Poles. With three million visitors a year, San Marino has the world's highest per capita tourist rate in the world.

'*Yob tvoyu mat!*' came a particularly nasty Russian curse from behind my back. It was like music to my ears. I turned round. A ruddy-faced man in a blue vest and baggy trousers was carrying half-a-dozen bulging plastic bags and was swearing under his breath. 'High quality chicken meat from the USA' was written on one of the bags in Russian. It probably used to hold American chicken legs, generously exported to Moscow in the late eighties and nicknamed Bush's legs by the Muscovites. I was somehow not too willing to start a conversation with this sweaty chicken carrier.

And there were Americans, of course. I spotted them while watching the changing of the guard in front of the Government House. Guardia di Rocca guardsmen, dressed in green jackets, red trousers and red and white feathered caps, looking very much like some exotic tropical parrots, were goose-stepping and brandishing their vintage rifles on a small patio of a city square. Suddenly there came a storm of applause: American tourists, watching the ceremony, had reacted in their usual teenage fashion.

The guards didn't actually guard anything. Their role was purely ceremonial and they all went home at six p.m., leaving the

Government House totally unprotected. That's probably why the ancient walls inside the building were covered with 'Giovanni loves Adriana'-type carvings. Immortality-hungry tourists seemed to ignore the strict 'No writing on the walls' sign next to the room where the Grand and General Council was supposed to sit. In that room there stood a funny double-barrelled wooden armchair for the two Captains Regent who, as I already knew, ran the country together. To me the throne brought associations with double beds, Siamese twins and Tyanitolkay, a fictitious antelope-like creature from a Russian fairy tale, with two heads and not a single behind.

The only other curious objects in the House were two ceramic urns, similar to the ones in which ashes of the deceased are stored. Here they were used for voting: the white one was probably intended for 'yeas' and the black one for 'nays'.

It was surprising how little San Marino, with its almost 1,700 years of history, could offer to a knowledge-hungry tourist. Apart from buying a pistol or a tacky postcard, he could visit two weapons museums – the museum of old weapons and the museum of modern weapons; he could pop into the Basilica del Santo where the skull of Saint Marino (alias stonecutter Marinus) was kept in the 'Holy Case' behind the altar; he could drop into the museum of curiosities to gape at the world's fattest man or even to pull at the world's longest beard (like all dwarfs, San Marino seems to have an obsession with things abnormally big or small); he could have a quick tour of the aquarium featuring a real cobra, an 'extremely voracious animal eating up to twenty small rats in one meal' and a strange fish called 'Piranha Vegeteriana' which probably meant a particular breed of piranha feeding on human vegetarians only.

There was not a single bookshop and only one newsagent, with no foreign and few Italian newspapers.

The museum of wax figures, à la Madame Tussaud's, proudly displayed a life-size statue of Jackie Kennedy, with horse-like face and long manicured fingernails, standing next to a pot-bellied Pope, extending his waxen hand in blessing. It looked like any moment

71

Jacqueline was going to scratch the Pope's face with those long nails of hers.

Napoleon Bonaparte in his ubiquitous cocked hat was flanked by the long-haired Garibaldi, who resembled John Lennon without his glasses. Other sets of statues showed Marconi, the inventor of radio telegraph, involved in a heated discussion with . . . Galileo Galilei, who died 240 years before Marconi's birth; Columbus, being told off for something (probably for having made the mistake of discovering America instead of India) by the angry Queen of Spain; Jose groping Carmen's breasts; Verdi playing the piano; and President Lincoln standing in a theatre box with the Bill of Rights in his hand, and the treacherous assassin creeping up on him from behind with a pistol. From Lincoln's expressionless wax-pale face, it was not clear whether he was meant to be already dead or still alive . . . The nearby exhibition of ancient instruments of torture featured cheerful prisoners in shackles being dutifully quartered and beheaded by even more cheerful executioners.

Having narrowly escaped beheading, I found myself alone in San Marino's only art gallery. The elderly, one-legged guard was so surprised to see a visitor that he kept limping after me all through the gallery with his squeaking crutch, lest I should steal something, I guess. There was not much to steal there, to be frank. Almost all the paintings were by a certain Titolo, probably the only real artist in the whole history of San Marino. His name made me ponder again over one inexplicable historical fact: that the names of all Italian painters end in 'o' and the names of all Italian composers – in 'i'.

The service was under way in the adjoining St Francis church. The priest, with his hands akimbo, was mumbling something about 'Nostro Papa Giovanni Paulo Secondo'. I decided I had had enough of San Marino for the day and took a bus to Rimini, where I spent a jolly fulfilling afternoon gaping at bikini-clad beauties on the beach and looking for the house of Frederico Fellini – without much luck. The bus driver was the same brown-eyed young man, only the girls chatting him up all the way to (and from) San Marino, were different.

I hereby declare that on the occasion of the antiques market to be held in Borgo Maggiore, the traffic is to be closed in Piazza Grande and Piazza Mercante on Saturday, 15 May and on Sunday, 16 May.

Antonio Volpinari, Secretary of State, Internal Affairs.

San Marino, 10 May 1993/1692 d. F. R.

This decree, in huge black letters, was displayed on notice boards throughout San Marino. I began to understand what kept thousands of government bureaucrats so busy: they were writing important decrees.

At least there was something happening. I wanted to visit the decree-making flea market, and early next morning took a cable tram from the city of San Marino down to the village of Borgo Maggiore. The walls of the cable tram cabin were covered with graffiti: 'Renato, '84', 'Valentino, '90', 'Laura, Aldo (Calabria)'. I was almost tempted to immortalise myself by writing 'Vitali, '93' on the submissive wall, but thought better of it: unlike Laura and Aldo from Calabria, I didn't want to state publicly that I was a fool.

In Borgo Maggiore I spotted a newsagent (or rather *the* newsagent, it was the only one in the country). I was craving a Sunday newspaper the way a heavy smoker craves his first morning cigarette. '*Giornali Inglese*?' I asked the newsagent. 'No!' was the curt reply.

The Ferrari Museum, the village's main (and only) permanent attraction, was closed and, frankly, as a driver who hit a fire-hydrant during his first driving lesson, I was not particularly interested.

At least four hours were left before the antiques market was due to open.

'When everything else fails, read notice boards' is another journalistic motto of mine. When an official is unable or reluctant to see you, make sure you read the papers clipped to the notice board next to his office; you might learn a lot.

This was exactly the case in San Marino, where the bureaucrats were not exactly falling over themselves to meet me, so I had to be satisfied with reading bills and posters in the deserted streets of Borgo Maggiore and thus improving my terrible Italian.

World Cup qualification game, San Marino versus Poland, will
be held on May 19 at the stadium of Serravale

The last time the San Marino football team scored an away goal was
in Turkey in 1961. Their home record was not particularly promising
either: earlier in the same World Cup qualification tournament they
were defeated by Norway 10–0. (Naturally, the team's fans were
overwhelmed with joy when San Marino lost just 6–0 to England at
Wembley in February, 1993.) The coming game with Poland did
not bode too well for San Marino.

Baseball Championship of Italy. San Marino versus Modena.
16–21 May. Baseball stadium of Serravale.

Were they playing baseball at the soccer stadium, or football at the
baseball stadium? There couldn't possibly be two stadiums in Serravale,
or in the whole of San Marino, I thought.

Republic of San Marino Independent State Board for Philately
and Numismatics announces that on May 26, 1993, the Postal
Administration of the republic releases the following series of
valuable postage stamps: 'Protected Animals' consisting of four
250-lira stamps with total cost of the series at 1000 liras; 'Great
Achievements of Our Times' ('The Village of Europe') consisting
of 12 stamps valued at 750 liras each in a unique folder at the
total cost of 9,000 liras.

Somewhat puzzled by the 'Independent State Board', I nevertheless
had to admit that San Marino stamps were among the most beautiful
in the world and had considerable philatelic value. With the sale of
postage stamps being one of the country's main sources of revenue
and the printing of stamps its main industry, it could be figuratively
papered over with them and, who knows, maybe one day it will. After
all, it would be much more pleasant for the eye than all these 'Gino
loves Adriana' inscriptions on the facades of all public buildings.

San Marino

Son Gastone, daughters Iolanda and Roseanna, nephew, sister
and husband (registered) mourn the first anniversary of the death
of our dear Emilia Peroni, born Pasolini. The memorial service
to be conducted at the Church of St Andrea in Serravale.

It looked like everything – from football and baseball games to
memorial services – was happening in the town of Serravale, and
nothing much (apart from the would-be antiques market) in Borgo
Maggiore, or anywhere else in San Marino. I felt like visiting this
exciting place on the spur of the moment and maybe even attending
the memorial service, which sounded more stimulating that the San
Marino–Poland football match.

The bracketed word 'registered' after 'husband' was a clear indication of how strong and persistent the Roman Catholic tradition was in
San Marino, where, just like in Italy, divorces and 'unregistered'
husbands and wives were obviously still frowned upon. For the poor
Emilia Peroni, born Pasolini, though, the fact that her husband was
indeed a registered one could not matter much one year after her death,
could it?

Every Sunday and every day Padre Marco receives confessions
from ten to eleven o'clock at the sanctuary

I looked at my watch: it was ten thirty, so I could go and confess.
Having given it some thought, though, I decided to drop the idea: thirty
minutes would not be enough to divulge all my sins. I would need a
couple of full working days for that. Forgive me, Padre Marco!

My unrepenting attention was drawn to numerous political posters
on houses, fences and trees. San Marino was on the eve of the general
elections and the country's political parties, all of leftist orientation,
were trying to woo the voters with their nice-sounding programmes.
There were six of them competing in the elections, and their names
spoke for themselves:
1. Partito Socialista
2. Partito Democrazia Cristiana

75

3. Partito Progressisto Democratico Sammarinese
4. Movimento Democratico
5. Alienza Popolare Democratico
6. Rifondazione Communista Sammarinese

As you see, almost all of them liked the word 'democracy', even the Partito Progressisto Democratico Sammarinese, which used to be called the Communist Party of San Marino until 1990. As to Rifondazione Communista Sammarinese, whose vociferous orator I overheard on my first night in San Marino, it was just a bunch of unreformed hardcore Communists, whose election list consisted of eleven candidates, all in their fifties and sixties. The rest of the parties were mildly belligerent socialists of the type who, according to Lenin's scornful remark (he hated socialists), were likely to buy themselves platform tickets before storming a railway station.

The parties' election programmes were as like as two (or rather six) peas in one pod. They all promised reform, social protection and democracy, of course. None of them were honest enough to promise bureaucracy, maybe because there was already more than enough of it in San Marino. The only programme that was slightly different and even mildly realistic was that of the Movimento Democratico (the Democratic Movement). 'Renovation of politics, reform of the state, independence, ideals and values.'

Ideals and values: this was what San Marino desperately needed. And there was no need to invent them. It took just a quick look into the country's history.

It was well past one-thirty p.m., yet despite the formidable decree, the traffic in Piazza Grande and Piazza Mercante was not showing any signs of being stopped, and cars kept speeding defiantly past.

Faded brass plates; greasy saucepans; giant antediluvian radios and music boxes; rusty keys and locks; old stoves, covered with layers of soot, were all being unloaded from vans and placed onto shabby stalls, or just onto the ground. Mercattino dell' Antiquariato, the antiques market, was gaining momentum.

It was all junk in different stages of decay. An old man in a tattered black sweater was selling Fascist paraphenalia: portraits, busts and high reliefs of Duce Mussolini, swastika badges, Nazi military orders. And on the opposite stall there was an impressive display of Soviet memorabilia: badges of Lenin; pins of a 'Communist Shock Worker' (my mother had one) and of a 'Five-year Plan Young Guard'; red banners of the Young Pioneers' organisations with the peremptory slogan: 'Be ready to fight for the cause of the Communist Party of the Soviet Union!' embroidered on them; red pennants 'To the best Oktiabryatsky unit' (Oktiabryata was the name of the Communist organisation for seven to ten-year-olds – I used to belong to it); congratulatory postcards on the anniversary of the 1917 revolution, the Day of the Tank Driver, or the Day of the Artillery Man – Soviet national holidays that invariably fell on Sundays.

The stern, narrow-eyed and slightly moronic face of a uniformed Soviet soldier was staring at me from one poster. His solid neck was craned towards me at an impossible angle, his fixed, piercing stare was full of blunt force and unspecified threat. There was no way to avoid this all-penetrating gaze. 'Be vigilant while on leave!' was written above his head in red Russian letters. And in the background of the poster there were numerous 'temptations' – a café, a cinema, a department store, a palace of culture – all of which the vigilant soldier on leave found easy to resist. No wonder: with a face like that, avoiding a palace of culture shouldn't be much of a problem.

'Breathing, body and muscle-gaining, use to improve your military training!' (my unauthorised translation) ran another poster showing a ruddy, muscled youth pushing up red weights . . .

'Armed personnel carrier, a toy for children, aged 6–14,' said the Russian inscription on a clumsy cardboard box. The box held a miniature copy of the BTR–60 PB armed personnel carrier, the one that was widely used by the Soviet Army in Afghanistan. Next to it stood a similar sized rocket truck, an amphibious rocket car, a mobile rocket launcher, etc. The same strict Russian instruction on every box specified that the toys were designed for six- to fourteen-year-olds exclusively. One must be fairly jingoistic to play with these toys at six and pretty iinfantile to keep doing so at fourteen, I thought.

And more: Soviet military uniforms; caps, shoulder-loops; a single-breasted jacket of an East German secret policeman; cards of Komsomol members; medals with the portrait of Stalin – odds and ends of the past epoch, never to be repeated. These knick-knacks used to mean so much for so many people, and there was a certain sadness in the fact that the only place they belonged now was a wobbly stall at the flea market in San Marino.

But it was also logical. The proximity of the Nazi and the Soviet stalls emphasised the two regimes' obvious similarity and made it clear that the only place where totalitarian states, with all their posters, banners and military toys – designed as a substitute for normal human values – will eventually end up is on the scrapheap of history. I wished the vociferous orator from the Rifondazione Communista Sammarinese was there to see the display; that would cool him down a bit. But there was no sign of him at the flea market. He was probably busy writing another fiery speech in defense of Communism in the comfort of his two-storied villa somewhere nearby.

The owners of the Soviet junk stall were Russians – two young men and a woman with a face that looked like an unwashed plate with leftovers of food on it. All three were clad in dirty Adidas tracksuits and Puma trainers – the uniform of Soviet racketeers and mafia minions. They kept chain-smoking and swearing in Russian, continually cursing f***ing San Marino where no one wanted to buy their f***ing goods. 'We should have brought the f***ing *matrioshkas* instead,' they were saying, not realising that I could understand their every word.

'Don't bother: no one will buy your f***ing *matrioshkas* either,' I told them in Russian before moving on.

Next morning I was solemnly introduced to the English-speaking woman (of course, she was young and beautiful) from the Ministry of Culture and (nonexisting) Universities which was also the Ministry of Justice, by the way. Although she did speak some English (to my surprise), she refused to answer my questions, saying that it was only Signor Di Pietro, the official press spokesman for the Ministry of Foreign Affairs, who was authorised by the Captains Regent to talk to visiting journalists. She could try to fix me a brief appointment with Signor Di Pietro, though it might be difficult since he was extremely busy.

She started making endless phone calls, trying to get hold of the evasive Signor Di Pietro. No luck.

During a short interval in her frantic dialling, I ventured to ask her about the reason for having such low-class tourist attractions in San Marino.

'Our country has to adapt itself to tourists,' she answered with a charming frown and added: 'Our tourists are not very high class, you see, and most of them come from East European countries . . .'

Who has to adapt to whom: tourists to the country or a country to the tourists? The answer, I always thought, was given long ago: when in Rome, do as the Romans do. By trying to cater to low tastes, not only do Sanmarinese officials lower their country's prestige: they do a disservice to the visitors, infecting them with mass culture and dubious values – hence the grafitti on the walls. 'You reap what you sow,' an old Russian proverb goes.

It took less than three hours to fix me a five-minute-long appointment with Signor Di Pietro. I was to see him next morning before lunch, 'because after lunch Signor Di Pietro goes home'.

In full accordance with Parkinson's Law, the corridors of the Foreign Ministry were brimming with activity: secretaries were running to and fro, telephones were ringing and faxes were beeping. I remembered with nostalgia the six modest and efficient government officials in Liechtenstein who brilliantly coped with the job of all the Sanmarinese ministries. Northcote Parkinson was right: each bureaucrat generates two more of the same. Bureaucrats tend to multiply like rabbits and constantly demand new offices, new secretaries, new telephones and new deputies. The same is true of diplomats who are bureaucrats of international standing.

Signor Di Pietro was both a bureaucrat and a diplomat. He was a slim, middle-aged man with the velvety brown eyes of a womaniser. His desk was piled with files (or was it filed with piles?), official instructions and invitations to cocktails and receptions: bureaucrats' favourite pastime is throwing receptions for each other.

Signor Di Pietro greeted me by looking at his watch meaningfully. I immediatley felt guilty for distracting such an important and busy official with my trifling questions. So I decided to ask only one.

'What is San Marino's main asset at present?'

'Beautiful women!' he snapped in English, looking up from the papers on his desk and feasting his sticky eyes on the lady from the Ministry of Culture, who was supposed to act as an interpreter. Her services proved unnecessary. One of the three telephones on the desk rang demandingly. Signor Di Pietro lifted the receiver and, with a not very polite gesture – as if sweeping away bread crumbs from his desk – waved us out of his office. (He was definitely hundreds of times busier than Hans Adam II, the Prince of Liechtenstein, who chatted with me for more than an hour at his Vaduz castle.)

The audience was over. And so was my trip to San Marino, this bureaucratic antiques market in the clouds. Even without Signor Di Pietro's help I knew what its biggest modern asset was: 'Vodka Imperial. Blue Label'!

I was flying back to London from Bologna, where I found myself after the exhausting four-hour-long train ride from Rimini. The train was running (or rather crawling at a snail's pace) two hours late, and I was worried I would miss my plane. The man in the seat next to me was reading *Corriere della Sera* and, looking over his shoulder, I learnt of yet another car-bomb explosion in Rome, and the Prime Minister's call for unity against the Mafia.

My observations show that the level of corruption in this or that part of the world is in direct proportion to its climate: the higher the average temperature – the more corrupt the country. Indeed, Italy is Europe's warmest place and by far the most corrupt. The same can be said about Queensland in Australia, Brazil in South America and the Central Asian and Caucasian republics of the former Soviet Union (Uzbekistan, Turkmenistan, Georgia, Armenia, Azerbaijan). On the other hand, I have never heard of a major corruption case in Finland, Sweden or Norway. To say nothing of Greenland.

The explanation might be that in the countries with warmer climates, people tend to spend more time outside their houses: in the streets, parks, open-air cafés, on the beaches, etc – where contacts, deals, conspiracies and unholy alliances are evidently forged with greater ease than indoors. Also, the residents of warmer countries are usually much more open and outgoing than northerners, who are calm, restrained and generally docile. So, Italy's biggest problem – the omnipotent Mafia – is probably a direct and objective result of its sultry Mediterranean climate, and the only way to eradicate it is to move the country some-where close to the north (or south) polar circle, to which most of the Italians would strongly object.

Bologna used to be a sister city of my native Kharkov (I am not sure whether it still is), and that's probably why all Kharkov men in the sixties and seventies (my father included) sported cheap bologna raincoats, rain or not. To own such an overcoat was in a way a status symbol, and I was very proud when my father gave me his old one to wear at the age of sixteen.

In fact, Bologna felt and looked very much like Kharkov – smokey and hectic. It was the most 'Soviet' place I had ever seen in the West. There were no luggage trolleys at the overcrowded railway station and a long queue for taxis was snaking all over the station square.

I was approached by a tout with darting eyes who offered me a ride to the airport for 20,000 liras – precisely Moscow style! I was running late and had to agree. The driver of the battered old Fiat was tearing along the streets at 150km per hour, completely ignoring road signs, traffic lights and pedestrians, who were ignoring him in return. Fluffy poplar seeds were floating in the air like snowflakes – exactly like in Moscow in June.

The aptly named Guglielmo Marconi airport was as unsophisticated as Marconi's first radio-set. Nothing worked, and the toilet was closed for repairs. There were no vacant seats in the departure lounge, packed and stuffy as a Moscow rush-hour tram, and instead of a snack bar there was a big sign: 'There is nothing to eat or drink after the check-in'. To those who were already in the lounge, the sign was totally superfluous – like a post mortem to a corpse.

I was about to lose my temper, but then recalled that Bologna had a Communist-dominated City Council, and smiled instead.

The first boarding call came shortly . . .

3. Mount Athos

The mountain path was steep and narrow. Strewn with rough, shapeless rocks and mule droppings, it wound mercilessly uphill along the edge of an abyss, and it seemed endless. Cicadas chirred deafeningly, as if they were laughing at us. The white-hot disc of the midday sun with several fluffy clouds around it – like a giant freshly cooked portion of bacon-and-eggs – glared at us from the blue sizzling frying pan of the Hellenic sky. Puffing like an early steam-engine, I trudged higher and higher up the track, scaring tiny agile lizards from under my trainers. My feet felt stiff and alien, as if I was walking on stilts, and streams of hot, salty sweat were pouring down my forehead.

At last, when I thought I wouldn't be able to take another step for a million pounds, I looked up and saw *him*. In his monastic *klobuk* hat he was standing on the path, blue robes and black beard flying in the breeze, and pointing at the square building of the nearby *skete*, resembling an obscure Cyrillic letter. In loose, worn sandals, he could have been mistaken for a mirage or an Old Testament apparition, were it not for the inscription on the fringe of the grey satin trousers showing from under his habit: 'Property of the Mount Sinai Military Hospital'.

It was Father Spiridon, the chief monk of St Anna *skete*, a small and secluded monastery. He came down to greet us, four London-based journalists turned hikers. He brought mules, one for each of us, and for the last several hundred metres to the *skete* we rode on their uncomplaining backs – a huge relief for us, if not for the mules . . .

This two-hour climb was by far the hardest moment of our three days at Mount Athos, the self-governing Orthodox monastic mini-state on the Halkidiki peninsula in Northern Greece.

The trip was organised by the Halkidiki Hotel Association in conjunction with a London public relations company. In journalistic jargon such trips are called 'freebies', since all the travel costs are carried by the sponsors.

The information booklet, sent to us in advance, promised long boat transfers, rides in trucks and on mules on very rough tracks, basic dormitory accommodation, frugal meals of bread, soup, olives, cucumber and fruit, and 'very early starts'. Among the useful items to be taken with us, the booklet listed insect repellant, torch, pocket knife and gifts for the monks such as 'a book, tea, coffee or a pen'.

As a heavy smoker, I was mostly put off by the smoking ban in the town of Karies, Mount Athos' capital, and in the monasteries. I even phoned the public relations company and said I was not going if not allowed to smoke. 'Don't worry,' was the reply. 'Most monks smoke.' 'And drink too?' I enquired sarcastically. 'Yes.' I thought it was a good joke.

It took us six weeks to get our *diamonitirions*, the official permits for visiting Mount Athos, from the Ministry for Northern Greece in Thessaloniki. The documents, signed by all five members of Mount Athos's ruling Holy Council, looked more like honorary diplomas or certificates of higher education than just visas. The Holy Mountain (another name for Mount Athos) is one of the world's most exclusive places, and the number of foreign visitors is limited to no more than ten a week.

ing to be any ladies on this trip. I hope it won't lead
ng,' Doug Goodman, the PR company director and
a... eller, who was to accompany us on the journey, told
us at Heau.... . 'By the way, there has been a small last-minute
change in our itinerary: we are not going to Mount Athos and shall just
look at some nice hotels in Halkidiki,' he added with a wry smile.

'Oh, no!' we moaned in chorus: Mount Athos was the only reason
we agreed to go on this trip, and Doug, who had taken hacks there
before, was well aware of this. Luckily, it proved to be just another of
his lovely jokes. He had a dry, if somewhat cruel, sense of humour.

Our Thessaloniki-bound aircraft finally took off after a long delay 'due
to the problems in Yugoslavia', as it was put by our Greek captain. 'But
the weather is nice, and we are going to see lots of beautiful places,' he
added apologetically.

The dark-eyed and sharp-nosed Greek hostesses were serving drinks,
and a buxom Greek peasant woman next to me ordered a beer. I had
three hours to think about the mysterious religious place I was going to,
and about religion as such.

I have never been religious, despite the fact that I spent the first three
years of my life in Zagorsk (now Sergiyev Possad), a town near
Moscow which was the centre of the Russian Orthodox Church. My
parents worked at a secret nuclear weapons factory located on premises
of the old monastery, where crosses on the gates were simply replaced
with red stars. My first childhood impressions were linked with the
chiming of church bells, the black-robed priests and the time-worn
icons displayed in the windows of log cabins next to portraits of Stalin.

My parents were at work all day and had to hire a childminder, an
old religious woman, to look after me. Once, coming home from
work, they saw her with me in a bundle in her arms standing near the
church and asking for alms to feed 'the poor little orphan' (i.e. me).
My parents didn't perceive me as an orphan, and the begging
childminder was sacked the following day. As she left, she boasted of

having christened me secretly, though no one knew if she really meant it.

This must be the reason why, though not a believer in any gods, I am nevertheless terribly superstitious. I constantly keep my fingers crossed, even in my sleep or when writing. Every five minutes I spit thrice over my shoulder. I touch wood whenever I see it. I never shake hands over a threshold, and if a black cat or a woman with empty buckets crosses my way, I go back home. Does it help, you might ask? It sure does! I am a very lucky man in a way. Not that I was born with a silver spoon in my mouth, it was more like a fork, I guess, but at least my mouth wasn't empty . . .

The Church in the Soviet Union was allegedly separated from the State. It was more a happy marriage, camouflaged as an acrimonious divorce, I would say. There was only one officially acceptable faith — with Lenin as a Christ figure, his mausoleum as a shrine, his bequests as commandments and the Communist party *apparatchiks* as priests to preach them. Anyone who was reluctant to adhere to this religion was bound to remain a secret agnostic in the best of scenarios, and a prisoner (or a corpse) in the worst. The few religious institutions that were tolerated were allowed to exist solely for window-dressing. There was only one practising Orthodox church in my native Kharkov, which also had a functioning Synagogue. It functioned as a gym.

I did enjoy a short association with the Church in the late seventies, when trying to find myself an interpreter's job in Moscow. This association lasted for one day only.

Having just come to the Soviet capital from my provincial Kharkov and lacking all necessary connections (or 'pull'), I had to face a stone wall wherever I went. It was then that I thought in desperation: 'The Church is separated from the State. The State doesn't want to give me a job, so maybe the Church would?' No matter how logical this premise sounded, in a system that defied logic it was bound to fail.

At the publishing house of the Russian Orthodox Church, I was given a short questionnaire to fill in. It had a space for religion. After some hesitation, I wrote honestly 'none'. The young priest to whom I submitted the completed form was rather taken aback. 'So you're an atheist,' he said. 'We don't employ atheists.' References to my childhood in Zagorsk didn't help.

At the office of the Baptist Order, where I was encouragingly addressed as 'brother', a man explained that to work with them I must be a member of their order. I expressed a readiness to join any kind of order, provided I got a job. The man didn't like my eagerness. 'It takes a long time,' he said. 'You'll have to undergo a test period of several years.' Suddenly he smiled. 'It's a good job we have here, travelling abroad all the time, so it's worth trying.' But several years of waiting – no, it didn't suit me at all. Besides, I could imagine how my parents would have reacted if they found out that I had become a Baptist.

And I went to the Soviet Muslim Board. It was located in a small wooden hut near Dinamo metro station. The hut was guarded by ferocious dogs, and there was a number of black Volga sedans parked in the courtyard. Inside, a middle-aged, narrow-eyed Uzbek sat under a huge wall-hanging with Arabic signs on it. He was trying to reach Tashkent by phone, and he couldn't get through, which made him angry. 'What do you want?' he snapped at me. 'I want a job,' I answered meekly. 'Are you a Muslim?' 'I don't think so.' 'All right, just leave your address with my secretary and go, I am very busy.' It was hopeless. I went to the Synagogue.

An old orthodox Jew in a *yarmulka* was washing his hands in the lobby. It was not a praying day, and he let me inside, where I saw a rabbi sporting an ordinary working-class cap instead of a *yarmulka*. He was sitting under the Yiddish and Russian (and not very promising slogan) 'Our Father in Heavens, bless the government of the USSR'. 'What does he want?' he asked my *yarmulka*ed escort, completely ignoring my presence. 'A job,' he replied. 'Then send him to the Council for Religious Affairs!' the rabbi screamed at the top of his voice. I was being sent packing again.

Following the rabbi's advice, I did go to the Council for Religious Affairs, which was in effect a branch of the KGB designed to supervise

87

religious institutions. I should have known better.

A polite, neatly dressed man with steel-grey eyes examined me thoroughly. 'So if I've got you right, you are an interpreter, aren't you?' 'Yes I am.' 'You've got no job, and you decided to go to the Council for Religious Affairs to ask for one, didn't you?' 'Yes, I did,' I answered nonchalantly. 'The idea of such a thing!' he shouted all of a sudden. 'Are you crazy or what? We don't know ourselves how we got our jobs here! And we don't take anyone from the street!'

Several years later, when I was already working as a journalist on a Moscow magazine, I was sent to the Krasnodar region to investigate the systematic embezzlement of church funds by a criminal gang posing as a team of restorers. The assignment was prompted by a letter I received from the church parishioners. At that time anything connected with religion (apart from lampoons or rampant criticism) was still taboo for the press, so I was instructed by the editor to get in touch with the chairman of the Krasnodar Council for Religious Affairs. I was told not to take any steps in my investigation without the chairman's approval.

A large roly-poly man was sitting at a huge desk with three telephones on it and the regulation portrait of Lenin above. He told me everything about himself. He was a KGB colonel, and his job was a kind of honorary retirement. His main duty was to curb and contain religious feeling in the region at all costs. He had extensive powers and was able to manipulate the believers by imposing exorbitant taxes on them, or by denying registration to this or that religious community. Without such registration, the believers had no right to attend the church.

He was obviously trying to impress me with how difficult it was to deal with 'these fanatics' as he called the clergymen. At one point he had a visitor – a broad-shouldered, bearded giant in a black suit and black collarless shirt. Looking at him, one could immediately see he was a priest. On seeing me, the giant wanted to come back later, but the chairman beckoned him in. 'You may trust this man!' he said, pointing at me. 'What do you have to tell me today?'

Throwing furtive looks at me, the priest started speaking: 'You know, comrade Chairman, the new Blagochinniy [a senior diocesan priest] in our district is rather a dark horse. Very persistent. People say he visits the houses of collective farmers and tries to convert them by reading from the Bible and so on. He also frequents the local youth club, persuading the young people to attend sermons.'

The chairman wrinkled his meaty red nose. 'Too bad. What shall I do to discourage him from this religious propaganda? I think I know what . . . I shall double the amount of the diocese voluntary donations to the Soviet Peace Fund. That will reduce his enthusiasm a little. And if not, we won't renew his parish registration next year and we'll have the church closed!' He made some notes in his jotter. 'Anything else you want to tell me?'

'That's all for the present, comrade Chairman.'

'OK. Now we owe you a fee for the last two months. Here's the authorisation. Show it upstairs at the window. And see you again next week!'

'Who is he?' I asked when the door closed behind the priest.

The Chairman dismissed my question with a quick wave of his hand. 'Scum. A petty crook in a priest's robe and also one of my secret assistants. They are all crooks, these clergymen, but I have to deal with them to know what's going on in the region.'

As you see, despite the much-publicised 'separation', the Soviet State was exercising tight control over the Church which was squeezed in the State's iron fist, squealing with pain.

At Soviet universities we had mandatory courses in Scientific Atheism and Scientific Communism, both asserting that religion would die out within a few generations. Well, two decades later it was the Soviet Union that died out, while religion is alive and well. And now I was flying to one of its main strongholds, Mount Athos, the place as important for the Orthodox faith as the Vatican is for the Roman Catholics, or Tibet for the Buddhists.

Prior to that, however, we were to spend several days in Northern Greece 'familiarising' ourselves with local holiday-making facilities.

The airport in Thessaloníki was called 'Macedonia'. People wearing

Little is the Light

'Macedonia is forever Greek' T-shirts could be seen here and there. All evidence of the ongoing dispute with the former Yugoslav republic of Macedonia, which the Greeks regard as part of their territory and therefore nonexistent.

We drove for about two hours to Sani Beach Hotel, where we were put up for the night. I drew up a curtain in my room and gasped: the full orange moon was shining in the velvety cognac-coloured sky above the ancient Aegean Sea, breathing heavily under my window. The serenity of the scene was slightly marred by the prosaic noises made by drunken British tourists in the hotel. They looked like a bunch of wild soccer hooligans, shouting and crushing everything around them. One of them kept methodically falling off chairs and tables in the lobby bar, and his slightly less inebriated compatriots were looking after him with extreme care – lifting him up from the floor and trying to keep him vertical by propping his body against the bar for a few seconds before he collapsed again. 'Are you all right, James?' they kept asking, while semi-conscious James brandished his fists in the air, trying to hit his well-wishers in the face. I thought that only in Russia could one encounter such a caring, almost parental attitude to drunks. Reserved and polite in their homeland, the Brits were routinely throwing away the barriers while on holidays abroad.

It was one of those promotional journalistic trips where you have to see the maximum number of things in the shortest possible time. Our next two days were spent galloping around Halkidiki, looking at beaches, hotels, restaurants and sights. We drove along blueish modern highways and yellow dirt-tracks; we passed through countless seaside resorts: little towns, where men sat in street cafés in the shade of acacia trees sipping their endless cups of coffee; and tiny sunlit villages, deserted, apart from the friendly dogs with kind, almost human eyes. Everything in Greece was old, even antique, and the dust of history lay everywhere. In one village shop they were selling ridiculously small straw hats that made you look like a turn-of-the-century Odessa gangster. And suddenly they

90

told us that Aristotle was born there, in that very village, almost 2,500 years ago.

The more I saw of Greece, the more I liked it. No wonder gods chose to live there. I felt I was gradually becoming an organic part of the place, like the trees, flowers and bees. And the Cyrillic road signs looked misleadingly Russian from a distance.

These two days were also like one long feast of Lucullus. Hotels and restaurants in Halkidiki were vying for our attention and falling over themselves to impress us with their hospitality. For us, all these *tzatziki, tiri, horiatiki, hummus*, washed down with *ouzo, tsipouro, retsina* and *krassi*, merged into one extremely delicious (and intoxicating) Greek salad.

I find Greek food and drink wonderful, but only when you have them in Greece itself. *Ouzo* (anise vodka) or *tzatziki* (garlic and yogurt dip) won't taste half as good in London, or anywhere else except from Greece. It must be some mysterious interaction of blazing sunlight, stupefying smells of bougainvillea, emerald sea on the horizon and the astringent taste of *retsina* (young, unsweetened grape wine) that adds a peculiar and unique flavour to the local food. 'They have everything in Greece,' one of Chekhov's heroes said. And he was right.

I remember attending the first ever tasting of Greek food and drinks organised by one foolhardy Greek businessman in Moscow in 1989. He invited all of the Moscow *beau monde* and the media in a vain attempt to get some publicity for his firm.

It was doomed from the start. As soon as waiters brought in food and wines, ninety per cent of the guests, as if on command, produced portable *avoskas* (just-in-case string bags) from their pockets and started loading them with the free grub and booze. When their bags were full, they would retire, or rather run away, taking their trophies with them. Trays and tables were decimated in no time. In vain did Yuri Kazakov, a famous Moscow film and theatre actor of Greek origin, appeal to the public to 'stop stealing Greek food'. In vain did the businessman himself try to deliver a speech about his company's achievements: no one was listening . . . Of course, not a single word appeared in the press about the banquet: those who did steal food were ashamed of themselves, and those who didn't were ashamed of those who did. All the parties concerned, including the hapless Greek businessman, who was left to count his losses, wanted to forget about the incident as quickly as possible.

At one hotel restaurant in Halkidiki we noticed a group of blonde busty girls, all clad in red bikinis, sitting at the bar, drinking beer and chatting loudly. 'These are our animators,' the hotel manager told us. 'We bring them from Austria and pay them salaries for entertaining our tourists.' All four of us pricked up our *retsina*-soaked ears and looked at the girls with renewed interest. 'Don't get me wrong,' the manager went on. 'By entertainment I mean ballroom dances, quizzes and beach-games, nothing else . . .'

We thought it was a good idea: these beautiful 'animators' had managed to animate us without any quizzes — just by sitting at the bar in their bikinis. They definitely deserved their salaries.

It was at the Costis restaurant in Nea Fokea village that we got our first glimpse of Mount Athos monks. There were three of them, all stout, bearded, black-robed, with warm brown eyes. One of them had his hair in a pony-tail under his hood. It was St Pablo's day, a religious holiday, and the monks were eating and drinking for all they were worth.

It was our last evening before going to Mount Athos, and we were the guests of Dr Andreas Andreadis, the President of Halkidiki Hotel Association, a forty-year-old millionaire with the looks of a Hollywood film star — slim, tanned, charismatic and impeccably dressed.

The food and drink on our table was especially plentiful that night, and I expressed my growing concern about the frugal vegetarian diet we'd have to stick to at Mount Athos. Andreas smiled. 'Look at them,' he said pointing at the vigorously chewing monks, with pieces of food stuck in their bushy beards. 'They are all fat. I've never seen a skinny monk in my life. So don't you worry: they won't starve you to death there!'

Had we been aware of the exhausting two-hour climb to the *skete* that was in store for us next morning, we wouldn't have stuffed ourselves with so much food and booze. Or maybe we still would: even monks, as we could see, found it hard to resist the temptations of Greek cuisine. And we were not monks; we were journalists.

In the middle of the night I was woken by bright flashes of lightning. Could it be that God was warning us against going to Mount Athos?

On board a steam-boat, taking us to Mount Athos next morning (the land border with Greece being closed, this is the only way to get there), we had to be revived by steaming hot Greek coffee, kindly provided by our skipper. We felt in pieces after three days of uninterrupted gluttony. To make things worse, our bodies were covered with red volcanic boils, caused by ruthless Halkidiki mosquitoes that made no noise, as if having tiny silencers on their stings, and always bit you – treacherously – on the back, where you couldn't reach them – probably the result of some age-long mutation.

Dolphins were playing in the transparent emerald waters of the Aegean Sea. 'My Black Sea, you are the bluest in the world,' a popular Soviet song went. Now I knew it was but another case of the all-permeating Soviet megalomania. It was the Aegean Sea that was by far the world's bluest.

The dark bulk of Mount Athos was already looming large on the horizon. Nikos, our interpreter, told us that in the fourth century BC there were plans to convert the whole mountain into an enormous statue of Alexander the Great. The statue was supposed to represent Alexander holding a town of 10,000 people in his left hand and a river falling into the sea in his right hand, no less. The 'Great leader' Kim Il Sung himself would have been disgraced by such a monument. Tribute has to be paid to Alexander the Great, who found enough common sense to reject the project and tell his sycophantic factotums to leave the mountain as it was.

The earliest records suggest that the first hermits, seeking refuge from the Iconoclast emperors, came to Mount Athos in the eighth century. In 1060 a monastic republic was established there as a self-administered area of Greece. At that time it had 180 abbeys, and now some 1700 monks and hermits live there in twenty monasteries (seventeen Greek, one Russian, one Bulgarian and one Serbian) and lots of smaller ones: abbeys, *sketes*, cells and huts.

Each monastery resembles a fortified medieval town, with turrets, moats and thick stone walls. There are two main types of monastic 'regime' on Mount Athos – the cenobitic, or communal, where everything is shared among the brethren, and the idiorrhythmic where each monk clothes and feeds himself.

The mountain-state has its own police – *serdaris* – and its own elected government – The Holy Synod, subject to annual rotation, which makes Mount Athos one of the oldest democracies in the world. One important element of a democratic state, though, has always been missing there. I mean female suffrage of course. The reason? Total lack of females!

From the year 1006, no 'smooth-faced person' (this phrase from the old chronickles can pass for the earliest known example of political correctness) has stepped onto its shore. Even the Queen of England, on a visit to Greece, had to be satisfied with admiring the monasteries from the sea. Naturally, Mount Athos is not an EEC member: at least half (and the better half at that!) of the European population is forever unwelcome there. Until recently some monasteries had 'No women or tractors' signs on their gates.

We disembarked at Karoulia, the northernmost point of Mount Athos. There was no one to check our *diamonitirions* there. In fact, there was nothing there at all, apart from a shabby pier and the ruins of a fourteenth-century house where travelling and unfrocked monks would stay overnight before setting sail to the real world. Vegetation was scarce and the surface barren, with solid rocks and volcanic boulders, the shape of our mosquito-induced boils, scattered everywhere.

'It's June the eighteenth, gentlemen,' Doug announced gravely. We thought he was pulling our leg again, since we knew it was the first of July. Doug had to remind us that Orthodox monks lived by the Julian calendar, which was thirteen days behind the Gregorian one. We shrugged and adjusted our watches.

Indeed, modern time did not exist on the Holy Mountain. As we found out later in the journey, clocks in some of the monasteries were set to midnight at sunset. In others they were set to midday at dawn. This made fixing any kind of appointment on Mount Athos a pretty hopeless business, which didn't seem to bother the monks, whose only appointments were with God.

A soft buzzing sound reached our ears from above. We looked up and saw a small cloud of dust moving downhill towards us and quickly growing in size. Soon we were able to discern a solitary truck with a pony-tailed monk behind the wheel. This was the legendary Father Makarios, Mount Athos' only driver, about whom we had heard plenty from Doug and our Greek hosts. His old Unimog truck was the only means of public transport available on the Holy Mountain, where monks and pilgrims travel on foot or by mules. The bumpy back of this truck was to become our second home for several days.

Father Makarios, a taciturn and (to my considerable relief) chain-smoking monk, was wearing a pair of greasy jeans under his grimy habit. His breath reaked of *rakia* and cheap Karelia cigarettes. His vehicle, with Virgin Mary icons instead of pin-up girls on the windscreen, had the character of a mule. It was capable of negotiating, grudgingly, the steepest and the bumpiest of dirt-tracks (roads in the true sense of the word do not exist on Mount Athos). The four of us bounced in the back, like table-tennis balls in an empty lunch-box. Just like a mule, our Unimog invariably travelled on the very edge of the mountain path. Occasionally, Father Makarios would switch off the engine and pop out to stone down an unwary snake luxuriating on the track.

Father Makarios, despite being a monk, was quite a worldly

character, with only one peculiar phobia: he hated being photographed. As soon as one of us tried to stealthily aim a camera at him, he would promptly duck down, covering his face with both hands and letting go of the wheel (he was probably convinced that only God had the copyright for his face). So, to stay alive, we had to give up our futile attempts to capture him on film.

The first monastery on our way was the 1,030-year-old Great Lavra, the largest on Mount Athos. In the sixteenth century it was inhabited by 700 brothers, whereas today there were just seventy, not counting 450 'dependent' monks living in cells and *sketes* under Great Lavra's jurisdiction.

A donkey was grazing near the monastery's ornate gates under the sign 'Forest is God's blessing. Protect it from fire'. There was no forest in sight. Businesslike monks kept arriving at the gates by mules, and Nikos, our interpreter, greeted them in Greek. 'In Mount Athos they say: "Your blessings, Father!" instead of "Hello" or "How are you today?"' he explained.

We were finally let inside and briskly led through a spacious magnolia-lined courtyard, where three duty monks were washing incense in bottles in a tub with soapy water, to the Abbot's quarters. The clock on one of the towers showed one thirty p.m.; by my watch, still set to Greek time, it was ten a.m.

Father Phillipos, the Abbot, looked wonderfully youthful and fit for his age: he was eighty-seven. His eyes emanated happiness, warmth and wisdom. He moved around with a crozier but it was part of his Abbot's outfit, not a walking aid.

'Welcome to Great Lavra!' he said in an unexpectedly high-pitched voice. 'You can see that God is here. He protects our monastery!'

We looked around the room dutifully: God was nowhere to be seen. Instead, a younger monk pushed in a trolly with tiny cups of thick Greek coffee, miniature glasses with *rakia*, a vase with rose petal jam, and a plate with sugary lumps of Turkish Delight (we had already been warned by Nikos that in Greece one was supposed to call this 'Greek

Delight': there was no delight lost between the Turks and the Greeks, as we all knew). This little feast was an obligatory part of the traditional welcoming ceremony in every Mount Athos monastery. Each visitor, be he a tourist, a pilgrim or a fellow monk, was greeted with these unsophisticated treats.

We were especially pleased with the *rakia*, since we all needed a hair of the dog.

'The Holy Mountain is the place of love and open-minded thoughts,' the Abbot continued after a quick sip of *rakia*. 'It stands beyond time, but accepts all people with the same love . . .'

'Apart from women,' I thought.

'We monks live outside the world with love and prayers for the outside world.'

'Love' was evidently the Abbot's favourite word. And he clearly meant it.

Having shaken the Abbot's withered hand, we went on a short tour of the monastery. Our guide was a middle-aged monk wearing a buckled leather belt on top of his robe. There was a parting on the side of his narrow and tight habit to make walking easier. His eyes, like those of the Abbot, were radiant and full of faith.

Besides the main temple (*katholikon*), there were thirty-seven smaller churches on the grounds of the monastery – more than in the whole of the former Soviet Union, I imagine. One of them, the Chapel of Forty Saints, contained the tomb of St Athanasios, the monastery's founder. The tomb was covered with fresh flowers, jewellery and watches – gifts from the pilgrims. There were lots of watches there, probably because they were not of much use in Mount Athos anyway.

Next to the tomb there hung a highly unusual icon of the Virgin Mary with her neck bared. Our guide said that they called her 'Economissa' at Great Lavra. I thought I understood why: the artist – Theophanes, from the island of Crete – was obviously a very practical person, fond of economising on paint.

The portrait of the flirtatious Virgin Mary was covered with glass, dimmed by kisses of the faithful. Her graceful bare neck was the most

97

opaque place of all: that was probably where the majority of pilgrims and monks were (inadvertently, I am sure) aiming their kisses. They were all men, after all, and the Virgin Mary was the only woman around them.

Nikos, himself a believer, planted a quick kiss on the icon. He struck the bare neck too . . .

At about midday, Nikos and Doug exchanged a couple of meaningful glances. We had no idea what they were up to, but felt trouble.

'Do you remember that particular part in my information package that warned you about transfers by foot or mule for up to one hour at a time?' asked Doug. We nodded. 'Well, time has come! Enough of eating and drinking, let's do some walking for a change!' he announced, cheerfully pointing his finger upwards, to the top of the mountain. There, partly hidden by a wandering cloud, we saw a tiny dot of a stone hut. As it turned out later, this was Doug's little ruse. We had to climb much, much higher, well beyond that abandoned *skete*.

The first several hundred metres were covered with ease. Fuelled by the monastical *rakia*, we were even trying to crack jokes. Lean and sprightly, Nikos was floating from stone to stone like a butterfly.

'You are like a mule, Nikos,' I said, in an earnest attempt to please him. In Russian there exists a simile 'as strong as a mule', and that was what I meant. But Nikos, who must have taken these words at face value, did not appreciate my compliment. 'Thank you very much!' he replied with utmost sarcasm and didn't speak to me until the end of the climb.

We all stopped talking in half-an-hour or so, and started puffing instead. It was the beginning of that nightmarish climb which ended with the appearance of Father Spiridon.

The chief monk of St Anna *skete*, Father Spiridon had an iron handshake and the lean, sinewy figure of a marathon runner. 'I can walk up and down the mountain several times a day,' he said to us on the way (he was walking and we were astride the mules). 'When someone is happy with himself, he feels no hardship . . .' Our looks must have betrayed profound dissatisfaction with ourselves. It took me more than an hour to fully regain my breath after the climb. Twenty-five years of smoking were not conducive to mountaineering.

Three *sketes* – St Anna, Thomas, and Danilei – were perched on top of the mountain, 400 metres above the sea level, next to each other, like three sisters. Each had ten to fifteen monks who rarely went down to the valley. Until 1963, no animals were allowed in the *sketes*, and everything – furniture, kitchen utensils and details of church interiors – had to be brought up by the monks. It took twenty of them eight hours to carry an electric power generator up to St Anna. I was beginning to understand why all the monks in the *sketes* were trim and broad-shouldered.

Each *skete* was like a little peaceful oasis – with branchy trees and gardenia bushes, with ivy-covered buildings and blossoming irises, with bees buzzing above the flowers. What a joy for a pilgrim to find himself in this cool paradise after a long and exhausting climb!

'This *skete* is the hardest place to get to at Mount Athos, and not many pilgrims make it here,' Father Grigorius, the chief monk of Danilei, told us. 'So, now you've got first-hand experience of monasticism which you can convey to your readers.' We were very proud, of course, our pride being only slightly marred by the prospect of walking all the way down soon.

Traditional coffee, *rakia* (or was it *tsipouro* this time?) and Turkish, sorry Greek, Delight followed.

'We are very happy to see you, because you are our brothers, and when you see your brother – you see God. To your health!' Father Spiridon toasted us.

I replied with my favourite Georgian toast: 'Once the highlanders were asked: "Why do you build your houses so high up in the mountains where it is so hard to get to you?" And the highlanders answered: "Good friends will get to us despite all the hardships, and we don't need any bad friends!" To friendship!' I thought it sounded very appropriate, if somewhat frivolous.

'We are the happiest people in the world,' Father Grigorius said.

'Without having anything, we've got everything . . . Had I a chance to be reborn, I'd become a monk again.'

I went out onto a terrace for a smoke. Monks' freshly-washed blue working robes were drying in the sun. Three black monastic cats (all tomcats of course) were sleeping in the shadow of a large geranium pot. The cats were as lean and sprightly as the monks themselves. Only the monks were much more hard-working. In summer, they would start praying at three a.m. in their cells, and then – at five a.m. – congregate for common prayer, to be interrupted at eight fifteen by a cup of holy water and a piece of bread – a monastic breakfast. After that – more prayers, and work, work, work – without holidays or days off. In winter, they would wake up at midnight, pray until seven a.m. and go to bed at sunset.

I quickly peeped through an open door of one of the cells: a bunk, a small bed-side table with an open Bible on it, several books on the shelf, that was all.

There was an icon-painting workshop at the *skete* of Thomas, where several young monks were sitting bent over drawing boards. And at St Anna the newly painted icons were supplied with sophisticated silver frames.

'The worst thing for a monk is lack of work,' Father Spiridon said, welcoming us to his domain. They prepared a 'special lunch' for us at St Anna: fish soup, potatoes, fruit and bread. The meal was served by a young, aproned monk who spoke excellent English and showered us with questions about London life. I thought I should leave him some English reading matter. Having rummaged through my shoulderbag, I found a rumpled copy of the *Sunday Times* 'Style and Travel' magazine and gave it to the monk. He took the magazine carefully, with two fingers, as if it were a frog or a snake. 'I have to ask Father Spiridon's permission,' he said with the trepidation of a teenager about to open the *Good Sex Guide*. The permission was granted (Father Spiridon must have overlooked the Lonely Hearts column), and the unremarkable 'Style and Travel' magazine, instead of ending up on a London rubbish dump or being recycled, took its place on a book-shelf in a monastic cell, next to the Bible. It was in for a very long life.

After lunch, Father Spiridon showed us a memorial cell of the late Gerasimos Gerasimakis (Father Gerasimos), a well-known Greek poet and writer of hymns, who spent forty-five years in this *skete* until his death in 1991. The prolific Father Gerasimos was the author of fifty books, at least 800 pages each, all written in longhand. He used to write spontaneously, without editing, and never came back to what he had written before. I wish that was the case with this book of mine . . .

At some point during the excursion, I heard a loud shriek of a mule from the adjoining cell. 'Do they keep animals inside the *skete*?' I wondered. But it was not a mule: it was a telephone with a bell that sounded exactly like a mule's neighing. Father Spiridon could not contain his joy, like a child showing his new toy to a friend. Like Father, like son, I guess . . .

Time was playing havoc with us again: it was four forty-five p.m. on the clock in one *skete* and five-fifty p.m. in another, while my watch showed two thirty-five p.m. I gave up trying to establish a system behind Mount Athos time. There was none.

'*Revenons à nos moutons*' – 'Let's come back to our sheep,' the French say. Whatever time it was, it was time for us to go back to our mules. With my legs still hurting after the climb, I firmly decided to make the return journey by mule and announced this decision to Father Spiridon, who took it without enthusiasm. 'You can have the mule, there is no problem with that,' he said. 'But, I think you might find it a bit uncomfortable . . .'

Riding a mule gives you a feeling of slow levitation. The animal is so small that you can hardly see it in-between your legs. It is as if some invisible force is carrying you slowly but surely up the hill. A downhill journey is much more precarious and feels like a slow freefall down the precipice. Stepping from stone to stone, my mule would bend his front legs, folding them up almost to his head, and my whole body would lean forward at an impossible angle (remember: mules always walk on the edge of the abyss) thus increasing the pressure on the poor animal's legs even further. 'Relax and let go of the saddle!' Father Spiridon, who was walking beside me, screamed. I tried to follow his instructions and came close to going head over heels down into the precipice, which would have been the quickest way to get to our boat, still moored at Karoulia 400 metres below.

After a couple of near-somersaults, I chose to get off the mule's submissive back and walk down. It was slower and much more tiring, yes, but at least it gave me a good chance of reaching the boat in one piece, not as a pack of mincemeat.

At one point during our slow and painful descent, we met a caravan of several mules, driven by two tired monks. One of the animals was carrying on its back a box with a computer monitor screen. The caravan was slowly moving up the hill, towards the *sketes*. Well, even Mount Athos probably cannot resist all the pressures of modern times.

Back on the boat, I collapsed on to a wooden bunk like a sack of potatoes dropped by a careless stevedore, and dozed off. I woke up at Daphnie, Mount Athos' main (and only) port of entry. It was just a cluster of houses: a pub; a deserted customs office; a shop selling sets of faded, fly-blown postcards and incense by the kilo; and a public toilet that I hurried to visit. Still groggy after the sleep, I stared at the toilet's only door, looking for a 'Gents' sign. It took me a while to recollect that I was in Mount Athos where there were no ladies and therefore no 'Ladies'. As they say in America, it doesn't take a rocket scientist to figure this out. I pulled the handle and resolutely went inside. The toilet was filthy.

We were to stay overnight at the monastery of Simonopetra, the fourteenth century skyscraper, sitting on a tower-like rock high above the sea. Thanks to Father Makarios, who drove his Unimog at the breakneck speed of twenty miles per hour, we made it there just before sunset, when the gates of all the monasteries are firmly locked for the night.

We were immediately taken to the refectory where the monks were already having their evening meal of pasta, green salad, water and peaches. A duty monk, standing on a small rostrum, was monotonously reading from the Bible as we ate. There was not enough time to savour our food (there was nothing much to savour, to be honest): the moment the monk finished reading everyone was expected to stop eating and leave. Obviously in a hurry to have a quick bite himself, the monk was literally chewing on his words, swallowing sentences and whole paragraphs.

Leaving the refectory was a curious ritual: the Abbot was the first to retire; three old, grey-bearded monks with hunched backs minced after him; other monks followed in strict hierarchic order. The procession was concluded by hatless and habit-less novices and trainee monks. We trailed disorderly after them as the last and totally unnecessary link in this chain. We probably looked ridiculously out-of-place in our dirty jeans and sweat-soaked T-shirts.

In the *Arkhondariki*, the monastery's guest quarters, where we were escorted by a grim and tight-lipped guest-master monk, we were provided with a pair of soft Old Testament sandals each. We were to sleep in one large cell with anti-mosquito nets on the windows.

The *Arkhondariki* were situated along the perimeter of the top of the monastery building. To get to the bathroom, one had to pass through a circular terrace, clinging to the monastery walls. This frail wooden scaffolding was precariously suspended above the bottomless precipice. It shook under your feet like an unsteady ship deck during a sea-storm. Through gaps between squeaky floorboards sagging under your feet, sharp black rocks licked by the foamy sea were clearly visible a hundred metres below. In short, it was an ideal place for committing suicide, even if you didn't feel particularly suicidal. It was also ideal for deterring you from using the bathroom too often.

The legend goes that when St Simeon was building this monastery, his attendant, monk Isaiah, slipped from the high scaffold he was walking on and rolled down the ravine. When he reached the bottom, he was standing on his feet, saved by his profound faith. It was plain that a convinced agnostic, like myself, didn't stand a chance of survival in case of a similar accident.

We were prepared to risk our lives for a hot shower however, and, despite all the dangers involved, ventured onto the terrace. In the bathroom, next to the shower cabins, we saw a puzzling sign proclaiming in English that 'Washrooms do not function as shower-baths'. In plain English this clearly meant 'Washrooms are not to be used for washing'. The sign next to it was even more contradictory: 'Washing or shaving is not allowed without bodily covering'. We decided to ignore the signs, but had to be satisfied with an ice-cold shower. There was no hot water in the monastery.

These forbidding bathroom signs were my first introduction to the *Typicon* – the code of conduct for visitors to the monastery. The full English version of it was prominently displayed on the walls of the *Arkhondariki*. It was one of the most amazing documents I've ever seen:

1. The hospitality to visitors is of one day's duration.
2. On arrival the visitors are obliged to be decently clothed.
3. Visits or circulation [sic] in the service areas of the Arkhondariki are not allowed under any circumstances.
4. The visitors pass the time quietly, and they go to and return from the washrooms [where they are not allowed to wash] decently clothed.
5. The visitors may converse in the hall of the Arkhondariki, but they do not visit the other areas of the Holy Monastery or the Monks' places of work. [Note the capital 'M in 'Monks' and the small 'v' in 'visitors'.]
6. Shanting [sic] or singing, noise and shouting, and the use of tape recorders and radio sets, especially at a loud volume, inside or near the Holy Monastery, is always not allowed.
7. After compline [the last service of the day] conversations are absolutely forbidden. Everyone goes to their rooms.

This bureaucratic San Marino-style *Typikon*, I must confess, did not prevent me from 'circulating' on the monastery's balcony, from where I was able to admire the most glorious sunset. The sky was gradually merging with the sea, and the sea with the shore, as if in the process of mutual mimicry. The night was falling upon Mount Athos like a giant black monk descending slowly from his heavenly *skete* and covering the earth with his black robes. The full round moon was this monk's face shining from under his starry *klobuk* . . .

That night I had wonderful technicolour dreams, the dreams where all my problems were solved.

'You snored!' Doug announced to me triumphantly next morning. 'No, I didn't!' I objected. It was a pointless argument.

We were awakened at dawn by the rhythmic sounds of *semantrons* — wooden drums — calling monks to the morning liturgy. To my great surprise, my body did not hurt after yesterday's climb and I felt beautifully rested. Maybe Mount Athos was indeed a divine place where miracles could occur.

The *semantrons* kept drumming monotonously, and the black-hooded monks were sliding across the monastery yard towards the church, like white-shrouded ghosts in a slow-motion picture, shown in the negative by the erroneous cinema operator of dawn. We followed them.

It was dark inside the church. Candles were burning, and the sweet smell of incense teased our nostrils. An invisible multi-voiced choir was singing psalms with amazing harmony and grace. Simonopetra had one of the best choirs on Mount Athos. The older monks were praying, half-sitting in special wooden high chairs with polished elbow-rests. They were totally immersed in prayer and kept moving their lips silently, as if in a semi-trance. We became so affected by the divine singing that we didn't notice how three hours lapsed.

The monks were leaving the temple, their eyes radiating joy and warmth. They greeted each other affectionately, taking turns to embrace one comrade who had just returned from a trip. They were like one big and happy family.

Among the bearded and hairy monks there was one whose

appearance stood out prominently. He was bald, bespectacled and completely hairless and perhaps because of this he looked much more down-to-earth than the rest.

After breakfast, he approached me on the *Arkhondariki* balcony.

'I noticed you in the church,' he told me in almost unaccented English.

'I noticed you too,' I said honestly.

'You have kind eyes. Are you a Christian?'

'I don't think so,' I replied, exactly as I had many years ago at the Soviet Muslim Board.

'Never mind. I know you will find God one day. Look at me. I used to be a very successful businessman in Athens, I travelled the world, but I was never happy. It was only here that I found the meaning of life. There are fifty-five of us in this monastery, all but five of us do not even have beds: we sleep on the floor. But we never quarrel, because we are happy with ourselves.'

'Are you asking me to take a monastic vow?'

'Nothing of the kind! I just want you to find faith and to save yourself. Human spiritual life is a constant movement. It can go up and down – like a thermometer. People become monks not because they are strong, but because they are weak. When you despair, you probably start drinking and smoking. When a monk despairs, he goes to the Abbot and gets his advice. The monastery helps you to take the right direction in your life. Monks do not have holidays. We do not need to see our relatives. When they come to visit us, we treat them no differently from other pilgrims. Our mothers, fathers and brothers are this holy community and God. We do not need women: all of them are represented here by the Virgin Mary.'

'What if someone gets disappointed with monastic life and decides to leave? Will you allow him?' I asked.

'It is easy to leave Mount Athos. It is like divorce. If you want to break your marriage with God, you are free to do it. Mount Athos is easy to leave, but it is hard to get to. Many young people these days want to become monks. Many more than we can accept.'

'How would you describe your main purpose of being here?'

'We are here to pray for you. And for the world. Someone has to.'

He nearly converted me, this bald, soft-spoken monk, who probably belonged to the monastery's recruitment unit. I never came to learn his name. For me, he remained Father Anonymous. Before returning to his prayers, he left a note in my memo-pad: 'Golden rule: do for others what you would like others to do for you!' And then added in his round, childish handwriting: 'East or West – God is best!' – a useful, if a somewhat belated, proverb for a vagabond like myself, who had no home and whose childish beliefs had been shattered beyond repair after thirty-six years of life in a totalitarian state.

Thanks anyway, Father Anonymous! My fourteen-year-old son would have probably found your advice useful.

Father Makarios's truck was waiting for us at the monastery gates like a faithful dog. Our bumpy journey continued.

I had two chances to speak Russian that day. The first was at the Russian monastery of St Panteleimon, the sight of which brought childhood memories flooding back. With its golden crosses and blue onion domes it looked very much like St Sergius monastery in Zagorsk. St Panteleimon, with its 3,000 cells, could have become the most populous on the whole of Mount Athos, had the Russian monks found it easier to come here in the last seventy-five years. As it was, it had just forty monks, of whom we saw only one – a red-headed and freckled Father Filaret, born in the Urals and still speaking Russian with a clear Ural accent. He showed us the world's largest bell on one of the belfries. It could easily cover all seven of us including Father Filaret himself. Father Makarios could probably have squeezed in too, if persuaded to leave his Unimog and join us. For me, this was the end of a yet another Soviet myth: we were always told that the Tsar Bell in the Kremlin was the world's largest. This one was not just bigger, it was still very much in use, whereas the Tsar Bell had never been rung.

* * *

We were in a hurry to get to Karies, the capital of the Holy Mountain, where we had an appointment with all five members of the ruling Holy Synod. This was a rare privilege that was bestowed on us thanks to Nikos, whose uncle, Father Lucas, was one of the Holy Synod members. Connections were important on the Holy Mountain too.

Karies was a soporific little village with several cafés and shops selling gardening tools, cheap icons and brochures denouncing Zionism. There was also a helicopter pad there, in case the Patriarch came on a visit from Constantinople. The golden domes of the Protato, Mount Athos' main temple, glistened in the sun.

We had some time before our meeting and popped into a shop-cum-pub for a quick beer. Inside there was only one customer, a skinny old monk sitting at a table covered with empty beer bottles. He was obviously drunk.

Father Tipsius (let's call him that) had a grey dishevelled beard and the quick darting eyes of a mischievous child. Fluent in English, German and French, he spoke with a dry intellectual chuckle. A physician by education, he was a graduate of the University of Grenoble and practised in Basel, where he became a professor of medicine. He refused to expand on his reasons for becoming a monk, but told us he was living in a *kellion* (cell) on his own and looking after 'someone who is very ill'. Father Tipsius was thoroughly enjoying our company, we could see that. He kept switching from English into French and back into English, with the same ease with which Father Makarios changed gear of his Unimog truck. Swigging from his umpteenth bottle of beer, he reprimanded me for smoking – first in German, then in French. *'Je vous remercie!'* he kept saying when we shook hands to leave. I thought there were tears in his eyes, but maybe it was just the effect of having had too much beer . . .

The Holy Synod building was clearly the loudest architectural statement in Karies. With its classical columns and oblong oval windows, from which the clatter of typewriters could be heard, it was a cross between a Byzantine shrine and a Soviet administrative building. The state flag of Mount Athos – a black two-headed eagle on a yellow background – fluttered on its roof.

The building was guarded by two sleepy *serdaris* in jeans and peaked cockaded caps.

We were met by Father Moisseus, the General Secretary of the Holy Mountain, who explained that restoration works were under way in the building and suggested we spoke to the Holy Synod members outside.

Soon they appeared on the porch, looking as grand and serene as apostles – five bearded men in long black robes. Father Mitrophanis, the First Abbot of Mount Athos (the equivalent of the Prime Minister), a bespectacled old monk with a snow-white beard on a kindly face and a crozier in his right hand, stood in the middle. Our open-air audience was short.

'The Holy Mountain is not what it looks, it is something you cannot see,' Father Mitrophanis said. 'We are here to keep the 1,000-year-old tradition. The past gives guidance to the future. Spiritual life doesn't change with the times. You don't want us monks to change, do you?'

Due to Nikos's connections, we were given yet another rare privilege – to take a photo of all the Holy Synod members. With the monks' notorious adversity to cameras (remember Father Makarios), this was on a par with the ancient Chinese honour of watching the emperor eat.

After a quick back-of-the-truck lunch of bread and olives, we visited the monastery of Philotheou, where Father Lucas, Nikos's influential uncle, was the Abbot. It was a neat and homely monastery, and all the monks were cheerful, young and relaxed. Some of them were wearing trainers under their robes. They clearly adored their Abbot and kept looking into his mouth when he spoke. We were beginning to comprehend what had made these handsome young men abandon our 'civilised' world, with its discos, restaurants, supermarkets and fancy cars.

Apart from being the Holy Synod member, Father Lucas was a

well-known writer and theologian. This became plain the moment he started speaking:

'It is very hard for someone who doesn't wear a black robe to understand what makes us monks pray and work so hard. We have to keep a distance from the world. The best way to admire a painting is from the distance, isn't it? We do not live for today, we look to the future. We follow not our own needs but God's needs. When a monk succeeds in something, he feels he works for the whole world. Our world is a circle with God in the centre, and all our life is a movement towards it. The closer one comes to the centre, the more charisma he acquires from God, the charisma that goes not to himself, but to others.

'The Holy Mountain doesn't answer any questions. It is the one single answer to the question of the meaning of life. All our visitors enter into a dialogue with this place, which allows them to spread their wings. Every human being has wings, but only very few of us can ever spread them. Here even the worst of sinners feel they can start changing.'

He looked at me with his tranquil grey eyes, and I suddenly felt a magic touch of the holy spirit, or whatever it was. I felt as if I had just taken a sort of spiritual shower which was making me, an incorrigible sinner, a bit quieter and a bit purer than I used to be – though it would undoubtedly take a couple of years to purify me completely. I was sure that my colleagues, the hardened London hacks, were feeling pretty much the same. The spirit of Mount Athos was definitely affecting us all, and we were slowly spreading our half-forgotten and feeble, rumpled and alcohol-stained wings.

The red-robed monk of the setting sun was leaving Mount Athos, heading for the sea, and our faithful Unimog, steered by Father Makarios, was doing its best to make it to the monastery of Vatopediou while its gates were still open.

We were running late, with no more than half an hour left before sunset, when we saw two hitchhiking monks at the turn of the track.

Their robes were slightly different from those of Mount Athos monks: they were grey not black.

Father Makarios pressed the brakes.

The hitchhikers were pilgrims from Russia, who had walked to Mount Athos all the way from Bulgaria. That's why their robes were grey: they were simply covered with dust after their long journey. One of them – Father Nikodim – was a monk of the recently re-opened St Daniel monastery in Moscow, the other was a first-year student of the theological academy in Zagorsk, the town where I spent the first three years of my life. His name was Maxim. It was a real miracle, not only for me, but for the tired pilgrims too.

'We thought we weren't going to make it to Vatopediou in time and would have to spend the night on the road,' Maxim was saying elatedly in Russian. 'The *batiushka* [little father] then started praying and – bingo! Your truck appeared. And, what's more, with a Russian in the back!' He was almost a teenager, with youthful pimples on his hairless face.

To complete the miracle, we gave the Russian pilgrims all the food we had in our knapsacks: dried fruit, biscuits, tinned meat and fish. We had brought these foodstuffs from London on Doug's advice, but after two days of healthy monastic diet were finding them superfluous. And heavy to carry.

Maxim was very pleased with our donations. 'We are not supposed to eat meat,' he said apologetically, while opening a can of meatballs and putting one of them into his mouth.

We arrived at Vatopediou one minute before a key-master monk locked the gates with a huge rusty key.

The monastery of Vatopediou was less spectacular in appearance than Simonopetra. Or maybe I was simply getting used to the sight of these medieval fortified towns.

At the monastery's temple there was a fresco of a dog-faced saint. The meaning of it, as explained by Father Lazarius, a young and handsome monk who showed us around, was that God was inside you and no matter how ugly you looked, you could still become a saint. This sounded reassuring.

On another icon, the Virgin Mary was depicted as a loving mother protecting her baby, whose uplifted finger was pressed to her lips as if telling her to shut up − a natural childish gesture. The icon looked like an old family photo rather than an object of religious adoration. There must have been realists among icon-painters too. Luckily, they were not socialist realists − the artists who draw not what they see or feel, but what they hear.

At the monastery's 1,000-year-old library-museum they had the original parchment manuscript of Ptolemy's *Geography*; the world's biggest precious stone, set into a chalice, a drink from which, supposedly, cured a snake-bite; and loads of other priceless treasures − all virtually unguarded.

Father Lazarius was a serious and unsmiling character. He told us a blood-chilling (from his point of view) story about some devious American TV crew who had somehow managed to get permission to come to Mount Athos. 'They filmed the monasteries, they filmed the monks, and then, back in America, inserted sex scenes into the footage!' He pronounced the word 'sex' with such genuine fear and disgust that it was clear he hadn't seen the film.

The *Arkhondariki* at Vatopediou were much better than at Simonopetra, though. Here we were allocated two rooms. At this point, Doug initiated a debate. Referring to the highly improbable (and unproved) fact of my snoring the previous night, he suggested that Nikos (another alleged snorer) and I were accommodated in one room, and all the (alleged) non-snorers − in the other. I objected by saying that this arrangement could work only in one unlikely case: if Nikos and myself could start snoring simultaneously. Otherwise, the one who fell asleep (and thus started snoring) first, would keep his room-mate from falling asleep, snoring or not. This iron logic could not fail to impress Doug (and everybody else) and I ended up alone in one of the two rooms.

The *Typikon* in Vatopediou was similar to that of Simonopetra, apart from a couple of additional regulations: one stating that 'Visitors who are naked and semi-naked in the corridors will be immediately expelled from the monastery,' and the other − somewhat mysteriously − urging the visitors to 'use sheets together with blankets'. On the brighter side, it didn't ask you to be fully clothed while in the shower-room, where you were not allowed to take showers anyway. The reason for this leniency was obvious: there were neither shower-rooms, nor showers in Vatopediou.

I spent a couple of hours chatting with Maxim on the balcony before retiring to the luxury of my private solitary-confinement cell, where I wrote my notes until eleven p.m., when the monastery's electric power generator was switched off and a duty monk shuffled in with a kerosene lamp. I kept writing in its treacherous light, throwing long vibrating shadows onto the cell's walls, and imagined myself a medieval chronicler or (heaven knows why) an alchemist, until my hand, holding the pen, and the pen itself, and my spider-like scribbles all started shaking and swimming in front of my eyes.

I had just enough strength left to blow out the light.

What foot do you usually get up from? You don't know? I do. I am always very careful to climb down from my bed right leg first. Why? Simply because, if you start your day from your left foot, it will be a disaster: you will be late to your office and quarrel with your boss; you will leave your lunch-box at home and stumble over your glasses, smashing them to smithereens; you will get three parking tickets in one hour; your wife will walk out on you and, to crown it all, in the evening you will be bitten by your own cat. And all of this because you got up from a wrong foot . . .

I got up from the right one on my last morning in Mount Athos − a clear indication of a successful day ahead. I was feeling as fresh as a cucumber, as they say in Russia.

They had fish and red wine for breakfast at the refectory. It was the last day before the start of the fast, when for two weeks monks would not be eating any animal products at all. They were clearly enjoying their final feast before the fast. With fasting not on our agenda, we nevertheless thought it proper to share this morning meal with them, although for us it was rather a feast before the feast: we were to go back to Halkidiki in the afternoon and had plans to celebrate our return to the real world at a good restaurant.

Prior to going back, we were to visit *kellion* Ravdouchou, Europe's oldest house. We were told that at present it was occupied by one of the Holy Mountain's most colourful characters – Father Ioannikios.

For me, this proved to be the best experience in Mount Athos.

Every morning at three o'clock Father Ioannikios starts his daily prayers. He prays for himself and for all of us. He prays for good harvests and for peace in the world. Father Ioannikios doesn't have to go far to get to church: he has a chapel in his own house, or rather his *kellion*.

Like other such *kellions* on the Holy Mountain, his cell resembled a farmhouse with a small tract of land. But Ravdouchou was far from typical. As a team of UNESCO experts established in 1966, this *kellion* was Europe's oldest dwelling, a house which has been inhabited continuously since the seventh century AD. Father Ioannikios lived there alone.

What drives people to solitude? Unfulfilled aspirations? Broken illusions? Religious ardour? 'Whosoever is delighted in solitude is either a wild beast or a god,' said Francis Bacon. Father Ioannikious, the only tenant of Europe's oldest house, was neither. Nor was he a misanthrope: he loves people and warmly welcomes any visitor to his remote isolated abode.

'I live here alone, but I never feel alone,' he told us in his excellent English. He also spoke Russian, Danish, Bulgarian, Albanian and German. And his native Greek, of course. He explained: 'I feel like being with lots of people – with every living being in the world. My goal as a monk is not just to save my own soul, but to save them all.'

Father Ioannikios had a tempestuous life. He was born Eustrakios Papakonstantinou in a small hamlet in Northern Greece in 1927. In

1943, at the age of sixteen, he joined the anti-Fascist resistance, and three years later, during the Greek Civil War, found himself in prison. There Eustrakios grew attracted to the Communist ideal, and on his release in 1953 he joined the Young Communist League. 'I was a true believer in Communism: that's why I joined,' he said.

Soviet tanks in the streets of Budapest in 1956, crushing the Hungarian uprising, crushed his ideal too. 'It was a great tragedy to have my beliefs shattered,' Father Ioannikios told us, pulling nervously at his ornate prayer rope. 'I suddenly realised that Communism was just a utopia: an insane dream that could be sustained only by tanks and bullets.'

Looking into his dark brown eyes, I remembered my own grandfather, an old Bolshevik and an activist of the 1917 revolution. In 1937, during Stalin's purges, he expected to be arrested at any moment. He was a robust and strong-willed man, but my mother recalled how he would faint when there was a knock at the door in the evening, or a late telephone call.

By the end of his years, my grandfather became deeply disillusioned with Communist dogmas, to which he devoted all his life, and his eyes had the same haunted, even tragic, expression as the one I found in the eyes of Father Ioannikios when he talked about the upheavals of his past. There is little more painful than belated awareness.

Having left the ranks of the Communist League in 1957, Eustrakios Papkonstantinou started travelling the world. He studied film-making in Bulgaria, then worked as a film director for Bulgarian television.

'It was the time of the so-called Khrushchev thaw,' he recalled. 'In Bulgaria they were trying to get rid of the party small fry, but never touched the big fish. In one of my films I showed a luxurious mansion where Communist top brass lived, and interviewed their serfs: cleaners and caretakers, the common people – the very people they were supposed to serve, but who in fact were serving them. Of course they sacked me,' he concluded with a sad laugh.

After Bulgaria he went to Africa, then to Copenhagen, where for several years he worked as a researcher at the Royal Library. Gradually he realised that capitalism was not ideal either. There was only one place he could go: Mount Athos. Despite his Communist past, he was accepted there with open arms. The rebellious 'red' intellectual Eustrakios Papakonstantinou became the pious black monk and hermit, Father Ioannikios Ravdouchos.

We were sitting at a huge oak table in the semi-darkness of his *kellion*. We drank his home-made *grappa* (he makes 170 litres of it a year in his own distillery), and ate a healthy monastic meal of beetroot, garlic, green salad and fish. Like all those Mount Athos monks who have chosen to live in cells, Father Ioannikios was almost self-sufficient: he grew most of his food himself.

After lunch he led me round the ancient house, which was in desperate need of restoration. The floorboards were rotten, the walls crumbling, and the spartan furniture was covered with the dust of history. But in the chapel Peter and Paul stared at us with unfading, wistful eyes from two amazing twelfth-century frescoes, fresh and untainted, only slightly touched by time. There was neither reproach nor reassurance in their eyes: only hope and forgiveness.

These frescoes were some of the most famous on the whole of Mount Athos. And underneath, in the cellar, there was another church, dating from the seventh and eighth centuries, the time of iconoclasm, with patterns of trees and flowers instead of frescoes or icons on its walls.

Who was it who said a house always resembles its owner? The *kellion* of Ravdouchou, which had withstood thirteen centuries of fire, flood, storm and frost, possessed the unbreakable spirit of its present-day dweller.

Do houses have souls? They certainy do. A house can breathe. It is capable of shivering in winter and perspiring in summer. It yawns in the morning and snores at night. A house can also die of old age — and this was what Father Ioannikios was desperately trying to prevent. He devoted all his exceptional energy to the restoration of Ravdouchou.

In 1966 the Ministry for Northern Greece decided to start restoring this unique *kellion*. But plans remained plans. 'The house has been caught in controversy between engineers and archeologists,' Father Ioannikios explained. 'The former wanted to renovate it; the latter to keep it as it was. As a result, nothing was done.'

Father Ioannikios saw us off to the gates.

'Communism is a utopia, but Ravdouchou is not,' he said. 'Here I have the chance to be on my own and think what I can do for other people.'

He closed the gate behind us. I looked back at the black-robed, white-bearded figure for the last time. A polyglot and film director, Communist turned monk, a man of the world who chose to live outside the world, trying to save it, he was standing on the path behind the gates, his hands folded on his chest, looking very much like one of the saints in the ancient frescoes of his *kellion*.

* * *

Several hours later – dirty, unshaven and mosquito-bitten – we were back in the real world. For the first time in three days we saw men not wearing black robes, and women – these strange creatures with round breasts and high-pitched voices. The world was as hectic and fussy as before, only we had changed. I felt as if I had had an anaesthetic against all worldly worries. Perhaps I even had a halo above my head?

Maybe it was *our* life, not the monks', that was unreal, after all.

I carried this anaesthetising feeling in my soul for about a week, before it got dissolved in the habitual whirlwind of daily routine, and the nimbus was transformed back into clouds of tobacco smoke above my head.

But now I know something very important: whatever we do and wherever we go in this world, the tireless monks of Mount Athos are praying for us, day and night. And we are never in solitude.

P.S. The story of *kellion* Ravdouchou had a happy ending. After I wrote it up in the *European* and after it was reprinted by several Greek newspapers, the government of Greece donated the money for the restoration of Europe's oldest house. As a gesture of gratitude, Father Ioannikios sent me an icon of the Virgin Mary. As I am writing these lines, she looks at me from the mantelpiece in my London flat.

4.   Isle of Man

Brian Stowell's profession is among the world's rarest; he is one of the two people on our planet teaching the ancient Gaelic language Manx. A physicist by education, he was born on the Isle of Man, a semi-independent state in the Irish Sea between England and Ireland. After a successful scientific career in Liverpool, he returned to his native island several years ago with the intention of devoting the rest of his life to the revival of the Manx language – a formidable task if we remember that the last native speaker died in 1974. Out of a population of 70,000, only about fifty islanders are fluent in Manx these days, and fewer than 700 can get by in it.

What is a language? Is it just a means of communication, or something more important? It was not by chance that the rulers of the former Soviet empire tried to subdue pro-independence feelings in their dominions by cracking down on native tongues. Ukrainian language was practically taboo in my native Ukraine. I remember how three of my fellow students were expelled from the Kharkov University for talking Ukrainian to each other. They were accused of 'Ukrainian bourgeois nationalism'. What was so 'nationalistic' and 'bourgeois' about speaking one's native language in one's native land? Only God (or Brezhnev) knew.

The death of a language destroys indigenous culture, kills national identity and ends a country's history. Preservation of a mother tongue is vital for any nation anxious to maintain its roots.

During my trip to the Isle of Man, I couldn't have had a better guide than Brian. Tall, stoopy and bearded, he looked unmistakably Nordic in his thick wool sweater – a reminder of the fact that the Manx people descend from the old Northmen (the Vikings) whose blood still runs in their veins. This semblance was further enhanced by his suave unhurried manner and his soft voice, in which he would hum melodious Manx tunes as he walked.

He met me at Ronaldsway Airport, where I arrived by the Manx Airlines flight from Heathrow. The flight took an hour and twenty minutes – longer than it would take to get to Paris, Berlin or Amsterdam. It felt like flying abroad, although, to my considerable relief, I didn't have to go through passport and immigration control; as a British dependency, the Isle of Man has open borders with the UK. There was a thorough security check, though: the flights to the Isle of Man were departing from the same lounge as those to Northern Ireland.

The English think they know everything about the Isle of Man: its Nigel Mansell, its tailless cats, its conservative legislation that still includes abortion ban and birching. Fewer of my London friends and colleagues were aware of the island's *de facto* independence, of its world's oldest continuously functioning parliament – Tynwald – or of its own indigenous language.

The sea breeze was sweeping through the airfield. An old castle could be seen in the distance. It was drizzling.

'Removals to UK and Northern Ireland' was written on the side of a trailer, parked behind the airport's window. 'See: we are not part of Britain,' Brian said triumphantly, pointing at the truck. 'We were totally independent until 1765, and now we have a similar status to Hong Kong.' Does this mean China is going to claim its rights for the Isle of Man one day? I thought, looking at the 'made in China' Manx cat pins on sale at the airport's souvenir shop.

Brian decided that a visit to Castletown, the former Manx capital, would serve as a good introduction to the island, especially as it was on our way from the airport to the present-day capital, Douglas, where I was booked into a hotel.

The village of Castletown was five minutes' drive from the airport. It was a sleepy and unimpressive place, dominated by Castle Rushen with triskeles, the three-legged Manx flag, on one of its towers. The flag's design was probably derived from the spokes of a wheel or from a pagan image of the rays of the sun. Roughly the same flag can be found in Sicily, and historians believe that Alexander III of Scotland, whose son-in-law, Edmund, was king of Sicily, adopted the symbol when he gained control of the Isle of Man in 1266. But if in Sicily the three-legged design can be explained by the island's triangular shape, on the Isle of Man, shaped like a dachshund, its exact meaning remains a mystery. Maybe it was supposed to represent stability? Hence the island's motto – 'QUOCUNQUE JEGERIS STABIT' which translated from Latin means 'whichever way you throw me I stand'. One facetious London journalist loosely translated it as 'Weebles wobble but they don't fall down'. Whatever the translation, the tiny Isle of Man stood firmly on its three feet throughout the Middle Ages: it was a major maritime power, and its fleet was able to compete with that of France. The Manx were very good at smuggling too.

There is no consensus as to the origins of the island's name either. One thing is clear: all connections with the human male are irrelevant. 'Man' in this case originates either from Mannanin Beg Mchir, the legendary wizard-king of the Vikings, or from 'Mona', the name given to the island by Julius Caesar himself. This seems to be the only reason why feminists and proponents of political correctness have so far failed to rename the Isle of Man 'the Isle of Person'.

There is nothing much left from the old times, when, according to a not very modest poster in Castletown's Nautical Museum, 'deep sea vessels were owned and sailed by the Manxmen, who by their courage and loyalty gained recognition for the Manx flag in the ports of the seven seas'. Only Castle Rushen, the former residence of Kings and Lords of Man (the present Lord of Man is a woman – Queen Elizabeth II) and the seat of Tynwald, still towers above the island as a reminder of those glorious years.

The Castle is now a museum, complete with wax figures and the intimidating 'Who goes there?!' sound effects. I was taken by the life-size representation of a prison guard emptying his bladder into a mediaeval loo and humming a Manx song, just like my new friend Brian. Yes, Castle Rushen also used to be a prison. Every significant castle in Europe used to have a prison on its premises, just in case. The purpose of such a layout was to enable tenants and inmates to conveniently swap living quarters from time to time: overnight, rulers could become prisoners, and prisoners rulers. The same transformation recently occurred in most of the former Communist bloc countries, which shows that the nature of power remains largely unchanged since the Middle Ages.

The prison of Castle Rushen used to accommodate such outspoken dissidents as Bishop Wilson, who had the temerity to translate the Bible into Manx; and James Brown, the editor of the *Isle of Man Times*, who printed an article criticising The House of Keys – the equivalent of the House of Commons in Tynwald, the Manx parliament. Well, the nature of crime and punishment, as well as that of dissent, has not changed much either since then.

The prisoners' ration consisted of bread and gruel, with one ounce of cheese for males, three quarters of an ounce for females, on Sundays. At the same time, the rulers behind the wall were hurriedly stuffing themselves with partridges and suckling pigs from crude wooden boards (plates and forks appeared later). They were not afraid of putting on weight, which they knew they would lose quickly after being thrown into prison and put on a healthy cholesterol-free diet of bread and gruel.

It was in Castle Rushen that the last execution in Manx history took place in 1872. A mentally demented young man was hanged for killing his own father with a pitchfork (forks had obviously been invented by then). A black flag was duly hoisted above the castle – the equivalent of the 'Silence. Programme On Air' indicator in a modern radio studio. It meant 'Silence. Prisoner In Air'. After that, all prisoners on death row were sent to England for execution. 'We always left the English to do the dirty job,' Brian Stowell commented with a cackle.

The last man was sentenced to be hanged on the Isle of Man in July, 1992. Tony Teare, an apprentice engineer from Ramsey, was found guilty of killing a twenty-two-year-old woman for a payment of £600. Deemster (judges are called 'deemsters' on the Isle of Man) Henry Callow told him: 'You will be taken to the Isle of Man jail and thence to a place of legal execution and there hanged by the neck until you are dead' – not a very promising perspective. The engineer turned contract killer, who needed the money to pay his bank overdraft, was not afraid for his life, though. He knew it was only a question of time for his sentence to be commuted to life imprisonment to be served somewhere in Britain. Had he lived a hundred years earlier, he wouldn't have been so sure.

The automatic death sentence for murder was removed from the Isle of Man statute book later that year. The move to ban birching for offences of violence, however, was abandoned by the Manx government as a result of an outcry among the islanders in April, 1993. It was mutually agreed that the birch, while kept in the statute book, would not be used to punish – a true judgement of Solomon.

For many years the Isle of Man remained the last country in Western Europe where homosexuality was banned. After 'homosexual acts by consenting adults over twenty-one in private' were decriminalised there in April 1992, the *Daily Telegraph* wrote: 'Which is more important: the rights of a few men, or the rights of Man?' The paper did not provide an answer to this largely rhetorical question.

Having come closer to the rest of the civilised world in its legislation, the Isle of Man still retains some peculiar regulations of its own. The Manx are allowed to drive at sixteen, breath tests are illegal, seat belts not compulsory, and there are no speed limits. All these taken together make the Isle of Man a young joyrider's paradise and an elderly jaywalker's hell. Luckily, due to the excellent system of secondary education, most of the Manx young men and women are serious people, not interested in joyriding.

From my very first minutes on the Isle of Man, I kept looking for its two main symbols — Manx kippers and Manx cats. I spotted my first Manx cat in Castletown. He was sleeping on the porch of a house near the port. 'Beware of the Cat' the plaque on the fence read.

The cat himself didn't look threatening at all. After meeting a number of his tailless brothers and sisters (Brian had one at his house), I came to the conclusion that the absence of a tail was not conducive to playfulness or liveliness of feline character. Most of them were either already asleep or preparing to go to sleep, only a few were in a reluctant waking-up mode. The reason for such idleness must be the Manx cat's broken genetic code. The creature is a genetic mystery in itself, and no one knows exactly how or why such a 'horizontally disadvantaged' animal came into existence. Some are inclined to think that it was the result of a cross with a rabbit. Had this been so, the Manx cats probably would have started multiplying like rabbits and would have been swarming all over the Isle of Man. In reality, there are only a couple of thousand of them on the island, and a special private cattery had to be established to preserve them. Perhaps they are just too lazy even to breed?

According to a more fanciful (and even less trustworthy) version, a pair of Manx cats were the last to enter the Noah's Ark, just in time as Noah slammed the door, severing their tails.

The only other place in the world where you are likely to see tailless cats is in the Bulgarian town of Gabrovo, where the locals are notorious for their pragmatism, bordering on greed, and their self-deprecating wit. One day they calculated that it would take a wee bit less time to let a tailless cat inside a house from the street in winter than a cat with a full-scale tail. In an attempt to save some precious warmth and to cut their heating expenses, they simply chopped their cats' tails off. Maybe it is there, in Gabrovo, that the solution of the Manx cat mystery lies, after all?

Having a house pet is like marriage. The only difference is that you can't get a divorce. Despite the obvious conveniencies and savings a tailless Manx cat offers as a pet, I always preferred dogs. In Russia I almost bought one shortly before I had to leave. Burglaries were on the rise in Moscow and, with most door locks being of the standard Soviet type that could be opened by any standard Soviet key, a guard dog was the only solution: the planned centralised economy had not gone as far as rubber-stamping one standard Soviet breed of dog.

I selected a puppy boxer, paid a deposit and, being an avid reader of James Joyce, named him Ulysses, or Ulka as a self-devised Russian diminutive for Ulysses. The pup was only a few weeks old and had to stay with his mother for a month before I could take him.

It was October 1989, and several days after the purchase I saw the start of the harassment that eventually made me arrive at the difficult decision to emigrate. The memories of the pup that had almost become ours haunted my son for many months. 'What's happening to our Ulysses?' he would ask moodily. 'He must have grown into a big dog by now.'

As soon as we were more or less settled in Melbourne, we started thinking of recreating our Russian Ulka in Australia. And soon it happened: a three-month-old mongrel pup, a mixture of German shepherd and blue heeler, was given to us by friends as a house-warming present. Despite his black skin, he looked rather like a white elephant in the beginning, since none of us had any experience of owning a dog.

The first thing the newly arrived Ulysses did was to wet the carpet.

The second thing he did was to wet the carpet again. The third thing he did was . . . You must have guessed already.

After a while we faced a dilemma: to turn our new house into a dog's loo or banish Ulysses to the back yard. We thought that he was still too little to be taught good manners. So we moved him to a tool shed.

Ulysses definitely enjoyed his new quarters. The back yard became his undisputed lawful territory. Any intruder was met with aggressive playfulness resulting in torn tights and trousers. Like Ilya Muromets, a fictional hero of a Russian folk-tale, Ulysses was growing not by the day, but by the hour. He was turning into a free Western creature without any of the complexes and inhibitions affecting his four-legged brothers and sisters in the Soviet Union.

Yes, pets also suffered from the constant ups and downs of the Soviet economy. Even now my Moscow friends often complain that they have nothing to feed their cats and dogs.

Ulysses certainly didn't experience any food shortages. Opening cans of dog food, I couldn't help but think that the quality of meat for pets in Australia was far superior to many foodstuffs for human beings in the former Soviet Union. The biggest difference was that it was easily available, back in Russia the very concept of pet food was missing: cats and dogs were fed refuse. I remember a beggar who would pick up food for stray cats from the bin at the door of our Moscow block of flats. She didn't have any house pets, by the way, simply because she didn't have a house.

I had suddenly entered the previously obscure world of pet shops and dog owners. The mincemeat they displayed at Melbourne pet shops would have sold like hot cakes at a Soviet *human* food market. They even had dog biscuits on sale; I wouldn't have been particularly surprised to see cats' caviare and dogs' champagne, too. And all these leashes, kennels, deodorants and nice-looking plastic plates . . . to say nothing of 'Mobile Dog Wash' vans. It even rained *cats and dogs* in Australia in winter! I read somewhere that in America they have special hotels, hairdressers and even brothels for pets. What can I say? It's good to be a cat or a dog in the West!

Daily walks with Ulysses were very entertaining. For some reason he became a special attraction for elderly ladies who liked to strike up conversations with him, or rather monologues interrupted by Ulysses's friendly growling as he attempted to grab his interlocutor by the skirt. One old woman with a walking stick stroked him for a quarter of an hour and called him 'darling' and 'cute little doggy'. Then she looked at her watch and announced solemnly: 'I am sorry dear. I must go now to have a nice cup of tea!' I thought she was addressing me, but in fact she was talking to Ulysses, as if a 'nice cup of tea' could soften for him the grief of separation. It was as if I didn't exist at all; she never even bothered to cast a glance at my end of the leash. I was just a speechless appendix to Ulka, a sort of walking extension of the leash itself. The only recognition of my presence was a sacramental question: 'Is it (meaning Ulysses, of course) a boy or a girl?' I don't know why it was old ladies who always showed a special interest in the matter of Ulka's sex.

While walking Ulysses in the park, I liked to watch other dog owners and listen to their esoteric vernacular: 'I am so worried about Sam. He started having dry faeces.' 'You know, my wife doesn't allow Linda into the house, but when she goes out shopping, I let her in and we play a lot.' The man spoke about his dear Linda with such genuine affection that it was hard to believe she was a terrier bitch, not his clandestine sweetheart.

Pets are great equalisers. They bring together people who would otherwise be as distant from each other as the earth and the moon: children and octogenarians, a destitute bag lady and a well-groomed gentleman. Walking a dog helps one forget about social prejudice, taboos and communication barriers, as though the dog itself jumps over them easily, as if over a garden hedge.

Watching dog owners often makes me think: who owns whom? Pets seem to completely subjugate the people with whom they live. Who said dogs usually resemble their owners? It's not true. It is the owners who resemble their dogs.

This makes totally irrelevant the notorious street sign I've seen many times in London: 'Owners who allow their dogs to foul the public footpath will be prosecuted'. Just try *not* to allow. This sign should rather read as follows: 'Dogs who allow their owners to allow them to foul the public footpath will be prosecuted.'

We have a lot to learn from our pets. The Russian poetess Marina Tsvetayeva said the biggest advantage of animals over people is that animals are never vulgar. On top of this, pets are never pretentious, unfaithful or hypocritical. They don't file complaints, join political parties or attend trade union meetings. Yes, sometimes they are a little . . . er . . . messy, but this is far from a major drawback.

Yet it was not always easy to be a dog owner (or rather to be owned by a dog), even in Australia. Due to Ulysses's playful demeanour, we have lost some of our acquaintances who were particularly keen on the inviolability of their tights and trousers. And those who were too smell-conscious. I didn't blame them. Ulysses destroyed beautiful flowers in our back yard. He burst into the house and nearly bit off a leg of the kitchen table. He ripped off the mattress from my bed.

Once, when he tore through a rubbish bag and scattered its smelly contents all around the garden, I started having serious thoughts about whether to return Ulysses to the friends who gave him to us. I shared my concern with my son, who was then eleven. His reaction was curt: 'I won't give Ulysses away, because I love him!'

And this was the weightiest argument I had ever heard.

Unlike Manx cats, Manx kippers were not so easy to spot on the Isle of Man. I saw them only once on the menu of a small café in Douglas and immediately ordered them. It was an ill-considered step (or rather munch): my hands smelt of Manx kippers for weeks afterwards. The smell was ineradicable: no amount of soap and deodorant was able to beat it. I probably brought it to London, since my colleagues and friends started avoiding me like the plague, while packs of stray London cats trailed me wherever I went, as if I was an over-sized, two-legged mouse. Even now, as I write these lines, I have the feeling that the keys of my word processor smell of Manx kippers.

* * *

Brian Stowell was driving me to Douglas. The road was empty and there was no one to test the island's lenient traffic laws. The Isle of Man looked like no-man's-land on that Sunday afternoon.

'Fastyr mie!' Brian suddenly said into the emptiness. I thought he was mumbling to himself, but he explained that we were driving across the Fairies Bridge where, according to one of the island's superstitions, one was supposed to greet the Fairies in Manx if you wanted your journey to be a success. So he said 'Good evening, wee folk!' to the Fairies.

He told me that other Manx superstitions included: always leaving the house by the same door you entered it and always moving to the island just before the start of the UK tax year, ha-ha.

Indeed, the maximum tax on the Isle of Man is under twenty per cent, and until recently this low tax bracket was applicable to anyone who died there. The island became a favourite destination for the wealthy British on their deathbeds, and Douglas funeral parlours were thriving, until the Manx government introduced a new law demanding several years of residence on the island before local tax laws could apply. Now people come to the Isle of Man to live, not to die.

The sea in Douglas smelled of Manx kippers (before I tried Manx kippers I thought it smelled of seaweed). The town looked like a typical English seaside resort, a smaller version of Brighton, Plymouth or Hastings, with piers, sea gull droppings on the pavement and Edwardian guesthouses along the semi-circular promenade.

There were a couple of things that were different, though. One was the horse-drawn tram. It was crawling along the rails, dragged by a muscular, businesslike horse, trotting lazily from one end of the embankment to the other and stopping dutifully at the traffic lights. The driver was munching through a sandwich, the conductor was whistling and collecting fares. It was like going a hundred years back in time, and I wouldn't have been surprised to see Sherlock Holmes and his faithful friend Doctor Watson jumping off the omnibus in their bowler hats and hurrying away to the spot of yet another mysterious crime.

Little is the Light

To the dismay of Manx animal rights activists, who like to shed crocodile tears over the plight of Douglas tram horses, the latter can easily be ranked among the world's equine élite. Each horse does only a short spell of duty each day, with four return trips set as a maximum. At one end of the two-mile seafront track is a water trough where the horses stop until a bucketful of water is brought to them by the driver. On the other end are the stables where they retire after their short working day for a meal of oats and hay. Come September they can look forward to seven or eight months of rest, grazing on fields reserved for them in various parts of the island. And when after several years of this debilitating work their career comes to an end, they go not to a slaughterhouse but straight to the Home of Rest for Old Horses in the outskirts of Douglas. I visited this unique establishment, run by the delightful seventy-four-year-old Mrs Dorothy Jones, who treated horses with zest and kindness, as if they were her own spoilt grandchildren. 'They are like people: all different – some are cheerful, others are shy,' she told me. The horses had everything there: from fresh grass and friendly vets to Christmas cards, sent to them by children from all over the world, cards to which they were not even expected to reply.

The one-horse-power-strong engine moved along the promenade with average reckless speed of ten kilometres per hour, overtaking some of the older pedestrians, especially those in wheelchairs. Rocking on a stiff wooden bench inside one distinguishing feature of Douglas, I had plenty of time to observe another – the town's terminal decline as a spa. Swarming with holidaymakers at the beginning of our century, Douglas had all but lost its touristic attraction by the late seventies. With flights from London to France and Spain costing less money (and often taking less time) than those to the Isle of Man, with inter-EEC travel formalities first eased and then scrapped altogether, no wonder the rain-soaked and sunshine-hungry English holidaymakers started opting for Costa del Sol and Côte d'Azur. There, at least, sunshine was guaranteed, whereas the only guarantee they could get on the 'Smile of Man' (that was how it was advertised by some resourceful travel agents) was of short sunny spells in-between never-ending showers. In a tragically ironic (or ironically tragic) twist, a £200,000 promotion campaign designed to sell the delights of the Isle of Man to tourists, had brought a mere eleven bookings in July 1992.

'All happy families resemble each other, each unhappy family is unhappy in its own way,' as Leo Tolstoy once rightly observed. The same can be said about towns. Douglas was definitely unhappy in its own peculiar way. Its unhappiness was in groups of teenagers, still under the driving age of sixteen, hanging around street corners and fiddling with cash dispensers to kill time. It was in countless small hotels with nice-sounding names (Windsor, Osborn, Marina, Melrose, etc) — all with either 'Vacancies' or 'Closed' plates in their windows and none with 'Full'. 'Licensed to Sell Ale', 'Colour TV in Most Bedrooms' and 'All Rooms with Private Baths' signs looked solitary and forlorn on their crumbling facades. I don't think these hotels would be able to attract many guests even if they started selling ale in most bedrooms and installing colour TV-sets in front of private baths.

The 'Smile of Man' turned out to be no more than the scowl of a dead man.

Disbelief was written on the faces of the staff at the seafront Empress Hotel, where I was booked for four nights. 'Are you sure you want to stay four nights?' they kept asking me. They would probably be less surprised to see a UFO landing in the hotel lobby than a lonely guest staying for four nights in September.

'I once went to Adelaide, but it was closed,' they say in Australia. Douglas had the atmosphere of being closed permanently. It was also locked, shut down and altogether cancelled. Signs and notices to this effect were everywhere. 'The afternoon tour is cancelled,' the sightseeing kiosk on the promenade informed. 'One horse tram cancelled,' echoed the horse tram station shed (that left only one other horse tram in operation, by the way). 'Sorry, we are closed,' the café near my hotel apologised. 'Closed!' the island's only 'Link' cash dispenser snapped curtly, spitting out my Abbey National card and leaving me cashless.

Little is the Light

The Peking Restaurant on the promenade was not simply closed. It was sealed. 'The locks have been changed today. Contact Lowey & Co if you require access. 2 February, 1993,' said the hand-written note on the door. Seven and a half months later, on 21 September, 1993, I was obviously the first person who 'required access'.

Rather than contacting Lowey & Co, I decided to settle for dinner at the only nearby restaurant that was open. It was called Rasputin, and, logically, I was hoping it would specialise in Russian cuisine. It proved to be Italian. The sweets menu had a cartoon of drunken Rasputin (or was it Rasputini?) spilling over a glass of something red – either blood or red wine. Among other puddings, it offered 'Rasputin's Whoppa – Eat it if you dare!' I dared not, having remembered that Rasputin himself died of poisoning.

In despair, I looked through the flimsy Calendar of Events, issued by the Manx Department of Tourism, Leisure and Transport and featuring such momentous happenings as 'Steam Locomotive Running on the Manx Electric Railway' (had it been the other way round – electric locomotive on steam railway – I would probably be interested) and 'Mountain Tram Ride' (I wanted to try, but it was cancelled). One event on the Calendar sounded promising, though: 'Billy Roberts – An Evening of Clairvoyance and Psychic Demonstration with Internationally known Medium. Villa Marina Garden Room'

A bit of psychic demonstration – that was what I needed to cheer me up.

I have always been suspicious of mediums. Suddenly at the end of 1989, TV screens in the Soviet Union were invaded by dubious gurus, home-made prophets and garrulous fortune-tellers predicting earthquakes, typhoons, nuclear wars and the end of the world, starting from next Monday. I remember how Pavel and Tatiana Globa, a married couple of astrologists, promised on TV that the British Isles would disappear from the face of the earth in a couple of years. Now, after five years, what do we observe? The astrologists themselves vanished without a trace, but the British Isles, strange as it may seem, are still there, and even the Isle of Man, though closed, is still alive and well. For the Soviet audience it was reassuring to know that someone else's future could be gloomier than theirs.

What made this invasion of paranormal phenomena into the Party-normal television surprising was that the official ideology, being purely materialistic, had always opposed occult sciences as opium for the people. But in the conditions of growing social unrest, the Soviet rulers, faced with the danger of mounting popular anger, thought it possible to forget their old dogmas.

They understood very well that there could not be a better means of distracting the masses from the real cause of their sufferings, i.e. the system itself, than ominous forecasts, sombre prophecies and paranormal phenomena. Indeed, what difference will it make for those who are destined (as predicted by a televised guru) to experience a twelve-point Richter scale earthquake next Monday, whether they will be able to buy some meat in the local shop on Saturday? Suddenly everyday life, with its incessant queues and unending injustices, looks like a paradise, when compared to the plight of someone who has just been buried under volcanic lava.

That autumn in 1989, a friend of mine, who worked as an ambulance doctor, told me of numerous emergencies in which people had to be taken to hospital after eating one of the same issue of *Vechernaya Moskva*, a Moscow evening newspaper. As it turned out, Alan Chumak, a healer, claimed on Moscow television that he had charged his own photo, published in that very newspaper, with his magic healing powers, capable of curing any imaginable disease – from a running nose to lung cancer. He certainly didn't tell the people to eat the paper, but you know how rumours start spreading: someone misheard, someone misunderstood.

In a later instance, another medium, Alexander Ilyin, claimed on Russian television (it was already after the collapse of the Soviet Union) that he was able to set objects on fire and to turn water into soup by the mere power of his stare. (His family, obviously, didn't suffer from food shortages. Their only problem was to make sure they were in time to eat the soup before it caught fire.)

It is bizarre when things like that happen at the end of the twentieth century but, on the other hand, when official medicine has nothing better to offer and when food is scarce, then having a newspaper for lunch can sometimes bring about a miraculous healing effect.

I thought that in the West where medicine can work wonders and newspapers (like the *Sunday Times*, say) though totally cholesterol-free, are still too heavy for dinner, people didn't have to dwell in the obscure world of the paranormal, since their everyday life was as a rule so full and normal. That's why I was so keen to see Billy Roberts.

Villa Marina, where the Evening of Clairvoyance was to take place, was locked. 'Available for Hire' and 'The premises are patrolled by guard dogs' signs were hanging on its plaster-covered windows. There was no sign of the internationally known medium Billy Roberts (or anyone else for that matter). Or, perhaps, I was simply not clairvoyant enough to see him through the firmly shut doors.

'The best thing about Douglas is the way out of it,' Brian Stowell told me from behind the wheel of his car. He was driving me to a country pub in the village of Laxey where a group of local enthusiasts met on Saturday nights to play Manx folk music and to speak Manx. Brian's old accordion was bouncing on the back seat. He called it 'my squeeze-box'.

We passed round a circular mound, topped by a canopy with a three-legged Manx flag on its roof. This was the famous Tynwald Hill, where each July 5th the island's parliament, in accordance with the ancient Viking tradition, meet in the open-air assembly to announce new laws – in English and in Manx. No law on the Isle of Man can become effective until announced from Tynwald Hill, and if it is not done within eighteen months after the bill is signed by both branches of Tynwald (the Legislative Council and the House of Keys) and got the Royal Assent, it simply loses force, or lapses, as legislators say. 'We are a typical Scandinavian parliament,' Professor T. St John Bates (his full name), the Clerk of Tynwald, told me in Douglas the day before. When the Millenium of Tynwald was celebrated on 5 July, 1979, with Queen Elisabeth II presiding over the proceedings, guests from several Scandinavian sister parliaments were present on the Hill.

The procedure of Tynwald is as cumbersome and pompous as it was a thousand years ago. Professor Bates showed me 'A Brief Guide to the Procedures and Practice of Tynwald' – a thick brochure, where paragraph sixteen ('Debate') started like this: 'A member who has been called must address his remarks to the President. Consequently, remarks which are directed to another member such as, "You know that you are being foolish", should be avoided. If a member feels obliged to make such a remark it should be phrased, "The hon member for . . . must know that he is being foolish." The brochure, as you see, left no stone unturned to ensure a fair debate. But, if I am allowed to say so, it must know that it is being foolish . . .

Unfortunately, I failed to get inside the graceful building in Douglas where the world's oldest parliament, started by the Viking king Orry, normally sits. You might have guessed why – it was closed.

The village of Laxey had only one sight: the world's largest water wheel. The wheel, used for pumping water out of a nearby coal mine, was named 'Lady Isabella' after a former Manx governor's wife who probably used to give her husband a hard time (maybe she was – figuratively, of course – pumping blood out of his body?). The first thing the ill-tempered 'Lady Isabella' did, when officially launched a hundred years ago, was to splash all those present with water. Women in heavy crinoline dresses must have been very displeased. At present, with the mine closed, the only thing the wheel was good for was dispersing rain, of which there was no shortage in Laxey: it was raining Manx cats and dogs when we passed through the village.

'Lady Isabella' reminded me of 'the devil's wheel', the highlight of the funfair in Kharkov's Gorky Park (for some reason it was fashionable in the Soviet Union to call 'parks of public recreation and rest' Gorky parks, hinting probably at the great proletarian writer's difficult childhood). It was a thirty-metre-high metallic sphere with cabins inside. People were always queuing to get on board. The wheel rotated slowly and screechingly, gradually lifting you above the trees into the sky. I don't have to tell you why 'the devil's wheel' was so popular in a society where in everyday life you couldn't raise your head above water without immediately being hit on the crown.

The White House pub was full of patrons. Brian led me to a small side room, where a handful of his friends were already sitting round the table, drinking beer and playing Manx music. There were two guitars, three flutes, one violin, a banjo and a harmonica, and the musicians were a local jeweller, a bank clerk, a teacher, a student on holiday from Liverpool, and a couple of others – all united by Manx music. Brian joined in with his accordion.

They played with amazing harmony and feeling, as if talking to each other. New musicians kept coming in from the street and joining the band. When someone got out of tune, the rest would smile at him, pause – and start again.

I felt genuinely moved by the Manx melodies which, to my inexperienced ear, sounded like a cross between Hungarian and Ukrainian folk tunes.

Conversation between songs was sparse and unhurried. *Traa dy liooar* – time enough – as they say on the Isle of Man. Indeed, there was no reason to rush and fuss and not much to talk about on this quiet isolated island. They were speaking the language of music, and never before had I seen people so absorbed with what they were doing.

Music is a mandatory subject in all forty secondary schools on the Isle of Man. It wouldn't be an exaggeration to say that every Manx person can play at least one musical instrument. On Saturdays and Sundays, whole families come to pubs and play there for hours, instead of bantering. Small play instead of small talk. Folk tunes instead of greasy pub jokes.

'This song was about bribing the jury. And the previous one was about smuggling and fiddling,' the man who played the violin told me in one interval.

I wished I could join in the next song, which was probably about tax evasion or money laundering, but it was impossible. My experience in music was limited to two weeks of compulsory piano lessons at the age of seven. My teacher had a rare patronimic, Nadezhda Adolphovna (meaning the daughter of Adolf). She was in the habit of hitting me on the tips of my fingers with a wooden ruler whenever I struck a wrong key. I was secretly convinced that her father was Adolph Hitler, and after a fortnight of torture, I told my parents that I would rather die than ever study music again. Even now, at the sound of a piano, my fingertips start aching.

But I do like music. Watching the players in the White House pub and listening to their iconoclastic songs, I realised that rulers (human or wooden) were helpless against the hands of a real musician.

Browsing through old books in a second-hand book shop in London's Cecil Court one day, I came across a bulky volume of *Observations of the European People* by Samuel Laying, Esq, published in England in 1850. It started with a colourful description of the author's cross-Channel journey on an early paddle steamer: 'What a world of passengers on our steamer! Princes, dukes, gentlemen, ladies, tailors, milliners, people of every rank and calling, all jumbled together. The power of steam is not confined to material objects. Its influences extend over the social and moral arrangements of mankind. Steam is the great democratic power of our age, annihilating the conventional distinctions, differences and social distance between man and man, as well as natural distances between place and place.'

I often feel nostalgic for the golden age of steam. Especially when travelling by British Rail. As a train buff of many years standing, I have always perceived human life as one long train journey. The train of life is running forward along the rails, rattling its wheels – clickety-clack – on the joints of days and weeks. It runs past the whistle-stops of childhood and youth, it slows down at the stations of maturity and old age, and there, on the hazy horizon, one can already discern the sad blinking lights of the terminal.

While on the Isle of Man I couldn't avoid one of its main attractions – The Isle of Man Steam Railway. The present sixteen-mile track from Douglas to Port Erin is a reminder of a railway network that once served the whole of the spacious (227 square mile) island. Of course, by now it has all but lost its economic significance and remains just an attraction for train buffs, like myself.

The first railway line from Douglas to Peel was opened on July 1, 1873. Despite lots of bureaucratic fretting about political and moral dangers of rail transport, narrow-gauge railways developed quickly on the island: at its height the Isle of Man Railway Company empire extended to forty-six miles of track, with a proud fleet of sixteen locomotives, around seventy-five carriages and dozens of assorted wagons. Two of the early engines, named Loch and Mona (not only water wheels had names on the Isle of Man, but steam engines, too), survive today.

The red-brick station building in Douglas had the aroma of the nineteeth century. Inside, there were wooden floors, a tiny coffee shop, an old clock on the wall and a ticket-window. A handful of my fellow train buffs were clicking their cameras while boarding 'The Manxman' – our little train. 'C.H. Wood' – a minuscule, almost toy-size engine – was spitting out clouds of vapour and puffing loudly, as if chronically short of breath. The driver was wearing greasy, oil-stained overalls, and the platform smelled of coals and steam – the sweet smell of journeys.

The carriages were equipped with window straps, wood panels and gas lampshades, now covering electric bulbs. 'Keep your head, arms and legs inside the carriage', the brass plate above the window warned. I always suspected that all warning signs like this were compiled by one and the same person: a little, bald and extremely boring bachelor, a retired tax inspector and a secret graphomaniac. Having failed to publish any of his boring works, he resorted to creating warnings and instructions and thus having his revenge on the whole of humankind, whom he hates. He probably writes them in longhand on small pieces of tracing paper during the night, when all normal people are asleep.

And when he comes up with something as brilliant as 'Keep your head, arms and legs inside the carriage', he starts giggling nastily into his inkpot and rubbing his little head, arms and legs in glee.

The engine gave a high-pitched whistle, the conductor slammed the door shut and the train started with a jerk.

Watching the island's pastoral scenery floating past the window, I made notes in my jotter. Tiny black coals landed on the page from time to time like fossilised fragments of the bygone epoch of steam.

Half-way between Douglas and Port Erin we stopped at the station of Ballasalla ('Balla' means 'farm' in Manx). The platform was empty, but I could almost see gentlemen in bowler hats and ladies in Victorian dresses strolling by. I was in 1893, and there were no reminders of our messy twentieth century.

The carriage was so compact that it reminded me of the Children's railway in my native Kharkov which I would board as a dromomaniac boy in search of travelling illusions. It also brought back memories of my trans-Australia journey by the Indian-Pacific Express a couple of years earlier. The journey across the Nullarbor plain took about three full days, and my first-class smoking compartment was a masterpiece of practicality: everything bent and folded. The washing tub, the sleeping berth and even the john were all collapsible. After spacious Soviet long-distance trains, this single sleeper looked (and smelled) like a medium-size snuff box without tobacco. I could hardly squeeze myself inside with my suitcase. What if I had been slightly bigger? I'd have had to sleep in the corridor.

Instead of tobacco, my snuff box was filled with ominous-sounding signs, warnings and instructions on how to flush the toilet and what to do in case of fire. ('Point one: tell the conductor and other people'.) Remember the little bald fellow . . .

Next to the door there were two plaques saying respectively 'Shoes' and 'Towels'. I started looking for one more saying 'Vitali' but failed to find it.

Trying to lower the sleeping berth, I faced a dilemma. The

compartment could accommodate either the berth or myself, but there wasn't enough space for both. I eventually went out into the corridor, lowered the berth through the open door of my compartment and quickly jumped onto it, slamming the door shut in my flight.

This little ruse was fine until I woke up during the night needing to go to the toilet. To use the loo, covered by the berth on which I slept, I had to: a) leave the compartment; b) lift the sleeping berth from the corridor; c) enter the compartment; d) use the loo; e) leave the compartment; f) lower the sleeping berth back into place; g) leap onto the berth from the corridor, shutting the door in my jump (see above). It was great fun.

Even without calls of nature, sleep was hard to achieve: the tiny compartment was brimming with the sounds of vibrating objects. Each vibrated with its own peculiar pitch and tone. The glass was clinking in its metallic holder, the Coke was splashing in the can like surf, the door hinges were squealing like two trams simultaneously turning the corner, the spoon in the glass was jingling like a conductor's bell calling the second shift of passengers to the restaurant car for dinner. Even my shoes, stuck according to instruction in the tiny dark closet in the wall, were rubbing against each other and making a muffled clattering sound as if they were either dancing or shivering with cold. A real railway symphony. Towards the coda, it was joined by some snoring sounds, I presume . . .

Port Erin was a nonedescript little town. It could be called a one-horse town, were it not for the fact that Nigel Mansell lived there. It could probably be called a one-formula (or rather formula-one) town nevertheless.

The train was to go back in forty minutes, and while other train buffs were pumping themselves with coffee at the station buffet, I went to explore the town. Like Douglas, Port Erin had its promenade (only a much shorter one) where everything was either shut or closed. The flower shop attendant was washing the pavement in front of her closed shop with soap and hot water – probably in order to make it slippery and to prevent any accidental passerby from wandering in and buying some flowers by mistake.

The Museum of Railways next to the station was open, though. It had an impressive exhibition of old cardboard rail tickets and train cancellation signs – 'Withdrawal of Trains' (1914); 'Late trains all lines' (1927); 'Partial Closing of Foxdale Railway' (1912). It looked like the island used to be pretty closed even in those distant times of burgeoning tourism.

The Queen's coach was missing from under the plaque saying 'The Queens' Coach', but a huge piece of coal from an early steam engine's fire-box was in place. It was chained to the wall . . .

The journey back to Douglas was uneventful.

There was one excellent museum on the Isle of Man – the Manx Museum in Douglas. Not being part of the UK, the Isle of Man is nevertheless a part of Great Britain, and The Manx Museum was British Museum of the Year in 1992. Among its beautifully arranged and perfectly designed exhibitions, I especially liked the one on the internment of Britain's 'enemy aliens' on the Isle of Man during World War II.

At the outbreak of war there were approximately 75,000 people of Germanic origin living in Britain. Roughly 60,000 were refugees from Hitler, mostly Jews from Germany and Austria who fled to Britain in 1939. All of them were branded 'enemy alien residents' and 'potential security risks' by Whitehall and hastily resettled. Some ended up in Australia, where they were taken by *HMS Duneira* having been robbed, beaten and grossly mistreated on the way. Others were interned on the Isle of Man, which had been turned into a vast prison camp housing 20,000 'enemy aliens' by the end of 1940. Nazi sympathisers (who were in the clear minority) and refugees from Hitler alike had to exist together behind the barbed wire. Contacts with the outside world were reduced to the absolute minimum.

The Museum displayed a pre-printed postcard that the internees were allowed to send to their relatives once in every two months:

Nothing is to be written here except the date, signature and address of the sender. Erase words not required. If anything else is added, the postcard will be destroyed.

- I am (not) well
- I have been admitted into hospital — sick
  - — for operation
  - — and going on well
- I am being transferred to another camp
- I have received your card dated
- signature
- camp address

At the time, when tiny Liechtenstein and San Marino were harbouring the outcasts fleeing for their lives, Britain — the superpower — was humiliating and persecuting them in the best traditions of Stalin or the Nazis themselves. Why? This is a hard question. The answer probably lies in the largely totalitarian mentality of the wartime British Empire, in its cannibalistic bureacracy and in fear, too. Faced with the prospect of destruction, the inept state machine, rather than consolidating its efforts to confront the powerful enemy openly, chose to vent its own frustration on the helpless and the unprotected, on those who came to Britain in search of a shelter and found themselves a target instead. 'The stronger always blames the weaker,' Ivan Krilov, the nineteenth-century Russian writer said in his fable 'The Wolf and the Lamb'.

History taught the British a bitter lesson. The 'Duneira Boys', having survived the camps, became the pride of Australian science and culture — doctors, artists, academics; many of the Isle of Man internees, among whom there were internationally renowned intellectuals, chose not to return to Britain after the war, thus depriving the country of their unique knowledge and expertise. So who punished whom in the long run? I think the answer is obvious.

Coming back to Britain from my frequent trips abroad and going through passport control at Heathrow or Gatwick, I sometimes can't help noticing the remnants of the old imperial mentality in the arrogant grin and rude manner of an immigration officer (generally, they are much nicer to you when you leave the country than when you arrive). He looks at you as if you are still an 'undesireable alien', and at moments like that I am proud to be one. There is nothing better than national pride. There is nothing worse than national conceit.

When the Manx Museum director received The Museum of the Year Award in London, the award-presenting official commended 'the efforts of the Isle of Man's local authorities in supporting the Museum'. The Manx representative in his word of thanks strongly objected to the expression 'local authorities'. 'We are a country in our own right,' he remarked.

This raises the question of the so-called Manx nationalism. Does it exist?

'Manx nationalism is not a danger, but its proponents do harm to our cause,' Miles Walker, the Chief Minister of the Isle of Man Government told me.

'If the people of the Isle of Man decide to be fully independent, the UK government, I am sure, will accept this,' His Excellency, the Lieutenant Governor Air Marshal Sir Laurence Jones, K.C.B. (I had to retype this several times, since I kept automatically writing K.G.B. instead of K.C.B. – old habits die hard), A.F.C. said.

(The Governor's plush residence was in turmoil: the Duchess of Kent was to arrive on a visit next morning, and it suddenly turned out that the private hairdresser on her party was a woman, whereas they were expecting a man – *Her* Royal Hairness instead of *His* Royal Hairness! 'We have already prepared accommodation for a man,' the Governor's aide-de-camp was moaning in despair.)

The following reader's letter, published by the *Manx Examiner* on 21 September, 1993, leaves little doubt as to the existence of nationalist feelings on the island:

Manxmen and Manxwomen, I call you to spring to the defence of all that you and your ancestors hold dear, to defend our nation and save it from almost certain doom!

Already, we, the Manx people, are a minority in our land. Our language has all but disappeared. Unless action is taken, we too shall vanish. Each year brings more and more immigrants from the adjacent Isles, house prices spiral way above the heads of the Manx worker, tied to low paid employment because of preference shown to foreign candidates.

I call the government to act now and introduce the following recommendations so this isle so beautiful may remain truly Manx for our sake and the sake of our descendants!

1. All non-Manx workers to be taxed at 30% and the extra revenue directed into Manx cultural projects.

2. Advocates and estate agents should give huge discounts on their fees to homeowners selling to Manx purchasers.

3. The financial sector should be made liable to create 200 jobs for Manx workers or be refused all government benefits.

4. The setting up of Manx areas similar to those Gaelic areas in the west of Ireland. In these places only Manx will be spoken and all street signs etc, to be in Manx only. Only Manx residents will be allowed to reside in these areas and others already there will be removed and rehoused in other areas or given assistance to leave the island.

5. All non-Manx residents be forced to swear allegiance to the Manx flag and nation and be made to carry identity cards.

6. Manx to be made the first language of all school children.

7. Anyone speaking ill of the Manx people or nation to be charged with treason and evicted from the Island without notice.

It is only by imposing such harsh laws that we can save our identity. It may already be too late . . .

S. Kermeen, Crogga Aignnay, Andreas

So, the Isle of Man for the Manx only? Familiar rhetoric . . .

I was not sure, though, how much credibility the letters page of the *Manx Examiner*, where other letters were signed 'Fuming', 'Perplexed', 'Let Live' and even 'Vested But Objective Taxpayer', could have.

Other news-making stories in Manx papers that week included: 'ESTRANGED WIFE SMASHED WINDOWS AFTER DOWNING TEN HALVES OF LAGER' and 'DOG JUMPS UP AND BITES BOY'S LEG' Or were they 'DOG SMASHED WINDOWS AFTER DOWNING TEN HALVES OF LAGER' and 'ESTRANGED WIFE JUMPS UP AND BITES BOY'S LEG'? But the biggest blockbuster was a 'mystery missile' which fell to earth from the sky at the village of Ballaugh. '"BOMB" FALLS NEAR HOMES' the front page headline of the *Manx Independent* ran. The 'bomb' was an oblong aluminium object measuring over two feet with 'Class One Laser Product' written on the outside. The paper quoted a Ballaugh farmer as saying: 'If it had landed on a house, it would have gone straight through the roof.' What a keen observation!

In the photo, the 'mystery missile' looked very much like a medium-size vibrator with a switch button on the side. It was probably dropped by an over-sexed female paraglider.

'We are like a funfair in the end of fun,' the Manx Chief Minister said to me. I thought it was a bit of exaggeration: economically the Isle of Man was not doing badly – with only five per cent unemployment, low taxes and good salaries. It hadn't experienced the economic recession which was rife in the United Kingdom at that time. With its excellent system of state education and healthcare, the island still remains a lucrative place to live, but the citizens of Great Britain who want to work there have to obtain a work permit from the Manx government. For me, the island's main attraction lies in the complete absence of political parties whose role is played by the so-called 'policy-making groups' within Tynwald. There are only four members of the British Labour party on the Isle of Man, and not a single Tory!

When I was on the Isle of Man, the government delegation from the Faroe Islands, another European semi-independent tailless cat of a state, came on a visit to study Manx experience in dealing with economic problems.

At the end of 1994, the European Parliament announced that the first ECU (European Currency Unit) coins were going to be minted on the Isle of Man and experimentally circulated there on a par with Manx pounds and pennies. Quite a strange decision if we remember that the island does not officially belong to the European Union.

This brings to memory the following Soviet joke. 'Who invented Communism – scientists or politicians?' a little boy once asked his mother. 'Politicians, sonny,' she replied. 'Had they been scientists, they would have tried it on dogs first.' Or on Manx cats . . .

Tourism on the Isle of Man has declined indeed, but tax-break incentives, investment and finance came in its stead. No longer a funfair, the Isle of Man is on its way to becoming an off-shore financial haven with well-developed niche industries. The local factories produce rollers for wall paper, ejecting seats and electric kettle switchers. So, when in the morning you hear your boiling kettle whistling and then switching off automatically, it might be the Isle of Man wishing you 'Moghrey mie!' – a very good morning.

I was going with Brian Stowell to one of the island's thirty-one state *scoills* (schools), where the Manx language was taught. When Brian and his colleague started the programme one year before, they received thousands of applications from parents who wanted their children to study it. 'We had to ask some of the applicants to wait,' recalled Brian. They had to do everything themselves: write text books, work out a curriculum and teach.

Manx (or Manx Gaelic) is an offshoot of Old Irish: its development reflects the island's tumultuous history. Before 5000 AD the Manx people spoke a Celtic language belonging to the same branch as Scottish. Under the Vikings, who ruled the Isle of Man from 800 to 1266, it coexisted with Norse, having incorporated a few Scandinavian words. After the Viking era, England and Scotland fought for control of the island, and England eventually won. The language adopted English spelling and some features of Scots Gaelic, but remained separate from both. In the seventeenth and eighteenth centuries, the Bible and the prayer book were translated into Manx by Bishops Phillips and Wilson. The eighteenth and the nineteenth centuries saw a sharp decline of Manx – dismissed by the island's aristocracy as low class and plebian. By 1871 only a quarter of the population could still speak it.

Manx is extremely poetic. The expression for swallow is *gollan ny geayee* – the fork of the wind. The name for the local religious feast of the annunciation of Mary is translated word-for-word as 'the feast of the whisper of Mary'. Manx is not an easy language to learn. It is marked by a great deal of 'mutation' whereby words can change their first letter or letters according to the ending of the previous word. Like in Scottish Gaelic, its pronunciation calls for the use of guttural and nasal sounds not found in the English language.

At present Manx is staging a revival. Road signs in Manx are now a common sight. A festival of Manx culture is held each July in Ramsey. A local radio station broadcasts a weekly programme in Manx.

Brian's official title is the Manx Language Officer. It reminded me of our local Tree Officer in London whom my neighbours had been trying to contact for months to get his authorisation to cut a branch off a tree in their front garden. He was nowhere to be found: probably spending all his time somewhere up a tree . . .

School corridors all over the world have the same smell of floor polish, gymnasiums and fresh paint. I sit at a desk at the back of a class at the Ballakermeen High School. Not even in my wildest dreams twenty-two years before could I foresee that my next time in a classroom would be at a lesson on Manx. Frankly, at that time I had no idea that the Isle of Man (to say nothing of the Manx language) existed.

'Don't worry, Mr Vitaliev is not a school inspector,' Brian announces to the pupils who keep turning their heads towards me.

'*Fastyr mie! Ta'n ennym Brian Stowell.* Good afternoon! My name is Brian Stowell.' He says it first in Manx, then in English, and asks the children what their names are and where they live.

He takes a huge plastic spider – or *duole* in Manx – out of his bag. Having asked one of the kids to leave the room for a moment, he hides it behind the blackboard. The pupil comes back and starts looking for the spider, while all the rest direct him by shouting 'Warm!' or 'Cold!' in Manx.

Time passes quickly. In just forty minutes the kids easily communicate with a couple of dozen Manx words. At the end of the lesson Brian tells the class a Manx legend about a black dog – *moddey doo* – near the ancient castle of Peel. 'Any one who sees this dog at dusk is going to die soon . . .'

A little girl raises her hand worriedly: 'Mr Stowell, my auntie often walks her black dog near the Peel castle in the morning . . . Is it all right?'

'It's OK in the morning!' Brian says reassuringly – in Manx of course.

I was leaving the Isle of Man from the sea terminal in Douglas. The building was a typical Stalinist wedding-cake with turrets and spires, but without red stars.

'I'd like to tell you a Manx joke,' Brian Stowell said while we were waiting for the ferry. 'Once an English visitor to the Isle of Man was catching crabs on the beach. He had already caught a bucketful. "Can you watch the crabs for me while I go and fetch another bucket?" he asked a Manxman who was passing by. "Don't you worry," the Manxman replied. "These are Manx crabs. If one of them wants to escape, the others will drag it back."

We shook hands.

'*Sura mie ayd!* – Thank you!' I said to Brian and started going up the gangplank.

5. Luxembourg

This chapter took a long time to write. When I was about to start it, my London flat was broken into and my PC and printer were taken. It was upsetting of course, but, having given it some thought, I decided that Western freedom of choice must spread to burglars as well: they simply took a liking to my computer (I don't blame them) and chose to steal it.

Or maybe, on the contrary, they were trying to teach me a lesson in primitive communism implying that everything is a common property, and my computer belonged to them as much as it did to me?

In any case, with my long experience of life in a so-called communal flat, I was not easily deterred.

For many years in Moscow we lived in one room only, having to share a toilet, bathroom and kitchen with three other families. So I had to write in a cupboard. Yes, in an ordinary closet, though a big one. The previous tenant of the room was a radio pirate and used the closet for storing his illegal radio transmitter.

Little is the Light

Although the cupboard was probably ideal for a radio, it was not that good for storing me (I am slightly bigger than a transmitter). Nevertheless, I could manage to squeeze into it with my Erica typewriter. Made in East Germany, the typewriter was good, but its keys tended to make so much noise, when pressed, that they sounded like a platoon of the Lenin Mausoleum guards goose-stepping on the cobbles of Red Square.

Inside the cupboard, I installed a small lamp and made a hole for breathing. Now I could type all night without waking my son, who was still a baby at the time. It was not very comfortable, as you may well imagine, but I consoled myself with the idea that a writer must suffer. (I think this was actually said by Tolstoy, who, I am sure, never worked in a cupboard himself.)

Certainly, I could theoretically flee from my closet to the communal kitchen, and try to write there, ignoring the small businesslike cockroaches commuting matter-of-factly between the rubbish-bin and the gas stove. It was more of a problem, though, trying to ignore my numerous neighbours, who would be very nice people were it not for their profound dislike of men of letters, which reached its height when they were drunk. And they imbibed on a daily basis . . .

With all these trials behind my back, rather than being devastated by the theft of my computer, which was, after all, just a machine that lets you make mistakes faster than any other invention in human history, with the possible exception of handguns and tequila, as one modern American writer put it. I simply went out and bought myself a new one.

To be more exact, I *limped out*: while shuffling around the room looking for my stolen computer ('It is very hard to find a black cat in a dark room, especially if the cat is not there,' Confucius said) I stumbled across an antique armchair, made of oak, and broke my little toe. Luckily, I am not in the habit of writing with my feet, and the chapter was finished in time.

'Jodie Paige, Director of First Impressions' was written on a business card I once saw at a solicitor's office in one of Melbourne's suburbs. I think that every travel writer should aspire to be a 'director of first impressions' which, although often misleading, are nevertheless always memorable and revealing.

My first impressions of Luxembourg, the largest European mini-state (population 370,000; area 2600 square kilometres), were very different from my expectations. I knew that this Lilliputian Grand Duchy was the wealthiest nation in the world, that it boasted Europe's highest per capita number of privately owned houses (eighty-one per cent of all homes), washing machines (ninety-seven per cent of all households), dishwashers (ninety-eight per cent of all homes), and a stunning ninety-seven per cent of satisfied citizens. The last figure made the place sound almost totalitarian (they always claimed a 99.99 per cent approval of the party course in the Soviet Union: 0.01 per cent of 'disapproval' was intended to make the overall figure more trustworthy), but at least, with all these washing machines and dishwashers, one could expect it to be reasonably clean.

The salon of the Luxair plane from Heathrow was clean indeed, with only a handful of Euro-bureaucrats, so immersed in their laptops that I wouldn't have been particularly surprised to see them eating floppy discs for breakfast instead of bacon and eggs; and several fidgety businessmen clinging to their briefcases at all times, as if they contained top secret codes for launching strategic nuclear missiles. The latter could have been money-launderers or tax-dodgers, attracted by Luxembourg's strict banking secrecy laws, which make the Duchy into a king-size (or rather duke-size) mattress, under which dirty money can be safely salted away.

The part of Luxembourg City where my hotel was located was dirty and rundown (they told me later it was the local red-light district). Two male tramps, dressed in rags, with faded expressionless eyes and month-old bristle on their cheeks, sat in the middle of Avenue de la Gare, next to a huge cardboard crate which probably served as their home. They obviously belonged to the insignificant three per cent of dissatisfied Luxembourgers who did not own either a dishwasher or a washing machine.

My hotel was called Nobilis, but 'Horribilis' would have been a better name for it. Its corridors were as dark as the bottom of the Black Sea on a moonless night, and coming out of the elevator for the first time, I had to grope the walls in search of an electric switch, which was almost impossible to locate without a special night vision device. Finally, having hit my head against the wall, I pressed the magic button with my forehead, and a dim, tired lamp reluctantly came to life under the ceiling. Before I could say Jack Robinson or Vitali Vitaliev, it went out, and I had to renew my search − first for the switch and then for my room, which I eventually reached after abandoning my suitcase in the corridor and dashing to the door with a speed close to that of light itself. The moment I inserted the key into the lock, the lamp went dead again.

This was my first introduction to one of Luxembourg's main character features which is called practicality, if you want to be polite, and meanness or miserliness, if you want to call a spade a spade. It was this very quality that accounted for the fact that the soap bar in my hotel bathroom could only be viewed through a microscope, and was stubbornly *not* replaced by the maid until it grew as thin and transparent as a razor-blade made of mica. It explained why a TV remote control could be only acquired from the receptionist for a healthy deposit. It somehow explained why the world's wealthiest nation, with the gross national product of three billion dollars a year, had neither opera nor ballet nor a single concert hall and only three museums, and why Luxembourg's Minister of Culture was simultaneously the Minister of Agriculture! And could it be that it had something to do with Luxembourg's homicide rate, one of the highest in Europe? 'Assassination is an extreme form of censorship,' George Bernard Shaw once observed. To slightly paraphrase Shaw, we can safely assume that murder is an extreme form of greed, too.

The first place I always try to visit in a new town (especially one that I do not particularly like) is the railway station, to make sure I can easily get away if there's a need. That was where my first walk around Luxembourg City started from.

The station building was utterly commonplace. Tramps, beggars, drunks and loitering teenagers hung around its main hall. But there were trains there too. Having estalished an escape route, I went out into the city and started along Avenue de la Liberté.

It was not long before I stopped at the first pedestrian traffic lights. There were no cars to be seen, yet the locals were standing on the pavement waiting for the green light telling them to cross to appear, and staring in front of themselves into nowhere. One minute passed, two minutes, three . . . No change of light. No change of expression on my fellow-pedestrians' faces. It was plain that if the green light did not come on until the end of this century, all of them would still be standing there in the year 2000 without a word of complaint (or any other word for that matter), apart from those who had died of old age while waiting, and even their dead bodies would not be taken across the road in breach of the rules.

Having lost my patience, I ventured to cross the road while the light was still red. Murderous looks burned through my back as I walked. They looked at me with inexpressible contempt as if I was a serial killer, a child-molester or a hired assassin, who had just made an attempt upon the life of His Royal Highness the Grand Duke Jean, Luxembourg's ruling monarch.

The farther away from the station, the cleaner the city became. There were more litter-bins around than people. Two workers in green overalls were digging in La Place de Paris, while the third one was standing nearby with a broom, sweeping the freshly excavated earth into a neat pile. They were speaking Portuguese. I recognised the language from one single word that I had at my fingertips: *saudade*. Gently melodious, this word has no direct equivalent in English and could best be translated descriptively as the nostalgia of an expatriate Portuguese for his motherland. I immediately felt sympathetic towards the diggers.

153

Little is the Light

Wide empty streets were lined with coffee shops and banks, of which, as I knew, there were 213 in Luxembourg. 'UNIAO DE BANCOS PORTUGUESES', the sign on one of the buildings read.

This sign, together with the Portuguese workers in the square, reflected the most interesting, to my mind, trait of present-day Luxembourg: the smallest state in the European Community, it was also Europe's largest immigrant nation. Proportionally, that is. Almost thirty per cent of its population were foreign nationals, and more than one third of those were Portuguese.

It has become a cliché to refer to Luxembourg as the melting pot of Europe. There is no other country in the world where so many different languages – Spanish, French, German, Italian, Portuguese, Flemish, Dutch, English and Letzeburgisch – blend so easily into a colourful cosmopolitan palette. It is hard for a tourist in Luxembourg to choose a suitable phrase book to get by.

To the Luxembourgers' credit, it has to be said that, with all their superficial pettiness, they are very tolerant of foreigners. In plain words, they like them. In opinion polls more than eighty per cent of locals describe themselves as incorrigible xenophiles. And for good reason: it was foreign workers who helped the tiny Grand Duchy to achieve the world's highest living standard, who were behind its postwar industrial boom, when many natives had gone off to America in search of wealth. Today, of every three workers in Luxembourg, two are foreign.

And yet all foreign nationals living in Luxembourg are still denied one basic human right – the right to elect or be elected. Only 'a Luxembourger, man or woman', says the constitution, enjoys that right. This leads to a paradoxical situation when in local elections municipal and village councils are either chosen by a tiny minority of the active population – as in the capital where forty-six per cent of the residents are foreign – or even by a clear minority, as in the village of Larochette, say, where sixty per cent of the villagers are Portuguese.

Why, then, don't the Portuguese take Luxembourg citizenship, which any foreigner can do after 'only' ten years of residence? This brings me back to *saudade*. 'We Portuguese are living with the unfading dream of going back to our motherland one day,' Jose Travao, the president of UNIAO, an umbrella body uniting more than a hundred Portuguese organisations in Luxembourg, told me. 'Unfortunately, Portugal doesn't recognise double citizenship. That's why less than one per cent of the Portuguese nationals in Luxembourg volunteer to become citizens of the Grand Duchy, which means loss of their Portuguese nationality.'

Jose Travao was a welder. He was forty-seven and had lived in Luxembourg for twenty-four years. 'Do you dream of going back yourself?' I asked him. 'Of course I do,' he nodded. 'But how can I? There are no jobs in Portugal, especially for someone of my age. And my children are already Luxembourgers.'

I envied Jose: he had a native land that he missed, and I had none. I could not possibly miss the Soviet Union, where our life was but a constant misery and humiliation. I couldn't miss the new Russia or independent Ukraine either, simply because I had never had a chance to live there. I am a 'rootless cosmopolitan' (Stalin's euphemism for a Jew), a cultural mongrel, a peripatetic Ukrainian-born Russian with an Australian passport living in Britain, and proud of it. I am at home everywhere in the world. I am a stranger everywhere in the world, too.

It is not always easy to be a cosmopolitan and to have a distinctively foreign name. Especially when living in England. Jose Travao, I am sure, doesn't have to go through the hassle of having to spell his name dozens of times a day.

'My name? Just a sec, I'll spell it for you: V-I-T . . . No, not "P" for "Peter". It's "T" as in "Tim". No, Tim is not my name, it's Vitali V-I-T-A . . .'

Living in London, I become engaged in such lively dialogues several times a day. It is a real curse to have a foreign name in Britain. 'Can I call a mini-cab please? My address is . . . What? My name? Let me spell it for you: V-I-T . . .

Depositing a shirt at the dry-cleaners, leaving a film to be processed at a local chemist, buying a travel card at a tube station, to say nothing of hiring a video – all these routine, everyday activities are a torture for the bearer of a foreign name in London. At times I seriously wish I were called Bill Smith, or Bob Brown. Or even John Major, in the worst of scenarios. But names are like parents: you don't choose them, they choose you. And unless you are a spy or a hardened criminal with lots of aliases, names stick to you for life like a birthmark.

Maybe all foreign residents in Britain should be assigned with personal numbers? 'This is Mr 1954/10 speaking. Can you send me a cab please?' The problem with numbers, of course, is that they have unpleasant associations with Soviet and Nazi labour camps, as well as with the British internment camps on the Isle of Man.

It could have been worse. I could have been called Trethewey, Vellenoveth or Ramsbottom, say. Had I been born in the Soviet Union in the thirties, my first name could have easily been Combine, Drive Gear or even Power Station (it was the time of industrialisation and therefore fashionable to name children after the new Stalinist realities). I heard of a man whose first name was The 23rd of February, after the Red Army day. Just imagine: The 23rd of February Vitaliev!

Or I could have been an offspring of the sixteenth century Zaporozhian Cossacks in Ukraine, who challenged the Tsar's regime by giving their scions bizarre and iconoclastic last names: Salo (Lard), Varenik (Dumpling), Neubiybat'ko (Don't Kill Me, Father) and even Lisakobilka (Bald Mare).

Once I decided to conduct an experiment, and introduced myself as Bill Clinton at a shoe repair shop, as Michael Jackson at a chemist and as George Eliot at radio rentals. It worked! Only the chemist got a bit suspicious and asked: 'Where does this Portuguese accent of yours come from, Mr Jackson?'

What's in a name? Not much, indeed! But getting rid of the spelling exercises saved me a great deal of nervous energy. The pills, prescribed for Michael Jackson, were as bitter as ever. The shoes, repaired for Bill Clinton, had the same gleam about them as the ones that would have been fixed for Vitali Vitaliev.

My only little concern was: what if one day Bill decided to claim his shoes back? Next time, perhaps, I had better introduce myself as Imelda Marcos.

Soon, the empty streets and the coffee shops of the City of Luxembourg gave way to woodland. I knew that pristine forest occupied one third of the country's territory, yet I was surprised at how tiny the Grand Duchy's capital, with a population of 80,000, turned out to be. There was not a trace of the Grand Duke's Palace, the Cathedral of Our Lady of Luxembourg or any other city sights, mentioned in my guidebook and clearly marked on the city map, generously given to me (without a deposit!) at the Horribilis Hotel. Puzzled to the extreme, I returned to La Place de Paris, where the three Portuguese workers were still digging the trench, and stood there for a while, shrugging and looking around helplessly like a troubled bird.

Suddenly I saw a small green steam engine, with three open carriages behind it, emerging from under The Grand Duchess Charlotte Viaduct. I pinched myself, but the vision, perhaps evoked by the excessive consumption of excellent Luxembourg coffee, did not disappear. I rubbed my eyes and noticed that the train was on wheels. Having made a circle around the square, it went under the bridge again and disappeared into the ravine. I followed it.

The mystery of the missing sights of the City of Luxembourg was solved: the whole of its historic centre was situated in a canyon and constituted a plateau whose steep cliffs plunged further down into the Alzette River valley. Luxembourg was like a mould of such uphill mini-states as Liechtenstein, San Marino and Mount Athos. Instead of sitting on a mountain top, it was built into a ditch which was supposed to provide a natural means of protection against invaders, but in fact, as history proved, only facilitated their task.

The place was chosen as a fortress by Siegfried, Count of Ardennes and founder of the Luxembourg Royal Dynasty, in 963. He calculated that the river valley could provide a natural defence, which didn't prevent the Burgundians, the Spaniards, the French, the Austrians and the Prussians from conquering this 'Gibraltar of the North' (that was what Luxembourg was called in the Middle Ages – heaven knows why). The fortress was besieged and devastated more than twenty times in just four centuries – passing through the hands of John the Blind, Philip the Good, Charles the Mad and heaps of other dictators, princes, potentates, knights, nobles and political adventurers. Indeed, one had to be blind, mad or too good not to try to conquer the submissive Duchy in the ravine, an easy prey and a tasty little morsel for any invader. A dominion of the Holy Roman Empire, it fell under the French Burgundian rule in 1443 before becoming part of the Hapsburg Empire in 1482 and of the Spanish-ruled Low Countries in 1555, next it was the French, the Hapsburgs (again), the French (again), the Dutch, the Prussians and the Belgians. During the French Revolution, when Luxembourg was annexed to France, the Duchy was humiliated by being turned into a 'Department of Forests', answerable to the French Forestry Ministry. Independence was finally bestowed on the long-suffering Duchy by the Congress of Vienna in 1815, but it took another fifty-odd years for all foreign troops to be withdrawn from its territory.

Yes, Count Siegried made a mistake by building a fortress in a ditch. Luxembourg's tempestuous history of submission is a proof of the simple fact that to climb a mountain is much harder than to descend. It also explains the country's linguistic versatility, tolerance of foreigners and a certain niggardliness of the locals: one had to be economic and crafty to live through all these never-ending invasions and occupations. The Duchy in the Ditch . . .

Ditches have always held an attraction for me. I spent most of my childhood in a ditch, or rather a crater, made by an erroneous air bomb that hit the centre of my native city of Kharkov during the 1918–1921 civil war. Rain and snow-falls kept extending the hole, and by the time of my birth in 1954 it had turned into a long and deep ravine, overgrown with wild grass. At the bottom of the ravine there was a puddle of rain water which gradually grew into a pond, fed by natural underground springs. We boys spent hours in the ditch (*Yar* in

Ukrainian) which served as a rubbish dump throughout the fifties and sixties until some local aquarium buffs jokingly released the fry of tropical fish into the 'pond'. Mysteriously, the fish started breeding happily in the *yar*, and soon we were able to catch some strange aquatic mutants with our primitive bamboo fishing rods there. The fish were small, prickly and utterly inedible, but we loved the sheer fun of catching a fish in the middle of a big industrial city, much to the contempt of uncle Igor, a Second World War veteran and an inveterate fisherman who lived in our block of flats.

Uncle Igor had the character of a child. A brilliant fabricator, he'd spend hours in the courtyard entertaining children with stories of his wartime feats and his fishing achievements. He would go to fish in the country once a week and would come back reeking of vodka and carrying a bag full of freshly caught fish that he proudly displayed to us. We all adored Uncle Igor, although our parents suspected that his catches had been secretly bought by him at the Tempo food shop round the corner. Of course, we kept asking him to come and fish with us in the *yar*, but he dismissed our pleadings with a wave of his rough fisherman's hand: 'What do you take Uncle Igor for? Uncle Igor will never deign to fish in that dirty bog where only small fry can be caught!'

He had a habit of referring to himself in the third person – as 'Uncle Igor' – like toddlers, martinets and Gorbachev do.

One day, being more tipsy than usual, he succumbed, and grudgingly went down to the *yar* with all his sophisticated fishing gear: spinnings, home-made spoon-baits and whatnots. We were most impressed by his special folding fishing-chair with a tarpaulin seat.

Having unfolded his magic chair, Uncle Igor sat down and solemnly threw three spoon-baited lines into the *yar*'s opaque, urine-coloured water. We all flocked around him, watching this performance with our mouths agape as if it was a religious rite. The fish started biting immediately, and all his three floats were diving and jumping like crazy. Uncle Igor raised his bottom from the chair, hooked and started pulling. The fish was obviously heavy and didn't want to give in. The silk Czechoslovakian line drew like a bowstring. 'See? It only took Uncle

Igor two minutes to hook the biggest fish in this bog!' Uncle Igor, red-faced and puffing, announced triumphantly.

Soon, the top of a rusty funnel emerged from the water. 'What's that?! A bloody steam engine?!' Uncle Igor cried out in disbelief.

It was not a steam engine he eventually ferreted out. It was an old and rust-eaten Tula *samovar* – a huge coal-heated metal urn for making tea – which had probably been dumped into the *yar* by its owners when electric *samovars* came into existence.

We did not see Uncle Igor at the *yar* ever again . . .

When I came back to Kharkov after many years of absence in June, 1994, the *yar* was no longer there. I was told it had been filled up after some drunk drowned there. A small park was in its place. And suddenly I felt a sharp pang of nostalgic pain for all those hard and joyful days, filled up by time, the days that could never be repeated.

I was standing on the grave of my childhood.

The train on wheels taking tourists through the historic ditch of Luxembourg was called *Petrusse Express*. Headphones providing 'a stereophonic account of the eventful history of the Fortress Luxembourg' in five European languages, were hanging from the cars' ceiling like stalactites. The tour was a disappointment and the 'stereophonic account' was not much of a help: the names of numerous invaders, accompanied by loud sound effects of gun-shots and explosions, could not fail to give a tourist a splitting headache. Fed up with an unending cannonade in my headphones, I removed them and started watching my fellow-sufferers on board *Petrusse Express*. Among them there was a young and skinny Asian girl who would have looked unmistakably Japanese, had it not been for the scruffy way she was dressed and her timidly assertive behaviour. When I stared at her, she didn't avert her eyes, as a Japanese would do (looking into a stranger's eyes is considered bad manners in Japan). She was shivering and wincing either with cold (it was late autumn in Luxembourg) or with the deafening din of battle in her headphones. From time to time she would produce a handkerchief from her pocket and blow her tiny nose gently.

Somehow, I could not place her, which was irritating.

'Do you speak English?' I asked her when the tour finally ended.

'Yes,' she whispered.

'Where are you from?'

'Brazil.'

My writer's curiosity was sparked off.

'You don't look Brazilian,' I remarked.

'Japanese,' she mumbled almost inaudibly.

The main difficulty of communicating with Alice (that was her name
– pronounced A-lee-che) was that, uncertain of her English, she only
said (or rather whispered) one word at a time. Perhaps she was just too
cold to open her mouth. It took me a while to find out that she was
born and lived in Rio de Janeiro, which boasts a sizeable Japanese
community. A computer programmer by profession, she had never
been to Japan and her mother tongue was Portuguese. It was her first
time in Europe (she was staying with some friends in Brussels) and her
first ('And . . . last . . .' as she herself pointed out) visit to
Luxembourg. She didn't like Europe in general. 'Cold,' she muttered,
when asked why.

I suggested we explored Luxembourg together. Not that I was
particularly interested in Alice's company (she was not a brilliant
conversationalist, as you might have guessed already), but the thought
of abandoning her in the ditch was almost sacrilegious: it was easy to
imagine her turning into an icicle there in a matter of minutes. Never
before had I seen anyone who suffered from cold as much as Alice. She
was a typical delicate bloom, cultivated on the beaches of Copacabana.
Her scruffy looks were due to the fact that she had put on all the warm
clothes available from her Japanese-Brazilian family: her grandmother's
shawls, her aunt's scarf, her sister's overcoat and her father's boots. It
was not all that cold, by the way – about seven degrees Centigrade.
For me, a northerner, whose ideal temperature is minus fifteen, it was
slightly too warm, to be honest.

We started our wanderings around Luxembourg City using 'Walk
A' suggested on the back of my map as a guide. Alice was following me

at a distance like a thread follows a needle. She was trudging along, robot-like, looking down at her father's heavy boots all the time, as if afraid of losing them. Whenever I stopped to look at the map, she would freeze behind my back, studying her boots and sniffing quietly. 'I think we must now turn left,' I would say authoritatively, not exactly sure whether it was left or right we had to turn. 'Left,' she would gasp obediently without looking up. She would stop at red traffic lights like a stranded Toyota Corolla that has run out of petrol, and would not move on before I told her 'Go!'. Maybe she was indeed a robot, the latest invention of Japanese technology being secretly tested in Luxembourg, I thought. I had just watched *Terminator II*.

We got lost at point seven of 'Walk A' — 'Monument of National Unity'. I discovered this when we passed by point six — 'Holy Ghost Citadel' — for the third time in a row. It was a haunted city: wherever we went we seemed to come back to the place where we started.

It was getting dark, and we popped into the Cathedral of Our Lady of Luxembourg to warm up. Alice held her frozen hands above a burning candle. 'Let's go and have a hot meal!' I said decisively. 'Meal,' she echoed as if in a hypnotic trance.

But first I had to drop my heavy shoulder-bag at my hotel. To my consternation, rather than waiting for me in the lobby, Alice sleepwalked after me to my room, and stood there motionlessly, looking at the floor intently, as if she was cross with it, while I used the bathroom and changed for dinner. Our moderately cool European autumn must have thrown her into the state of profound hibernation, with all her thoughts and reactions greatly slowed down.

Our modest dinner in an empty pizza parlour near the station failed to wake her up from prostration. As you can imagine, it was not a very exciting experience for me.

With relief, I accompanied Alice to her hotel. She was to leave Luxembourg next morning. 'Thank you,' she murmured as we parted, and something that could pass for a smile lit up her impassive Asian face. She was probably not a robot, after all: robots, even if made in Japan, cannot smile.

On the way back to my hotel, I bought myself a bottle of incredibly cheap Moskovskaya vodka. To tell you the truth, after half a day with frozen Alice, I needed a bit of warming up myself.

The orange juice they served for breakfast at Horribilis Hotel next morning foamed and bubbled like champagne. Having champagne for breakfast is like doing a bungee jump on a full stomach, so I refused to drink it. A family of local peasants at the table next to mine didn't seem to mind, though, and were drinking the bubbling orange juice for all they were worth (they were probably familiar with the main motto of Russian alcoholics: if you don't have a drink first thing in the morning, your day is ruined). As a result, a toddler of the family was already banging his blond curly head against the table, but his parents pretended not to notice.

My destination for the day was Kirchberg, a suburb of the City of Luxembourg housing several mysterious European Community institutions such as the European Court of Justice, the Court of Auditors (?), the Statistics Office of the EC (Eurostat), the Office of Publications (?), the European Investment Bank, the European school and several departments of the General Directorate of the EC. The list alone was enough to give anyone a big yawn.

A supporter of unified Europe, I am an ardent opponent of unified European bureaucracy. Unfortunately, the Maastricht Treaty and the whole much-publicised process of 'European integration' have brought little to most Europeans, apart from Euro-bureaucrats themselves. This insignificant, yet ever-growing stratum of European population remains their main, if not only, beneficiary.

Sitting in their plush offices in Brussels, Strasbourg or Luxembourg, the extremely well-paid Euro-bureaucrats are busy issuing directives, of which they produce more than one million a year. It was they who were allegedly responsible for classifying carrots as fruit and cucumbers as mushrooms, for forbidding the sale of fresh yeast throughout the European Community; it was they who invented paternity leave, forbade children to have pocket money, demanded cultivating standard-size bananas (which would, supposedly, make them easier to transport) and prohibited trade in certain traditional seeds; it was they who — for ten years — had been trying to introduce a universal telephone code for Europe — without any success so far. Luckily all these directives were born and died inside the EC bureaucracy and were totally ignored in the real world.

Luxembourg alone is now home for almost 10,000 Euro-bureaucrats (out of the overall 'army' of 100,000), living and working in Kirchberg. Not a Euro-bureaucrat myself, I didn't have a company car as a perk, and hence I had to take a bus there.

Kirchberg reminded me of Canberra: equally modern, artificial, soulless and windswept. The plush glass-and-concrete skyscrapers of the EC buildings were scattered around in clusters, like mushrooms in a forest, and wide expanses between them were bare and lifeless. If architecture is music in stone, then Kirchberg was a noisy military march. There was something soporific about the air there: I felt like yawning all the time. No pedestrians could be seen in the streets, only Euro-bureaucrats dashing by in their fancy cars. They had to rush to be in time for countless briefings, receptions and board meetings.

The European Court of Justice occupied a huge rectangular building — a cross between army barracks and a stadium. They demanded my ID at the reception desk, and it took the receptionist half an hour to find someone who could take me around. ('They are all busy: you should have made an appointment,' he said.)

My escort was a cheerful Greek woman, an employee of the Court's public relations department. She said she spoke nine European languages. It was hard for me to check, since I myself speak only four.

We went through endless corridors that looked and smelled like catacombs. The ceilings were low: they pressed down upon you and made you feel small and helpless. People passing by us (my guide told me there were 800 staff employees at the Court) were not walking, they were all running, and, without noticing how, we started running too.

164

We looked at several courtrooms, all named after European artists and poets, with wood panels and abstract paintings on the walls. They were all empty.

As we walked, I picked up a pile of neatly stapled sheets of paper from a coffee table in one of the foyers. It was a document entitled 'Judgment of the Court of the First Instance in Case T–83/92'. I opened it at random at paragraph 5 which read:

> In that request, the applicants claimed essentially that the Commission's conclusion in its decision of 19 December, 1991 that the notified operation did not fall within the scope of Regulation No 4064/89 resulted from a fundamental misapprehension as to the essential facts concerning the extent of the influence and control exercised by Mediobanca, both by itself and in conjunction with Lizard, prior to the increase in its shareholding by the notified operation which in the view of the applicants could be attributable only to manifestly incomplete or incorrect information regarding the terms of the agreement and in particular regarding its effect . . .

I had to stop reading immediately; if I'd gone any further I would have fallen asleep on the spot. Instead of throwing the 'judgment' out, I decided to take it with me in case I ran out of sleeping pills one night.

'Have you got many cases in progress?' I asked.

'Not at the moment,' the woman replied. 'It is Thursday today, and the Court doesn't sit on Thursdays. And Fridays. And weekends of course.'

She explained that the Court only considered several cases a year, and these were mainly claims of European Commission employees haggling over better pay and complaining of lack of promotion (only rarely did they have a more exciting case, like Phil Collins suing bootleggers who made a fortune selling unauthorised recordings of his music). She remembered that a decision on one such case was to be pronounced in Fernando Pessoa courtroom shortly and offered to take me there.

Little is the Light

The courtroom was half empty. A flock of ubiquitous Japanese tourists with their Nikons abreast sat in the public gallery, watching the proceedings with their habitual lack of interest. It was plain that no matter what they had to watch – the launching of a space shuttle, a blooming sakura tree, the eruption of Fujiyama volcano or a violent sado-masochistic show – they would remain equally poker-faced. Their unwritten code of conduct did not allow them to show their emotions under any circumstances – an admirable quality.

I have always found it hard to contain my emotions, which is probably why I always wanted to go to Japan. A couple of years ago my dream came true. My Australian newspaper sent me to Cairns, the town in north Queensland that could be called the entertainment capital of Japan. No, it's not a misprint – I was one of the very few non-Japanese people in this formerly Australian town, one of the most favoured places for Japanese holidaymakers. The passersby (all Japanese) eyed me with curiosity, throwing at me the sort of furtive glances an Eskimo would get in the streets of Abu Dhabi.

My newspaper assignment included taking part in rafting. It was raining so heavily in Cairns on that winter morning in July that one could almost go rafting in the town's main street. I was nevertheless told to go to the Barron River. Using a Japanese–English phrase book, I found my way to the river easily. There I was introduced to my raft-mates, two of whom were from Tokyo, another two from Osaka, and the last one an Australian expatriate from Perth. We had to put on orange plastic helmets and tight water-shoes and were ordered by the instructor to carry our own cross, sorry, raft, to the river. Luckily, unlike the one of Jesus Christ, it was made of rubber.

As soon as the raft touched the water, it started bouncing precariously, trying to throw us off its back like an obnoxious stallion. The instructor sat astern and gave commands – in Japanese first, then in English.

Since the English commands came a moment later than the ones in Japanese, it was rather hard for our international crew to achieve the required synchronisation of movement. Due to the discrepancies in our paddling, at one especially nasty set of rapids the raft listed and scooped water. As a result an elderly Japanese businessman fell out, and for a while we could see his helmeted head floating on the surface of the water like a buoy. He didn't utter a single sound and his face remained calm, as if he was mentally perusing the business section of the *Asahi Shimbun* newspaper. Only his distending pupils, which soon filled his eye-sockets to the brim and started spilling out onto his cheeks, were indicative of his fear. I couldn't help admiring his appearance of sang-froid. We fished him out eventually, of course.

At one point, our raft was thrown up in the air, and for a moment I experienced the incomparable sensation of free-fall. I had no time to savour the feeling, since almost simultaneously I received a mighty blow on the back of my helmet with what I thought was the paddle of the Aussie woman sitting behind me.

It was pretty mean of her to do this to her compatriot in an almost foreign land. My head was tolling like a church bell at Easter, and as soon as we were in quiet waters, I looked back and said to the woman: 'I am so glad I am wearing a helmet.' 'I wish you weren't, since I hit you with my nose,' she muttered, covering her face with her hand. Then she removed her hand, and I saw that her pretty nose was bleeding.

Our instructor told me afterwards that such accidents were common. 'Once we had a Japanese lady's nose stuck in the helmet of a man in front of her. Her nose was so tiny that we had to cut the helmet to free her,' he said and added: 'Believe it or not, she behaved as if nothing had happened all the way through: despite being in terrible pain, not only did she not cry – she literally didn't bat an eyelid!'

'What a remarkable nation!' I thought then, feeling secretly happy with the fact that an average Australian nose was slightly larger than an average Japanese one.

But here, in the Fernando Pessoa courtroom of the European Court of Justice, even some of the Japanese tourists – in total breach of the samurai code – were nodding off.

I sat next to the Japanese tourists in the public gallery. Each seat was equipped with headphones: the interpreters, sitting in glass cabins at the back of the room, were simultaneously translating the hearing, conducted in French, into five languages. 'Application for the annulment of the decisions of the appointing authority of the Commission of the European Communities of 26 March, 1992 and 21 May, 1992, rejecting the applicant's candidature for the post of Head of Unit IX.A.7 and Head of Unit IV.D.3, for the annulment of the decisions appointing T. and F. to these posts, and for awards of damages for the harm allegedly suffered by the applicant through his staff reports being drawn up late and their not being consulted when the above-mentioned posts were filled and through his receiving no reasoned reply to his complaint . . .' a monotonous male voice was droning on in my headphones. Suddenly it was replaced by an equally monotonous female voice. The interpreters kept changing every five minutes, probably replacing their colleagues who had died of boredom. As a former interpreter myself, I didn't envy them their job.

The whole case, that had been dragging on for a couple of years already, could be easily summarised in one sentence: an EC commission official was denied promotion because he was often late with filing his reports.

'My client asks for material damage. He lost his chance of promotion,' the applicant's Belgian attorney confirmed in French.

'Stand up! The verdict is about to be read!' the court's secretary announced sternly. My Japanese neighbours woke up, sprang up from their chairs synchronously and stood still, with their hands pressed to their stomachs, as if about to commit *hara-kiri*.

'The decision is postponed!' the judge blurted out and turned away to retire. He was wearing a black robe and resembled a Mount Athos monk without a *klobuk*.

'The judges will now deliberate for two or three months,' my guide explained. 'So if you want to hear the final decision, come back at the beginning of the next year.'

'I certainly will!' I promised. 'Only what if they decide to deliberate a bit longer? To be on the safe side, I'd rather return at the beginning of the next century, which is not that far away, after all . . .'

Having thanked my helpful escort, I ran out into the street. The clouds in the sky were deliberating annulment of the sun's candidature for the post of the luminary. It was drizzling.

The international exhibition of office equipment was under way at Kirchberg's new exhibition complex. It should have been called 'INTERBUR' – everything for a bureaucrat. There couldn't be a better venue for it than Kirchberg and I had the impression that all 10,000 residents of this bureaucratic enclave came there with their families to gape at all those computerised folders, electronic filing cabinets and remote-control paper shredders. It was not uninteresting, even for someone like myself, whose routine working day at a Moscow magazine used to start with begging for a staple at the letters department. For some reason, all Soviet editorial offices suffered from chronic shortages of staples, to say nothing of photocopying machines, of which there was only one in our building, which housed a dozen newspapers and magazines.

You were supposed to collect three signatures from the bosses of the publishing house for each item you had to copy. The last signature was to come from the so-called 'first department' – a KGB office existing at every factory, school or institution. If you were lucky enough to collect these signatures, you had to go to the basement and shove the letter or the article to be copied through a tiny barred window where three women in dirty overalls, looking no less important than editors-in-chief, were operating the building's only copying machine.

As a rule, they would tell you to come back at the end of the day and collect the stuff, but their working hours remained a mystery, or possibly a state secret, I don't know. What I do know is that the window of their copying sanctuary was as a rule closed, although through the doors you could discern the muffled characteristic hissing of the exploited photocopier. What were they copying there behind the bars? A collection of Gorbachev's secret speeches? The Constitution of the United States? Or a popular hard-to-get book, *All You Should Know about Sex*, translated from Bulgarian? No one knew.

It was not by chance that photocopiers, typewriters and other copying devices were always treated in the Soviet Union as a threat to the very existence of the country, comparable only to subversive plots by the CIA, FBI, ICI, Mossad and Mitsubishi together. Communists never underestimated the importance of the printed word.

Which is why I found it hard to tear myself from all these automatic and semi-automatic, full-colour and black-and-white photocopiers at the INTERBUR exhibition. It all looked so simple. Want to copy something? Go to the machine, put your document under the cover, press the button and after a short friendly hiss you have your copy. Freedom . . .

I also liked the machine called 'The Böwe 507 Inserting System' (no dirty innuendoes, please). It was automatically inserting sheets of paper into envelopes, sealing them and typing addresses. Its output was 'up to 7,200 insertions per hour', as assured by the German pamphlet describing this 'ideal inserter to process leaflets, circulars, advertising letters, brochures, postcards, reply cards or return envelopes'. I wouldn't be particularly surprised to hear that the clever machine was also capable of writing love letters and reading them too.

A thick crowd of visiting bureaucrats gathered around a TV monitor through which a serious business woman in London was speaking to her business partner in Luxembourg. It was called 'video conference' – a truly revolutionary invention, designed to replace costly international conventions, congresses and general assemblies. It allowed bureaucrats of all countries to communicate with each other without leaving their offices. From the sceptical expressions on the visitors' faces, it was clear they didn't like the idea: a bureaucrat without travel expenses is like a TV set without a screen.

One place in Kirchberg that I really wanted to visit was the European school. It was founded in 1953, the first of its kind at the time. The main principle of the school was to provide multilingual education in all

European Community languages.

A child who enters the school at the age of five starts being taught in his (or her) mother tongue – any of the twelve languages of the EU member states. Soon he chooses his second language, which is going to be his main studying tongue: history, geography and most other subjects will be taught to him in it (maths is always taught in a mother tongue). At year five, a second foreign language is chosen, and at year seven, a third.

'We try to mix the languages whenever we can. The philosophy is to go across the language and to stop treating it as a barrier. On leaving the school with the Diploma of European Education at the age of eighteen young ladies and gentlemen have four European languages at their fingertips,' Antonio Pino Romero, a native Spaniard and the school's principal, told me in French. His right hand was covered in plaster, and I wanted to ask him whether he had broken it while banging his fist on the table trying to pacify some obstreperous students, but thought better of it: I hadn't quite overcome my fear of teachers fostered in me by my Soviet school.

They were all normal Western kids – these future citizens of unified Europe. In the schoolyard they were greeting each other in different languages during the break. 'Hello! *Salut! Hola! Ciao!*' echoed in the school walls. They didn't look like all-knowing goody-goodies and seemed to carry the burden of multilingual education well. There was a good deal of necking and kissing (among older kids, of course) in the schoolyard which proved again that love and friendship had no language barriers. At the back of the yard there was a modest obelisk to a Dutch boy, killed in a car accident. It was overlaid with fresh flowers.

'What is your best school friend's nationality?' I asked a ten-year-old Luxembourger girl. 'I am not sure,' she answered in English. 'She is either Italian or Spanish, but we speak French with her.'

'I am Flemish. I speak French, Danish and Spanish,' a shy sixteen-year-old girl told me with her eyes downcast.

A list of the school's junior football team displayed at the main

171

entrance spoke for itself: 'Navarro, Van Eenennam, Brunetti, Hedegaard, Mackay, Pabst, Sorensen, Cabeza, Costa, Biancarecci, O'Connel, Da Silva'. The whole of the European Union was represented there.

I wished my son Mitya could study at this school, but it was hardly possible: most of the pupils were children of EC workers. For them the tuition was free, whereas for the few 'outsiders' it was exorbitantly expensive. Another Euro-bureaucrats' perk . . .

I attended a Natural History lesson for year five, where kids were discussing in English – their second foreign language – how to save the Brazilian rainforest. At the Literature lesson for year seven the pupils were studying *Catch–22*. English was their third foreign language, but their command of it was amazing.

'Is there a word for "paranoia" in your languages?' Mr Edwards, the teacher, asked them.

I openly envied these kids. And contrary to the principal's warning to avoid such clichés as 'melting pot of nations' or 'the tower of Babel' while writing about the European school, I want to say here: yes, it was the Tower of Babel, it was the melting pot of Europe, it was the best achievement yet of the fragile European Union. No matter what these European-educated kids were going to become, one thing was certain, they would never be racists or xenophobes – not a little thing in our cruel, hatred-ridden world.

My own European education was gained not from school, but from life and travels. As to my complicated relationship with the English language, which, after five books and hundreds of articles written in it, I sometimes call 'my second mother tongue', it deserves a separate story.

'How did you learn your English?' I am often asked by my British, Australian and American friends. 'Was it normal to have a good command of a foreign language in the former Soviet Union?' I hope the answer to these questions might be of interest to those of you who have by now managed to digest half of this strange travel book. As to those who haven't, they won't read the following lines anyway.

It is hard to imagine what my life would have been like if I hadn't started learning English in 1962, aged eight. I did it under duress, since, like all normal boys of my age, I didn't feel like learning a foreign language. I felt like playing soccer, making snowmen, fishing in the *yar*, or just dashing aimlessly around the streets.

But my parents insisted.

My first teacher of English was an old mustachioed man who had been educated in a pre-Revolutionary grammar school and was fluent in several European languages. His methods of teaching were brilliant but at times a bit painful – in the true sense of the word. I'll never forget how he introduced to me the verb *to pinch*. Well, what can I say? No pain, no gain – as a good English saying goes.

After the Pincher I had a number of other English teachers, no less eccentric and resourceful. Because of the lack of English-speaking people in my Ukrainian city, one teacher encouraged me to practise my basic spoken English by talking to a wardrobe or to a fridge. I had no problems with the wardrobe, a nice taciturn character, but the fridge proved a poor interlocutor: it kept making indecent guttural noises in response to my uncertain: 'How are you today?'

Besides, at that time I was dead sure that there was either a *Baba Yaga* (a hook-nosed witch from Russian folklore) or a polar bear hiding behind it – a belief that was not conducive to easy-going verbal exchanges.

What about school? you might ask. Yes, they taught English in Soviet schools, but in a strange manner. They started with grammar, and there's no surer way to kill a child's interest in a language than making him memorise tedious grammar rules, when his knowledge of the language as such can be best described by two Latin words *tabula rasa*.

That's why it's not uncommon among my former compatriots, who have spent a dozen years 'learning' English at schools and universities, to retain in their brains the same *tabula rasa*, only occasionally sprinkled with such grammatical terms as *Present Continuous* or *Subjunctive Mood* without the slightest idea of what on earth they could mean.

Teaching grammar first was not just an innocent attempt to put the horse before the cart. Such a method of teaching was imposed by the Soviet system, whose aim it was to create an impression of English being taught on a wide scale, while at the same time curbing the students' ability to master it.

Why? I got the answer from a bored KGB man, who, during my last year at university, came to question me about my girlfriend's alleged propensity for wearing imported clothes. He himself was dressed in a well-tailored Belgian suit and glossy Finnish shoes — a ridiculous attire for someone investigating the crime of sporting Western togs.

'Of course, we watch you guys from the Foreign Languages Department with special attention,' he declared gravely. 'You know a foreign language and have access to Western literature. You can even strike up a contact with a foreigner.' At this point, his steel-grey eyes filled with genuine horror of all imaginable international contacts, which his fearsome establishment tried to minimise.

Indeed, my early knowledge of English automatically turned me into a suspect, even a *bête noire* in the eyes of the system. As to the access to foreign publications, this was an obvious overstatement. The only foreign newspaper I read regularly was *The Morning Star*, the organ of the shrinking British Communist Party. Not that I was especially pro-communist. It was simply the only Western periodical available at newsstands. Even so, it used to disappear from the stalls from time to time, when the stand of the British comrades on this or that sensitive matter (like the 1968 invasion of Czechoslovakia, say) deviated from the Soviet Communist Party line.

The possibility of 'contacts with foreigners' was an even bigger exaggeration. We language students were strictly forbidden to go anywhere near the city's only Intourist Hotel, and even there the only foreigners you could bump into would be squiffy Bulgarians.

The first real Englishman I saw was a teacher. At least he claimed he was one. He had a serious speech defect (a heavy slur, aggravated by a stutter) and came to our university from Britain on an exchange scheme, allegedly to teach English. In reality, he spent all his time playing the flute and chasing local girls, who would run away from him because he was a foreigner, and therefore not supposed to be contacted.

We students, whom he was supposed to teach, hardly ever saw him (our Soviet teachers took turns taking him out for meals, and he had a strange habit of eating leftovers from their plates). But his presence in itself was at least irrefutable proof that England (and the West, for that matter) did exist.

The English we were taught at the university, by teachers who had never met a flesh-and-blood Englishman, apart from the flute-player, was at best old-fashioned and Dickensian. Sometimes it was worse. Our lecturer in the Methods of Teaching English had a nickname – Mr Moonface. He was ruddy, round-faced and bald as a snooker ball. His knowledge of teaching English was much better than his command of English as such. 'How would you introduce to your pupils the verb *to jump*?' he would ask menacingly. Without waiting for an answer, he would start bouncing heavily on the sagging floorboards, shouting: 'Does I jumping? Does I jumping?' We hoped he would fall through the floor one day . . .

When, after graduation, I finally became an interpreter, I had to face the reality: my spoken English was as distant from the real thing as Mr Moonface's jumping was from normal teaching methods. I had to brush it up on the road.

Once I was assigned to work with an American woman, an impresario and pianist, touring the USSR. She was young and good-looking. One day in Baku she came to my hotel room to discuss the details of her schedule. 'You can undress here,' I offerred hospitably. She blushed and took a step back. In Russian, *razdet'sya* means both to undress and to take off one's coat. I certainly meant the latter, but she took the words in their English sense and stopped talking to me for a couple of days (which was a certain bonanza for me as her interpreter, by the way).

I will remember this lesson in colloquial English for the rest of my life.

'What language do you think in, English or Russian?' I am often asked. The answer is: I don't know. I just think. What linguistic dressing my thoughts will eventually acquire – Russian or English – is purely the product of opportunity. Who said that one is as many times a human being as the number of languages he knows? That's the whole pleasure of being bilingual: you can live two lives at a time. And for this I am ever grateful to all my teachers of English, Mr Wardrobe and Mr Fridge among them.

Back in Luxembourg City, ASTI (The Association of Immigrant Workers in Luxembourg) invited me to attend a musical evening in the town of Dudelange. To get there, I had to take a toy CFL (Chemins de Fers Luxembourgois) train from the City's railway station. The journey took ten minutes. Perhaps it would have been easier (and quicker) to walk.

The *soirée* took place in the town's Hotel de Ville. In the basement they had an anti-racist exhibition of racist posters 'From White to Black – Images of Black People in Western Mass Culture'. The posters, mainly from France, America and Nazi Germany, showed black people as crooks, gangsters and prostitutes. It was an impressive demonstration of human meanness and stupidity.

In the assembly hall upstairs, two virtuoso musicians from Cape Verde (there is a sizeable community of immigrants from this African country in Luxembourg) were performing African, French and Luxembourger songs. With childish smiling faces, they kept switching from piano to accordion, from guitars to African drums. It took me some time to realise that they were blind.

The audience reacted with genuine oomph, chanting and singing with the blind musicians. There was an intense feeling of warmth, togetherness, and cosmopolitanism about the evening, and my general impression of the Luxembourgers was improving by the minute. The tiny nation that was willing to accommodate so many immigrants and was treating them with tolerance and respect (even if the government denied them the right to vote) deserved admiration. It showed again that discussion of national characteristics can only work on a jocular level; the moment it grows one hundred per cent serious, it becomes far-fetched, xenophobic and irrelevant. To quote one British quality newspaper, 'generalising about nations is a tricky and not entirely respectable business, even though whole careers are built on it.'

On the train back to Luxembourg City I got into conversation with an expatriate British businessman residing in the Grand Duchy. He was travelling with a girlfriend who kept trying to kiss him on the lips, which was not easy, since there was no sign of these 'two fleshy folds surrounding the mouth' (here I had to consult Collins Dictionary to avoid tautology) on his John Major-like face. They were both tipsy.

It didn't take him long (the journey was very short anyway) to plunge into an angry diatribe about the vicissitudes of his life in Luxembourg.

'It is an extremely Bolshevised country, run by the mafia,' he said. 'Everything which is written in black and white here is irrelevant. It is whom you know and how you behave that matters. They have state censorship, and any criticism of the system is frowned upon. Divorce is not encouraged (he looked at his Luxembourg girlfriend meaningfully), and government employees who get divorced lose their jobs. It's a dictatorship. My friend had his computer files scanned by the police. And the local newspapers are pathetic and strictly controlled: if you want to find out what's happening in Luxembourg, you have to read German or French newspapers. You only have to come to the central station on a Sunday morning to see all British expatriates waiting for the *Sunday Times* to arrive. It is also in deep shit economically; the steel industry is only twenty per cent of what it used to be, and there's no more ore . . .'

I felt that, even if most of this was true, there were a couple of contradictions in what he was saying: firstly, this seemingly 'totalitarian' system that could not stand criticism somehow didn't stop him from verbally destroying it in front of a total stranger; secondly, if the country was indeed so awful, why on earth was he still living there?

People in the West tend to abuse the words 'dictatorship' and 'totalitarianism' simply because they are lucky enough never to have experienced them. Had my travel-companion lived in Stalin's or Brezhnev's Soviet Union, he would have been much more careful with his choice of words. Otherwise, this ten-minute train journey could have cost him up to twenty-five years of his life. Or his whole life, in the worst of scenarios. Everything is relative, as proved by Einstein.

I told the businessman (his name was Derek) of my desire to visit the village of Schengen, and he volunteered to drive me there next morning. Frankly, I was not sure he really meant it.

He got off the train a free man, and there was no one at the station to arrest him.

Needless to say, next morning Derek called me to cancel his kind offer. He spoke in a peculiar way, swallowing most of his vowels: ' . . .'m srry, . . .dn't feel trrbly well . . .' It was plain he was suffering from a severe hangover.

The phone was then snatched from his unsteady hand by his girlfriend, whose name was Erna. She told me in French not to listen to her '*petit chéri*' who had a bit of a headache and needed some fresh air. She volunteered to drive both of us to Schengen, which was only half an hour away from the city.

A recent European survey listed the favourite Luxembourg pastime as sleeping. The second favourite was resting.

It looked as if half of the Grand Duchy of Luxembourg was asleep on that Sunday morning. The second half was obviously at rest.

We were driving across the valley of the Moselle, Luxembourg's main (and only) river. The historical land that had seen thousands of years of territorial disputes, wars and invasions looked quiet and pastoral, as though all the atrocities of the past had been erased from its surface like a long and unnecessary file from a computer disc.

Erna was behind the wheel, and Derek was sitting next to her, wrapped in half a dozen woollen scarves, which didn't stop him from shaking violently — not with the atmospheric cold, but with an inner chill coming from his alcohol-tormented body.

I noticed a number of neat round holes in the ground at one of the road bends. Erna explained that these were frog-tunnels, built by the local animal lovers in a campaign to stop the migrating frogs from being squashed. The frogs were not using their man-made road-crossings that morning: in full accordance with Luxembourg's laid-back lifestyle, they were probably sleeping and resting. Or reading a Sunday newspaper.

We stopped in the village of Tramm to have a look at the cemetery of the American soldiers killed at the battle of Ardennes during World War II. Hundreds of simple wooden crosses and obelisks, some of which had the Star of David painted on them, stretched to the horizon in even rows, like soldiers on parade. Each of the crosses marked a young life – with dreams, aspirations and unfulfilled ambitions – squashed like a migrating frog by a heavy truck. No one bothered to build road tunnels for the soldiers to bypass their fate.

The starred-and-striped US flag was fluttering in the wind. 'Silence and Respect', the sign at the entrance read. The great powers have always thought it proper to make lots of patriotic noises while sending their sons and daughters to die in their thousands on battlefields, and then to erect memorials for them calling for 'Silence and Respect'. Something was definitely wrong with a world where frogs were a better protected species than humans.

Having driven past some more vineyards, churches, impassively grazing cows, country houses with tiled roofs, and pubs – all named 'The Moselle' – we soon reached the village of Schengen.

Why do politicians always choose boring and unremarkable places for signing important treaties? Maybe it is because such places suit these mostly boring and unremarkable people.

The sights of Schengen, this sleepy Luxembourg hamlet, tucked away between the Moselle River and vineyards on the border with Germany and France, were restricted to a thirteenth-century watchtower, an old castle and a French brasserie (called 'The Moselle', of course), where a visitor arriving by accident could have a German

179

sausage with *sauerkraut* and wash it down with a glass of local Luxembourg wine.

And yet the name of Schengen is known all over the world, since it was there that the new borderless Europe first came into being on 14 July, 1985, when the Convention of Schengen was signed. In actual fact, the signing took place not in the village, but on board the *Marie-Astrid* yacht, the only 'battleship' of the Luxembourg Navy (!) which, as a local *gendarme* once put it, was built 'to fish the corpses out of the Moselle River, a job hitherto left to the Germans'.

Representatives from Luxembourg, Germany, France, Belgium and the Netherlands agreed to dismantle internal borders. All other EC states (with the exception of Ireland, Denmark and Britain, of course) joined the Convention later. To mark the occasion, Schengen's village square, with an old water-trough in the middle, was proudly renamed Europa Plaza and the blue EC flag was installed on the roof of the village's *Mairie* building.

It was lunchtime, and Derek had to take his usual morning-after dose of anti-depressant pills, so we headed for the nearest 'The Moselle' eatery. All of them — both in Schengen and in the nearby Luxembourg town of Enhen — were closed for lunch, just like in the old Soviet Union, where restaurants also used to close down for breakfast and dinner. I came to realise why Luxembourg was sometimes ironically referred to as 'Luncheonburg'.

'Let's go to Germany for lunch!' Erna suggested. Derek gave a nod (or was it just another big shiver?) of agreement.

I knew that with an Australian passport in my pocket, I didn't need a visa for Germany, but couldn't escape that peculiar ticklish feeling as we drove across the bridge towards Germany. Convention or not, who knows what these border guards had on their minds? Besides, mine was a distinctively Russian, hard-to-spell name, and Luxembourg, due to its proximity to NATO headquarters in Brussels, had always been a hotbed of Russian spies (in 1976, out of the thirty-six staff members of the Soviet embassy in Luxembourg, twelve were engaged in espionage). I knew for sure I was not a spy, but who could guarantee that the hardened frontier guards were equally aware of this fact?

The brand-new border post was decorated with turrets and spires, which made it look almost like a smaller version of the Kremlin. Not a single human being was inside, which, strangely enough, made comparisons with the Kremlin even more apposite. Before I could get seriously frightened, we saw a '*Welcommen in Saarland*' road sign. We were in Germany!

Passing through an unguarded border was such a relief that I asked Erna to drive across the bridge over and over again, until Derek protested feebly. It gave me a sense of freedom a native Westerner would find hard to understand. The Convention of Schengen started making sense to me at last.

Germany was as neat and quiet as the Duchy in the Ditch across the bridge, the only real difference was that the cars, cottages and even cows were all bigger than in Luxembourg. It was also much more dynamic, this great country in the throes of reunification — like a strong sinewy athlete recovering after a knee injury. The wound was healing quickly, and the athlete was ready to jump and sprint again.

We stopped at Schlossberg Inn in the village of Schlosshof. Or, maybe, it was Schlosshof Inn in the village of Schlossberg — I can't remember. Not only did the restaurant have its own helicopter pad, more importantly for us, it was actually *open* for lunch.

Several dozen patrons, all serene and well-dressed, were sitting by the fireplace and speaking German. In a country whose language I don't understand, I always feel as if I am inside an aviary surrounded by happily chirping exotic birds.

Erna spoke fluent German and immediately asked a fast-moving tuxedoed *kellner* to bring Derek a cup of tea. She had to hold the cup in front of him, while he frantically tried to take a sip. The moment his lipless mouth came close to the cup, his shaking would increase manifoldly, and the tea splashed all over the tablecloth. I suggested he used a straw. It helped, and, having grabbed the plastic tube with his teeth, he finally managed to suck some liquid into his mouth, where pills were already melting on top of his tongue like snowflakes on the bonnet of a racing car. After several sips, his tremor subsided considerably and colour returned to his face. He ordered himself a *shweinencotletten* and started castigating Luxembourg with renewed energy, just like yesterday on the train.

The inn was so clean one could have eaten from its wooden floor, and the bathroom, smelling of wild flowers, was all electronic: a tiny portion of liquid soap was released from a special steel tube by a hidden photo-element the moment you brought your hands to the tap, and water was switched on and off automatically.

After almost five years in the West, I had got used to Western toilets, but my first ever toilet on the ferry from Hook of Holland to Harwich in 1988 was rather a shock: there were so many mirrors there, and the smell was so nice that I thought I had gone into a barber's shop by mistake. I leave it for you to imagine what the toilets were like in the former Soviet Union: they were simply beyond description.

It's interesting that during my last visit to the democratic 'capitalist' Ukraine, I noticed that the toilets in their new stock exchange buildings and casinos were even filthier and smellier than those under the Communists. They have obviously got their priorities wrong: democracy starts with cleaning filth, not with building casinos.

After lunch, we drove to Saarbrücken to see a Salvador Dali exhibition in the city's *sporthalle*. Dali is one of my favourite artists, although in the Soviet Union he was only mentioned in monographs criticising 'decadent Western art'. I admire his settees in the shape of lips (Derek could use one), his *Drawers of Memory*, his time-dripping clocks, his elephants on flies' legs, his *Geopolitical Children*. At the exhibition in Saarbrücken, I especially liked the painting called *Ruins of a Car Giving Birth to a Bespectacled Horse*. What an image!

Several weeks later, I read in London newspapers that the Saarbrücken Dali exhibition had been robbed, and several paintings, including *Ruins of a Car . . .*, had been stolen. The thieves were probably as mesmerised by it as I was.

After Dali, we all felt like a cup of coffee, though I suspected that Derek felt like a cup (or a glass) of something else. 'It is ridiculous to drink coffee in Germany, when France is just around the corner,' he said. 'The French make the best coffee in the world.' 'And the best wine,' Erna added sarcastically. She knew Derek better than I did.

'Yes—yes! Let's go to France for a coffee!' I cried out enthusiastically. I was greatly enjoying my newly found freedom of movement. Unified Europe was not such a bad thing, after all.

I had my first real (in fact, it was rather unreal, as you will see) experience of unified Europe on board the *Pride of Kent* cross-Channel ferry, carrying 500 revellers from Dover to Calais and back on the first night of 1993, when the so-called Single Market was supposed to come into existence (it actually didn't, but this is not the point). My trip was a newspaper assignment, and I was hoping for a couple of exclusive interviews.

Having marked the New Year in Calais with fireworks and champagne, we sailed off back to Dover to be in time for the British New Year celebrations (Britain, as you know, is one hour behind France, and the crossing time in that part of the Channel was just forty-five minutes).

The mood on the ferry was growing jubilant. A juggler was squeezing himself through the drinking and dancing crowd spitting out table-tennis balls as he went. My hopes for a good interview were evaporating by the minute: everybody on the ferry was drunk. To be frank, I myself was not entirely sober.

'Ladies and gentlemen, this is your captain speaking. I'd like to remind you that we are now back in 1992!' Listening to this discouraging announcement, I realised suddenly that on her way back to Dover the *Pride of Kent* found herself in the no-man's-time-zone — the one-hour time loop between Central European Time and GMT. This black hole could not fail to attract a couple of ghosts from the past.

With renewed hope, I started looking for two of them in particular, without whom the Single European Market celebration guest list would not have been complete. Both tried to unify Europe by force in their own times, and both failed.

After another glass of Château Tourbier I spotted the first. With a cocked hat on his head, he was standing on the upper deck looking at the receding shore through an old-fashioned spy-glass, his black mantle flying in the wind.

'What do you think of European Union?' I asked him, switching on my dictaphone.

He lowered his telescope. 'I've always said that this Channel is a mere ditch, and we'll be across as soon as someone has the courage to attempt it.'

'But aren't you pleased that England and France have become much closer?'

'*Ha! L'Anglettere est une nation de boutiquiers!*' (England is a nation of shopkeepers) he chuckled.

I decided to change the subject. 'You look amazingly fit for your 223 years,' I said.

'The bullet to kill me has not yet been moulded,' he muttered.

'Shall we drink to that?' I suggested.

'Not tonight, Josephine,' he replied, turning away and pressing the spyglass back to his eye.

I found the second ghost in the Club Class lounge. Throwing back a fringe of black hair from his forehead with twitchy movements of the head, he was frantically tossing coins into a slot machine. He was dressed in a grey semi-military service jacket and gleaming high-boots with jodhpurs. From the angry look on his face, with a dot of a moustache under the nose, it was plain he was losing.

'Sorry to interrupt you,' I said, 'but what do you think about the Single European Market?'

He turned back sharply. 'It's a big lie,' he barked, piercing me with his beady, fierce eyes. 'The great masses of people will more easily fall victims to a great lie than to a small one.'

'But didn't you try to unify Europe in your own way?'

'This is the last territorial claim that I have to make in Europe,' he answered sadly, pointing to the gambling machine area. 'I go the way that providence dictates with the assurance of a sleepwalker!'

'But don't you agree that this is a historic night?' I persisted.

'*Jetzt ist die Nacht der langer Messer!*' (This is the night of long knives), he screamed suddenly, and snatching a long SS dagger from his pocket, he chased me round the ship.

I was saved by the sound of Big Ben. We were back in 1993, and my persecutor vanished into the thin wintry air.

Euro-drinkers and Euro-dancers and Euro-Lovers and Euro-bureaucrats on board the *Pride of Kent* mingled into a boisterous multi-lingual Euro-crowd. We had boarding passes, not border passes, in our pockets; we had glasses, not guns, in our hands; we had Europe, our native land – with all her pros and cons, with all her proms and wars – in our hearts. We had a common history, common ghosts and a common future. We were all in the same cross-Channel boat.

Next day I left Luxembourg and flew back to London, where my newly discovered sense of European Unity was dealt a blow at Heathrow airport. I had to queue for more than an hour with a crowd of equally hapless Australians and Americans, Swedes and Swiss, under the humiliating sign 'All Other Passports'.

The po-faced immigration officers questioned us about the purposes of our visits. I was tempted to say: 'To set the Thames on fire,' but decided not to test their sense of humour.

Borderless Europe may have started at the Luxembourg village of Schengen, but it certainly ended at Heathrow.

6.   Faroese Flashes

The Faroe Islands

In all my wanderings around the world, never have I seen a country even distantly similar to the Faroe Islands, a self-governing Danish dependency of eighteen barren volcanic islands far out in the North Atlantic.

When visiting a new country, one inevitably compares it to places one has been to before. With their mountainous terrain and 80,000 sheep – almost twice the human population (*forer* is the Nordic word for sheep), the Faroe Islands could resemble a smaller and cooler New Zealand, were it not for total lack of trees and flowers ('Flowers do not grow because of the wind, and trees because of the sheep,' as one local explained), constant rain and unattractive grey beaches, good only for killing pilot whales.

Countries, like people, have faces. Some are those of smiling young beauties, others of worn-out ageing peasant women. The Faroes' face is that of an old fisherman, wrinkled and weather-beaten, yet proud and attractive. A smile is a rare guest on this face, but when it comes, and the sun suddenly breaks through the clouds at the end of a long summer day – lighting up multi-coloured lego-land houses scattered along harbour fronts, graceful Lutheran churches, and ubiquitous football fields – you can't help smiling back.

This remote Nordic country is a constant alliteration: the Faroes – ferries – far-away – fairies – frescoes – fjords – fish. It is also a succession of crisp morning frosts and transparent winter sunsets at four o'clock in the afternoon, when rocks and cliffs are silhouetted clearly against the pinkish sky, like a huge appliqué work created by Odin, the supreme God of the Vikings. It is a soft unruffled impression of boat masts, doubled in the glassy waters of the fjords. It is a multiple repetition of timid and translucent snowflakes falling silently, almost regretfully, and melting instantly on your face.

Nothing is certain about the Faroes, where you can experience all four seasons not in one day – like in London, not even in one hour – like in Melbourne, but in ten minutes. 'The Isles of Maybe' – this is what the British RAF pilots stationed there during the last war called the country: maybe grim or maybe cheerful; maybe grey or maybe colourful; maybe boring or maybe exciting; maybe old or maybe new. And the white summer night above Tórshavn, the capital, is but a long twilight Maybe: is that the sun or the moon in the low satin sky? Who knows . . . And who cares . . .

The shifting between sparkling light and resounding shadows, the never-ending natural *chiaroscuro*, is one of the most characteristic features of the Faroese landscape. This is probably why my impressions of the country are hazy and not at all chronological. They can be best described as Flashes. Flashes of light and darkness. Flashes of memory. Faroese Flashes . . .

Football

Pal Gudlaugsson is one of the hardest men to get hold of in the Faroes. The former national football team manager, he divides his time between coaching and running three sport shops that he owns. I finally managed to talk to him over the telephone. 'Faroese football is not what it used to be several years ago,' he said with a loud, deep sigh that made my eardrum vibrate like a goal post hit by a powerfully kicked ball.

It is not easy to find a more football-crazy nation than the 49,000 Faroese. The country has 400 men's and twenty-five women's football teams. A sand or an articicial turf football pitch can be found in every single village, no matter how small, together with the regulation church and primary school. To build such a space in the Faroes, where the only natural patch of flat surface is reserved for the country's airport, with the world's shortest runway, is not an easy task. In many cases, nearby mountains had to be excavated by the determined villagers.

The biggest day of fame in the history of Faroese football, if not in the whole of the country's history, was 12 September, 1990, when the Faroese team of amateurs defeated Austria 1–0 in their first European Championship qualifying game. This victory, which was later called one of the biggest shocks in international soccer history, was achieved on a neutral field in Landskrona, Sweden, although officially it was supposed to be the Faroes' home game: the other three members of the qualifying group refused point-blank to play in the Faroes, despite the fact that the first real grass pitch (it cost the country one more mountain) was especially built for the tournament in the village of Toftir. The excuses varied from difficulties of travel to the capricous weather (with changeable wind making the players kick the ball in one direction and run in another).

The reverberations of the sixty-third minute victorious shot were heard throughout the world. For the Austrians, it was the biggest humiliation since the Anschluss. 'Resign, Waldheim!' the headlines in all eight Faroese newspapers yelled. It was hard to imagine that one of the world's best professional football teams could be defeated by a bunch of part-timers from the top of a cliff in the middle of the Atlantic Ocean.

Eventually, it was not Kurt Waldheim, but Josef Hickersberger, the Austrian manager, who had to resign (Waldheim had to resign later after his Nazi past was revealed).

In the Faroes, a National holiday was declared. 5,000 chain-dancing (not to be confused with chain-smoking, this is a long and monotonous Faroese folk dance, in which the dancers gradually whip themselves up into a trance, making associations with chain-smoking not that far-fetched) Faroese came to meet their heroes at Vágar airport. 'Now it's the turn of the Danes,' the triumphant and belligerent Pal Gudlaugsson told the cheering crowds, having in mind his team's next qualifying game with Denmark. But miracles do not happen twice (otherwise they wouldn't be called miracles): the Faroese team didn't make it into the finals.

Once was certainly enough for the game's two protagonists: a timber-office clerk, Torkil Nielsen, who scored the winning goal, and a lorry driver and part-time goalkeeper, Jens Martin Knudsen, who prevented the Austrians from scoring a good dozen of theirs. Overnight, they became the country's most popular figures, and Knudsen's bobble hat, worn during the match, was elevated into a national symbol on a par with the Canadian maple leaf, Russian vodka and the British laxative pill.

This bobble (or pom-pom) hat had an interesting history of its own. It was knitted by the future hero's granny at the suggestion of a doctor, to protect the fourteen-year-old Jens Martin's head from being kicked by his junior soccer team-mates, who often confused it with a football. Knudsen was seldom seen without it (I mean his bobble hat) on a football field. 'Once, early on, I forgot to wear it and had a bad match,' he confessed in one of his interviews.

A couple of months after the game with Austria, two Norwegian wrongdoers stole the pom-pom mascot from Knudsen's unlocked house (they don't have locks on the houses in the Faroes — on some heads, yes, but not on houses). Luckily, the thieves were apprehended at Vágar airport, and the hat was duly returned onto the locks of its legitimate owner. This was the third recorded robbery in the whole of the Faroese history.

Drinking

Having opened the mini-bar in my Hafnia hotel room, I found the following three items:

1. A bottle of mineral water.
2. A bottle of Fanta.
3. A rusty bottle-opener.

I was not particularly surprised by this more than meagre choice. The government information brochure that I had perused on the plane warned against 'importation of disposable cans and/or non-returnable bottles' which was 'strictly prohibited'. Small amounts of alcoholic beverages could be brought to the Faroes 'in regular long-necked bottles only'. Another, no less strict warning stated that 'driving under the influence of alcohol in access of 0.80/00 is punishable by a fine and a loss of licence at the very least'. I especially liked 'the very least' bit of it. What punishment could be in store for a mildly intoxicated driver in the worst (or in the 'least best', as they say in America) of scenarios? Life imprisonment? Beheading? Quartering?

All these limitations were a hangover from the 'restrictive law and regulations on selling and serving alcoholic drinks' (another quote from the brochure), or near-prohibition, introduced in the Faroes by the 1907 referendum. It is significant that the referendum took place a couple of months after the Faroes women got the right to vote. So it can be assumed that near-prohibition expressed a natural desire of fishermen's wives to keep their husbands sober in-between their fishing expeditions – far from an easy task, especially in the Faroes, where cold climate and hardship made booze one of the main joys of fishermen's life. 'The joy of Russia is in drinking,' the Russian eleventh-century Prince Vladimir used to say. The same could be said of twentieth-century Faroes.

Not that alcohol was made illegal in 1907, but it was severely rationed. The Faroese had to order it from Denmark, and delivery would take place eight to ten days later. The maximum ration was twelve bottles of liquor every three months per person, provided he (or she) could prove that all local taxes had been paid. Tax dodgers had to remain teetotallers – an ingenious idea which, I think, could be borrowed successfully by any other country. As to beer, it could be bought locally, but had to be ordered one day in advance (by regular tax-payers only, of course).

The truth was that despite (or rather because of) all these restrictions, the Faroese people started drinking much more than ever. Forbidden fruit is always the most coveted. Also, having got the twelve rationed bottles, a drinker would empty them in a couple of days and would start looking for a way to get himself (or herself) another supply. And the way is always there, provided there's a will (or a bill), as we all know. After 1907, travellers to the Faroe Islands recorded an unprecedented growth of dypsomania in the country.

'Nothing was an adequate preparation for sitting in a hotel in Tórshavn and being told that it was illegal to have a glass of wine or beer with dinner, while out of the window I could see hundreds of people, and teenagers especially, staggering around absolutely pissed, rat-arsed, out of their brains,' Matthew Engel wrote emotionally in the *Guardian* in September, 1991, one year before the 'restrictive regulations', to quote the useful government brochure once again, 'underwent a radical and long-awaited change'.

In short, the near-prohibition in the Faroes did not work. It *could not* work, to begin with, as proved by the sad experience of Sweden, the United States and Gorbachev's Soviet Union.

Gorbachev started his crazy anti-alcohol campaign shortly after coming to power in 1985. Only instead of trying to eradicate the social roots of alcoholism, he and his flunkies decided to fight . . . spirits.

The production of all alcoholic beverages, including beer, was cut sharply. The relict vineyards in the south of the country were razed and a leading winegrowing expert, a professor of agriculture, commited suicide.

A new rubber-stamp organisation, the Sobriety Society, was formed and people were coerced into joining under threat of losing their jobs.

The entrance fee was simply deducted from pay packets. It was a typical Soviet thing to do: to try to solve a problem by creating another bureaucratic structure to be blamed in case of failure.

Did these measures reduce the amount of drinking? Not in the very least! On the contrary, statistics showed that people started drinking more than before, only instead of having good wines and vodkas (both of which were next to impossible to get) they were imbibing shampoos, perfumes, hair lotions and terrible stinking homebrews. In 1988, this resulted in more than 17,000 deaths due to poisoning.

It is dangerous to ignore the lessons of history, showing that drinking is a socially based phenomenon and cannot be stopped by bans and restrictions.

Liberalisation of the Faroese drinking regulations in November, 1992, was 'long-awaited' indeed, yet far from 'radical'. Rationing and red tape were stopped, and two state monopoly liquor shops were opened in Tórshavn and Klaksvik. Despite the fact that now one can have a glass of wine or beer at a couple of restaurants and brewery outlets, public drinking remains restricted. You have to belong to a special club to be able to have a serious drink in the evening. I was invited by a Faroese contact to be her guest at one such club in Tórshavn.

The establishment was called:

Kaggin Club

My contact opened the thin plywood door with her own key. It was semi-dark inside, and it took me a while to discern a long bar, a piano in the corner, and a handful of melancholic men sitting at tables with batteries of empty bottles on them. One of the men was tickling the ivories lazily and humming in a discordant falsetto: 'Let it be! Let it be!' 'He is a famous Faroese musician,' my contact said.

Another patron (they were all males, apart from my escort) was swigging beer from the bottle and puffing like a hippo emerging from the bottom of a lake for an intake of air: 'Oo-ff! Oo-oofff!' A minute later, a couple of men from the neighbouring table, having got fed up with his huffing, grabbed him by his shirt collar and threw him out. He continued to ooff as they frogmarched him to the door.

The barman, a Scotsman from Glasgow, nearly fainted when I orderd a glass of mineral water.

'How does one become a member of the club?' I asked him.

'Well, you have to provide a couple of written recommendations from the members and prove that you know how to drink.'

'Do the applicants have to undergo a drinking test, similar to a driving test, to be accepted?' I wanted to ask, but thought better of it. From the behaviour of most of the members it was clear that, even if the test did take place, it was either not serious, or both the examiners and the examinees were completely legless.

Another man, drinking at the bar, would give out piercing shrieks: 'A-aa-a! A-aa-a!' – similar to those of a pig about to be slaughtered, at fixed intervals. No one seemed to mind. Perhaps he was a Faroese version of the talking clock?

The Musician stopped playing the piano, came up to our table and, without any prelude or greeting, tried to make contact with my contact by grabbing her breast. She slapped him in the face matter-of-factly (it was obvious she was used to this Farose-style foreplay) and he let go of her. He was drinking Cognac and washing it down with beer, which reminded me of my student days when, in our constant striving to get pissed as quickly and as cheaply as possible, we would add vodka to beer or to champagne. The first cocktail we called 'Ruff' and the second 'Starlit Night'.

How on earth could he pass his drinking test? I wondered.

'You know, I just like to drink!' the Musician said in heavily accented English.

'Really? I thought you hated it,' I remarked. He was too drunk to appreciate my irony.

A broad-shouldered, pot-bellied man stumbled to our table. 'I am a flower man,' he introduced himself, drowning his words in a good swig from a whisky bottle, which he was holding in one hand gently, as if it was a watering can (it *was* in a way, only instead of flowers, it was used to 'water' his own liver which, judging from his brick-red face, was about to start blossoming).

The Talking (or rather screaming) Clock gave out a piercing: 'A-a-a!' again. The barman looked at his watch and started cleaning away the bottles.

'Tomorrow is a public holiday, that's why he has to stop selling alcohol at eleven forty-five p.m., instead of three a.m., as he normally does,' my contact explained, brushing off the tenacious hands of the Flower Man, which were stretching towards her poor breasts like two sunflowers towards the sun.

The Musician yawned. 'Goodbye, Crocodile!' he said to me amicably. He probably wanted to say 'See you later, Alligator!' but alcohol was playing havoc with his uncertain English. Or perhaps he somehow knew that I used to work for *Krokodil* magazine in Moscow?

We started towards the door, but the Flower Man blocked my way and tried to poke me in the eye with his dirty, soil-stained finger. He missed of course.

'I am a bloody Communist!' he shouted all of a sudden.

'And I am a bloody anti-Communist!' I shouted back and went out. I was fed up with this particular side of Faroese culture.

The pale drunken Moon was mooching about in the whisky-coloured Faroese sky.

Løgting

I am sitting in the Speaker's chair in the Løgting, the Faroese ancient parliament, the origins of which can be traced back more than 1,000 years, when a shipload of Vikings stumbled upon the umbrella-shaped Faroese archipelago on their way to Iceland. According to some sources, they were simply too seasick to continue their journey, and chose to settle on the islands, driving out the wandering Irish monks who had lived there since the seventh century AD.

The Løgting now sits in a black log cabin with a turf roof in the centre of Tórshavn. Like so many other Faroese buildings, the parliament house looks deceptively shabby and derelict from the outside, while its interior is quite spacious and modern.

Papers are strewn all over the empty room, where, in line with the Home Rule Act of 1948, only Faroese internal matters are supposed to be debated by thirty-two local MPs (foreign policy and executive power are in the hands of the Danish crown). There is a strong smell of crisis in the air.

And a crisis was indeed unfolding in the Faroes. On the day of my arrival (I know I tend to attract trouble), one of the MPs resigned, thus depriving the ruling centre-left coalition led by Prime Minister Margarita Petersen (a former teacher and the Minister for Education) of the fragile parliamentary majority of seventeen. Early parliamentary elections were to be announced any moment, and the ruling party had very little chance of retaining power.

The last couple of years had seen an unprecedented decline in the Faroes' economy and well-being. Throughout the eighties, the Faroese enjoyed the world's highest living standards and fast economic growth, largely due to the abundance of fish and generous subsidies from Denmark. In the early nineties, all this prosperity was ruined by two natural disasters: the fish that had accounted for ninety-five per cent of the country's exports left the Faroes' waters (only God – or rather Neptune – knows why), and the left-wing Social Democratic coalition came to power in November 1990.

As in all other Scandinavian countries, the Social Democrats started enlarging the public sector, giving out social benefits right and left (mainly left, I think) and increasing the number of government bureaucrats (i.e. themselves). It all went well for a while, until the day of reckoning came: someone had to cough up to maintain this socialist Utopia. To make both ends meet, they had to raise taxes and beg Denmark for more loans, which they knew they had no chance of ever paying back. The country turned into a beggar, still relatively prosperous but plunging deeper and deeper into economical and political despair, aggravated by chills of the pan-European recession which started reaching the Faroes, infecting them with transient pneumonia. For the first time in the Faroese history, unemployment benefits had to be introduced, and the official number of the unemployed reached twenty per cent of the working population in 1993 (unemployment had never existed in the Faroes before). The real figure, I was assured by an influential MP, was forty-five per cent. All this resulted in massive emigration from the islands (3,000 left in 1993 alone), soaring real estate prices and the closure of half of the country's fish factories, the backbone of the Faroese industry. With tourists as scarce as fish (or even more so), national debt of about one billion pounds and the Danes reluctant to play kind uncle any longer, the islands found themselves wallowing in financial, economic and moral backwaters.

'We now have to import frozen fish from Russia to process at our remaining factories,' Margarita Petersen, the Prime Minister, confessed during our earlier meeting in her shabby turf-roofed hut of an office. Compared to this, carrying coals to Newcastle or coming to Tula with one's own *samovar* (the Russian equivalent) sound like ideas worthy of the Nobel Prize for Economy.

There is no denying the facts: the much-praised Scandinavian socialist model crumbled together with its infamous Soviet counterpart, and the Faroes serve as another brilliant example of this global collapse. Alas, people in many countries are slow to learn and, seduced by nice-sounding populist slogans of equality and prosperity, keep bringing socialists back to power.

Sitting in the Speaker's chair, I wished the Faroese MPs were at their desks and I could convey this message to them. But would they listen?

'The Prime Minister tried to run our society as if it was a teacher's room,' said Oli Breckmann, a Sean Connery lookalike member of both the Faroese and the Danish parliaments who was showing me around the empty Løgting. 'The public sector has eaten its way into everything, but she has to understand that money does not fall down from the sky. And, what does she do? She appoints the former Communist party official to resurrect the economy!'

Mr Breckmann's People's Party stands for complete independence from Denmark which, as he himself put it, was only achievable through economic self-sufficiency.

'The world's social democrats have lost their *raison d'être* and refuse to accept it,' he concluded puffing at his cigar

I found it hard not to agree with him.

On the Speaker's table, next to a timer-clock (to regulate the MPs) and a silver bell (to cut the MPs short), lay a beautiful whale-bone hammer (to hit the MPs on the heads?) – a gift from the government of Iceland.

'This hammer went missing recently, but after we advertised its loss in a local newspaper, it magically reappeared,' said Oli Breckmann.

This was probably the country's greatest robbery since Knudsen's famous bobble hat was nicked in 1990.

It takes a big effort to ruin a country like this.

Souvenir Shop

P/F Heldin gallery next to my hotel had the most bizarre collection of souvenirs on offer. Its shelves sagged under skilfully made effigies of puffins, ravens and magpies. Gold-plated puffins' feet were displayed on the counters. Some poor crow's severed feet, made into earrings, hung on the wall. Just imagine a flirt wearing these feet, with every claw meticulously preserved and covered with varnish, in her ears.

In the corner there stood a sack full of sheep's horns, and next to it a bucket full of sheep's skulls, with gaping eye-holes and yellow teeth sticking out.

'What are these for?' I asked Karin, the shop's owner.

'We eat the sheep's head and use the skulls as decorations - pretty, aren't they? And our children play with jaw bones like with toy pistols,' she replied.

'Do tourists buy all these pretty skulls and horns?'

'Ya . . .h,' she said in an inimitable Scandinavian gasping manner as if choking on her own uvula. 'Ya . . . h . . . Especially Germans. They like using horns as bottle-openers.

'We eat everything in the Faroes,' she went on. 'Whales, puffins, crows. There is only one bird we don't eat – *tjaldur*, the oystercatcher, because it is our national bird.'

What is this? Cruelty, inherited from the Vikings who used to carry their enemies' heads on pikes? Or something else?

I addressed these questions to Professor Jóan Pauli Joensen, rector of the Faroe University in Tórshavn and the ultimate authority on Faroese customs, traditions and ethnography.

'There is no tradition of cruelty in the Faroes,' he said. 'We are an old peasant and fishing culture. All these birds and animals have not just been an essential part of our diet since time immemorial, killing and eating them has always been part of our national identity. There was no ritual involved in these killings. It was a necessity. Living on these barren islands with no resources and little vegetation, we had to be satisfied with what we had. We Faroese are children of nature . . .'

Well, it's not that uncommon for children to milk their parents dry these days. The Faroese have simply made one little step forward by choosing to eat them. But perhaps they simply had no choice?

Pilot Whaling

'Don't mention the whales,' my omniscient London friends advised me before my trip to the Faroes. This valedictory sounded pretty much like Basil Fawlty's proverbial 'Don't mention the war.'

Pilot whaling remains the Faroe Islands' most sensitive issue. In almost all the sources on the country that I could dig up at a London library, the Faroese were portrayed as uncaring whale-slaughtering savages – the image created by animal rights zealots and Greenpeace activists. It is largely due to this stereotype that the Faroes have not become a popular tourist destination: they are boycotted by a number of European tour operators.

I don't believe in stereotypes. The 49,000-strong little nation with a hundred per cent literacy, the nation publishing eight daily newspapers and 150 books a year, hardly corresponds to the image of 'blood-thirsty barbarians'.

But back to *grindadráp*, as they call whale-hunting in Faroese.

To begin with, pilot whales are *not* an endangered or a protected species, even Greenpeace had to admit this. Their number in the waters of the North Atlantic is huge and keeps growing.

The killing of whales has never been commercial and whale meat was always intended for family consumption only. Trade in it is illegal in the Faroes.

The Faroese started hunting whales more than 1,000 years ago. They braved the ocean to drive whales ashore in their traditional wooden rowing boats. When a school of whales was sighted, an intricate system of smoke signals was used to send the message from village to village, before the whale was jointly driven to the beach.

A pilot whale drive would bring together people from all levels of village community, people would 'dance themselves warm' on the shore after a hard day's work. So it was very much a social and a cultural event, too.

Whale meat has always been one of the most important local sources of food, even now representing one fourth of the islanders' overall meat consumption. I tried it once in my hotel restaurant, and, believe it or not, I found its taste disgusting – like that of a shoe sole soaked in salty water. You wouldn't eat whale meat, *if given a choice*, I assure you. The problem is that eating meat is essential in the islands' climate, and there has never been much of a choice of it in the Faroes.

There are strict rules as to how the beached whales must be killed. It is done by severing their major blood vessels in the neck with a knife (spears, grapnels and harpoons are strictly banned). Blood pressure drops rapidly and the whale loses consciousness in a matter of seconds. Naturally enough, this fairly humane killing turns the sea quite red with blood.

The catch is shared between the villagers by the district sheriff, calculating the size of a share for each person.

'I have killed many whales,' Palli Lamhauge, an old whale-hunter and birdwatcher from the village of Vestmanna on the island of Streymoy, told me proudly. 'I still do it. Every man in our village does. We have always lived like that – hunting birds and whales and sharing them. I don't understand why tourists boycott us. They have bullfighting in Spain, but no one wants to boycott Spain because of this.'

And no one boycotts Britain because of fox-hunting, I could add.

Cruelty in any form is appalling. Hypocrisy – even more so. How many of those who write angry letters of protest against whale hunting to the Faroese government after a good English breakfast of *bacon* and *eggs*, have a *lamb* (or a *chicken*) kebab for lunch and a sizzling *beef* steak (or a *pork* chop) for dinner? Why is slaughtering a sheep, a pig or a cow OK, and killing a pilot whale with a brain much smaller than that of a pig a crime?

A whale is a part of wildlife, you might object. But so are rabbits, partridges, pheasants, shrimps, crabs, squid, fish and hundreds of other species that we humans consume for all we are worth without the smallest pangs of remorse, and even call delicacies. As to the Faroes, the only wild animal you can find there is a feral rat – a creature not exactly suitable for a steak.

One day in the future, when the world community becomes a hundred per cent vegetarian, when the ruthless slaughtering of sheep in England, cows in Holland, pigs in Germany, fish in Spain and chickens in France comes to an end, then – and only then – we'll have the moral right to tell the Faroese: 'Stop killing your whales, or else.'

I sincerely hope that this day will never come.

Local Madman

After a couple of days in the Faroes, I started noticing familiar faces in the streets of Tórshavn: a woman from the bookshop, a waiter from the restaurant, a local madman. Encounters with the latter were frequent. Toothless and dishevelled, he would follow me everywhere, giggling and showing his bare gums amicably. He would watch me from the street as I had my morning coffee in Tórshavn's only café, his grinning face glued to the window. He would burst into the lobby of my hotel, grab a couple of pamphlets from the reception desk and dash out, mumbling to himself.

In a way, he was a strange symbol of the place, with all its complexes and idiosyncrasies. The people of Tórshavn, a town where a crowd of three causes interest, treasured him as a living local sight. The café's chef would carry out a piece of cake for him on a plastic plate. At the tourist office, they always had a stack of old pamphlets that he could grab.

'Who is this man?' I asked my hotel receptionist, when I saw the madman for the first time.

He waved his hand condescendingly: 'Ah, he is mad. He lives with his mother!'

Mikines

The national art gallery in Tórshavn was my biggest surprise in the Faroes. This small country had a real constellation of brilliant artists, all of whom were represented there. The most striking feature of all the paintings was colour – red, blue, green and yellow spots of joy screaming from the sombre grey and black background of everyday gloom. I understood why all the houses in the Faroes were brightly and cheerfully painted – to disperse the darkness of the landscape, to beat boredom and suffering, to defeat the hostile climate and hostile sea. They desperately needed something to please the eye on the islands.

'We have only a dozen professional artists in the Faroes, all the rest are amateurs,' Bárdur Jákupsson, the gallery's owner and himself an artist, told me. He was a typical painter: bearded, long-haired and smoking a pipe. 'Life here has always been hard, and it is reflected in the paintings,' he continued.

The works of one artist – Sámal Mikines – stood out among the rest. They could grace any museum in the world. At a first glance, they all looked gloomy and depressing: grieving fishermen's wives clad in black, murky seas, funerals. The titles – *Grief, North Wind, Before the Burial* – speak for themselves. Yet in every painting, no matter how lugubrious, there was always a tiny spot of light and hope: a patch of sunshine on a grieving face, a speck of moonlight on the water. These tiny bright flashes dominated the canvasses, making them hopeful and even optimistic.

'Mikines lived in a typical Faroese fishing village, where men often died at sea. In 1934 alone, nine of his relatives died – some of them drowned, others died of tuberculosis. Mikines took it upon himself to give expression to suffering, but he tried never to give in to it.' Bárdur Jákupsson explained.

Pilot Whale Hunt, an oil, painted in 1942. Dark silhouettes of whale hunters with their spears ready (spears were still legal at the time) standing up to their knees in torrents of crimson, blood-coloured water, with the burning disk of the setting sun behind their backs, as if they are holding it on their shoulders. The sun is pierced by the tops of the hunters' spears like a huge red pilot whale on the yellow beach of the evening sky.

In one of his letters, Mikines wrote of the colours in the Faroes:

. . . a few more words about the colours. Here in the islands they are broken in a wonderful way by the dampness of the air, which often creates a diffuse sensual impression, the likes of which I have experienced when the sea and sky meet together in pink and grey tones with the gleam of a conch shell, or in cascades of light which are suddenly cast out of huge dark cloud masses, lighting up the sea, the cliffs, the green grasslands and the black village houses. In both cases, it is a strong but also a gentle light. It is fascinating . . .

He was a poet as well, Sámal Elias Mikines.

There are no icons on the altar of the old white-walled and lead-roofed church in Kirkjubøur, the Faroes' oldest village. Instead, there is just one painting showing a flimsy boat with fishermen (or whale-hunters) in the rough sea at night. The boat, tossed around by the waves, is about to sink into the cold black nothingness, but all of a sudden the luminous figure of Christ in long robes appears in the background. This is not a fisherman's vision: the figure of Christ arises from behind their backs, and they cannot see it from the boat. But somehow it is clear that their ordeal is over, that from now on they are safe, and are going to make it back to their homes.

I've never seen an altarpiece more powerful than this painting by Sámal Mikines, created shortly before his death in 1979.

No artist can dream of a better recognition than having his work displayed in the altar of a village church where people come and pray looking at it.

Without Mikines' oils you can't understand the Faroes, these distant and colour-hungry islands.

Driving

The biggest dilemma I faced in the Faroes was 'to drive or not to drive'. In my case, it could easily reach Shakespearean proportions ('to be or not to be'), due to my very basic driving skills (if they can be called skills at all). My 'probationary' Australian driving licence was acquired with lots of sweat and drama a couple of years before (in Australia, they put you on probation for three years, which means that you are not supposed to have a drop of alcohol in your blood while driving). For you to understand the full scope of my doubts, I have to tell you about my first driving lesson.

Melbourne was invaded by fire hydrants. Wherever you went, you saw lots of them standing nonchalantly at the curbs, dragging you towards them like powerful magnets. Their short vertical statements were almost pagoda-like, but I didn't feel like praying in these little roadside temples. I hated fire hydrants: there were far too many of them in Melbourne. They made it look like a city possessed by pyrophobia and inhabited exclusively by pyromaniacs, thinking of nothing else but setting everything on fire.

I started suffering from this peculiar disease — firehydrantphobia — after my first driving lesson.

Yes, having suddenly remembered the old French wisdom — 'mieaux veux tard que jamais', better late than never — I decided to overcome my inborn handicap and learn to drive a car. I even successfully passed my traffic rules test, only slightly embarrassed to be doing this in the company of giggling teenagers: at thirty-seven years of age I was by far the oldest contestant, a sort of a patriarch figure.

I couldn't wait to be able to sit behind the wheel of my brand-new Mazda 121. Never before have I felt so passionate about an inanimate object. My Mazda was not inanimate though. She was gleaming, and young, and beautiful, and looked almost feminine from behind. I was sure she winked at me coquettishly with her left headlight when I first approached her.

Her insides smelled of leather and plastic. She was bright-yellow from the outside, the safest colour, as I was told. Her engine worked with short flirtatious purrs, which were driving me mad with desire to drive her.

At last, I was sitting in Mazda next to my knowledgeable instructor. Yes, that was the sad reality of my driving status: I had to share my mechanical sweetheart with him. An eternal triangle . . .

Given the choice, I would have preferred to have my first lesson in the desert. But the closest desert was too far away, so I had to satisfy myself with a fairly deserted street in Port Melbourne.

Gee, I never knew driving was so easy. The most difficult thing so far was to adjust the mirrors properly. And see: I am moving, faster and faster, I am keeping my hands on the wheel, I am looking triumphantly around, I am driving my Mazda crazy with driving her, I am making a left-hand tu . . .

Crash! Bang! Bam! . . Oh, God . . . I think I pressed the accelerator instead of the brake by mistake. Mazda leaped forward and landed beyond the curb. The instructor had no time to react . . . But it seems to be all right . . . We are both alive . . . Only where is this angry hissing coming from? . . Have I run over a red-bellied black snake?

I looked over my shoulder. A thick fountain of pressurised water was beating from under Mazda's boot. My first thought was that the water was coming from Mazda herself (I read somewhere that the engine needed some water for cooling), but there was too much of it. And the ominous hissing continued, as if a hundred rattlesnakes were writhing under Mazda's rear wheels. 'What if the car explodes?' I asked myself, and without answering fell out onto the ground through the open front door.

For an outside observer it all must have looked absolutely hilarious: a portly man falling out of a car which was sitting on top of a bubbling and fuming fire hydrant. There couldn't be a better sequence for a comedy film, but for me, the reluctant star of this film, it looked rather like a slow-motion horror movie. Here I was, standing next to my beloved Mazda, who was being violated by the stream of water from beneath, and laughing nervously.

The fountain, beating from the smashed, almost flattened fire hydrant, was watering generously the nearby palm tree, the house and the pavement on the opposite side of the road. It was at least twenty metres high, its firing range was twice as big, and two agile rainbows were already shining above the sea of mud created by the stream.

Suddenly, from the corner of my eye, I saw another palm tree, just twenty centimetres from where the car stopped. The tree was tall and solid. I realised what a close shave it had been. And it was only then that I got really frightened.

It was like a bad dream: the instructor trying to soothe me down; the water board people arriving about 20 minutes later, when torrents of water were already flooding the street; the tow-truck lifting my poor Mazda on its back and carrying her away.

I could hardly believe that I was the source of all this fuss. After all, I was just trying to turn the corner, the first corner in my car-driving life.

The injured fire hydrant was lying on the ground like a desecrated obelisk on the grave of my illusions that driving was easy. It probably saved my life by slowing down Mazda's thrust a little and stopping her from hitting the palm tree. Maybe it was also an obelisk to me as driver?

My driving had certainly improved since then, though occasionally I would still try to park my car into a pole, or into a Hungarian (there were plenty of both in Melbourne).

I knew that driving in the Faroes had many hidden hazards. The roads were good, but the road signs scarce and misleading. The numerous tunnels were narrow and unlit. The ferries connecting all eighteen islands were tiny, and considerable parking skills (which I didn't have) were required to accommodate a car on their decks. It was impossible to get out of Tórshavn: wherever you went, you came back to a modern Lutheran church with a tall spire, the haunted town's only milestone. On top of it all, if you ran over a sheep (it was pretty hard not to, considering these reckless animals' sheer quantity), no matter how small a lamb, you were in for a 1,000-krona fine. Besides, such an accident was bound to make 'BLOODY FOREIGNER KILLS OUR LAMB' front-page headlines in all eight newspapers of this crime-free (and event-free) country.

There was one positive side to Faroese driving, though: the chance of your car (locked or unlocked) being stolen was practically nil. How far can you drive a stolen car on the islands, where everyone knows each other (and each other's cars) and where you are never more than three miles away from the sea?

So, having weighed all pros and cons, I wisely chose *not* to drive in the Faroes. I had to deviate from this decision only once, on my last day in the country.

Vágar on Sunday

Vágar (which means 'the bays') is the third largest island in the Faroes archipelago. It is separated from Streymoy, the main island, by a two-kilometre-wide stretch of water.

The country's airport was on Vágar, and, since my departure day (Monday) was a public holiday, which meant no ferries, I was advised to spend my last evening there. It turned out to be the whole day: the last ferry from Streymoy to Vágar left on Sunday morning.

The guesthouse I was booked into for the night was in the hamlet of Bøur, at the end of the island's only eighteen-kilometre-long road. The road began at the ferry terminal, so there was no alternative to renting a car and driving there.

To my great relief, there were practically no other cars on the road, and I was able to get away with swaying from its left side (they drive on the left in Australia) to the right one (they drive on the right in the Faroes) and back without a dreaded head-on collision. A couple of times, however, I narrowly escaped head-on collisions with the sheep, who, like me, were not exactly sure which side of the road to choose.

It was sunny for the last hour or so (it rained heavily in the morning), and the countryside, with murmuring waterfalls, yellow marigolds and green meadows extending to house tops, looked cheerful and pristine. An abandoned NATO radar station that was used to intercept Soviet radio traffic in the times of the Cold War was bristling with now useless antennae and resembled a giant dead cat on top of the mountain.

I passed through a couple of villages, each with rainbow-coloured houses, a school, a football field, and a cross to those lost at sea near the church where Sunday mass was under way.

Near one of the villages I saw an old car moving towards me at a snail's pace. I quickly returned to the right side of the road (I was forgetfully driving on the left side again) to let the car pass. When it came alongside me, I saw an elderly, neatly dressed gentleman behind its wheel. As he slowly drove along, he was looking not in front but to the sides, turning his head right and left, like a leisurely pedestrian admiring the landscape. I suddenly realized that he *was* admiring the landscape and that he *was* a pedestrian, only *a pedestrian behind the wheel*. He was out on a Sunday walk in his car!

* * *

When I arrived at Bøur, the liturgy in the local church was over, and the villagers, dressed in their Sunday best (men and boys wearing bowties, women wearing shawls and long woollen skirts) were coming back to their turf-roofed homes for the Sunday's chunk of whalemeat. At the guesthouse, hymns were still played over the radio, their soporific sound mixing with the monotonous bleating of the sheep grazing outside.

Bleating and praying. Isn't there something in common between the two? They both put you to sleep promptly.

The only two other guests at the guesthouse were a skinny, long-nosed and permanently angry Faroese man, looking like an oversize mosquito, and his chain-smoking wife, with a low masculine voice that sounded like a trumpet of Jericho, capable of causing stone walls to fall. It was clear why her husband had such an angry face.

The couple has just returned from a two-hour walk to the hamlet of Gásaldur, the most isolated village in the country, which can only be reached by walking over the hills. Going to Gásaldur is a popular family sport in the Faroes, like climbing the Fuji Mountain in Japan.

The company of the Mosquito couple did not seem particularly enticing, and I drove back along the road, hoping to have some lunch at the airport's restaurant, the only public catering establishment on Vágar. I was driving slowly, turning my head right and left and admiring the landscape. Like the old gentleman earlier on, I strolled around in the car.

I stopped in Midvágur, noteworthy for a strange custom practised nowhere else in the world, except for this Faroese village. At Lent, a couple of young people, dressed up as monsters and with seaweed in their hair, go round the houses screaming wildly and trying to frighten the children (I am sure they usually succeed). The actual purpose of these black-faced (and poor) mummers is begging for meat.

Another local curio is the so-called 'minister's widow house' – an isolated hut where a woman called Barbara lived in the eighteenth century. This woman was married to two clergymen (not simultaneously, but one after another, of course) both of whom died mysteriously (one after another). My guess was that she poisoned them for trying to drag her along to their Sunday services. Or, more likely, all of them, including Barbara, simply died of Sunday boredom.

My lunch at the airport's restaurant was spoilt by a tall Viking-like Faroese man drinking at the neighbouring table. From time to time he would come up to me and say: 'I can help you!' I would tell him I didn't need any help, thank you very much, and he would piss off, only to return two minutes later with the same drunken mantra: 'I can help you!'

Having lost patience, I finally said: 'OK. You will help me tremendously if you get your arse out of this restaurant this very second!' To my surprise, he enunciated: 'Yes, sir!' and stumbled towards the door, chased by a waitress whom he clearly didn't feel like helping by paying his bill. From the window, I could see him getting into a car and driving away. I wished him good luck in avoiding a head-on collision with the nearby mountain. Or with a landing aircraft . . .

Having watched a solitary plane balancing on the edge of a cliff before taking off, I drove back to Bøur.

Bored (or rather 'bøured') out of my mind, I spent the rest of the afternoon watching the sheep who seemed to be the only creatures in Bøur who had something to occupy themselves with on a Sunday evening. My observations revealed that the sheep lived according to some tribal laws of their own: the rams sat together on the grass gossiping, like old men in a Greek village (they needed only cups of steaming coffee in front of them to make the resemblance complete), while the ewes looked after the kids.

One horny ram was chasing another along the grass, trying to sniff his behind. Perhaps he was gay.

I soon felt like bleating myself, and went inside the guesthouse.

I slept badly that night. The Jericho Trumpet of a woman kept nagging her Mosquito husband in her thunderous voice behind the wall (or maybe they were just having sex and she was roaring with pleasure).

The waterfall was murmuring outside, and the sheep bleated tirelessly all night through.

One could certainly have a sleepless night in the bleating village of Bøur, but hardly a *sheepless* one.

Bird-watching

'Are we going to see puffins?' I asked Palli Lamhauge.

'Maybe . . .' he answered in an uncertain Faroese manner.

He stood astern his old motorboat, chugging along Streymoy's indented coastline. This was the first bird-watching expedition in my life.

We entered fjords and grottoes, bypassing phallic and cathedral-like rocks sticking out of the water. It was raining. The sky above our heads teemed with birdlife: gulls swooping and squawking, fulmars gliding, guillemots standing shoulder to shoulder on the cliffs like miniature penguins. It was a real birds' bazaar, resembling the Queen Victoria market in Melbourne: same hubbub and ethnic versatility. But there were no puffins in sight.

'You can't shoot a puffin, it is not allowed. You can only catch it with a long stick,' Palli said. Shooting (or even catching) a puffin was not on my agenda. What would I do with it? Eat it? Stuff it? Take it to London?

The day before I had a chance to try an 'underdone puffin breast' at my hotel restaurant. It tasted like calf's liver — much better than whale meat.

I kept looking up worriedly. One traveller to the Faroes warned bird-watchers of the dangers of being attacked by an Arctic skua, a bird who defends its eggs and young by dashing at any potential threat, including humans. He wrote that the best way to protect yourself was to carry a chair leg above your head: if the bird attacked, it would be the leg, not your head, that would get the bashing. Unfortunately there was no chair leg in my luggage.

I could also do with a large, round tray, a medieval knight's shield, or anything else to protect my head from torrents of birds' droppings, mixed with rain, falling down from the sky. Thank God sheep cannot fly . . .

Palli pointed his huge oar-like palm to the top of a distant rock where a long-beaked oystercatcher (*tjaldur*), the Faroese national symbol, was nesting, and explained that this bird was in the habit of looking after other birds' fledgelings, as if they were its own. What a caring altruistic creature! Completely unlike the cuckoo who abandons its eggs and nestlings for other birds to nurse. That's what they call a promiscuous and irresponsible woman in Russia – a cuckoo.

On one of the cliffs, we spotted two men and a boy, crawling up the slippery mountain slope ant-like, with long sticks and buckets in their hands. They were collecting guillemots' eggs – another traditional Faroese pastime. Like mountain-climbers, they were tied together with a thick rope. This occupation involved lots of dexterity and hair-raising acrobatics. Food must have been really scarce in the Faroes, if people were prepared to risk their lives for a couple of small spotted eggs.

No matter where you go in the Faroes, you can't escape the sheep. I was hoping that at least here, among the cliffs, I would be spared their irritating toneless bleating. Nothing of the kind!

A pitiful 'Be-e-e!' sounded from the sky. I looked up. On an almost vertical moss-covered cliff, half a dozen sheep were grazing peacefully, oblivious to the fact that their hooves were sometimes precariously dangling in the air, a good hundred metres above the sea. It was amazing to watch a tiny newborn lamb running up an almost vertical rock effortlessly, as if it were a flat green meadow somewhere in Devon. This must have been a special Faroese mutant lamb – a cross between a sheep and a lizard.

'They bring the sheep here in May and leave them to graze until October,' said Palli.

'How do they take them back?'

'They throw a lasso around their necks and bring them down.'

I thought it was not such a bad idea, after all: to leave the sheep to graze and bleat among the birds for half the year. The sheep were guaranteed against premature slaughter, the owners could give their long-suffering ears some coveted rest, and the birds, preoccupied with their own volatile interests, didn't seem to mind.

Salmon Farm

Do you like smoked salmon? I adore it! Prior to my visit to the Faroes, I hadn't given much thought to where this delicate red meat came from. A total technological ignoramus, secretly convinced that rubber is extracted from galoshes, I could be forgiven for thinking that salmon grew in the trees, together with bagels.

The Vestmanna bay smelled of salmon, like a Jewish delicatessen in Golders Green. Here and there one could see circular enclosures, marked with colourful floats, on the surface of the water. These cages (and this was what they were – salmon cages) lived their own life, quite separate from the rest of the bay: water in them was turbulent and maelstromy.

'We have 106,379 young salmon in this cage,' Sigtór Andreassen, the young marketing manager of Vestsalmon fish assured me.

Come, come, I thought ironically. Did you count them or what?

'Are you sure there are that many of them?' I said aloud, looking intently at the cage's wavy surface. 'To me, it looks rather like 106,378.'

My irony was quite unnecessary. It was not Sigtór himself, but a computer that counted and even fed the fish. Food was pumped into the cages through long computer-operated rubber pipes snaking all across the bay.

We went to inspect other cages by boat.

'Here we have year one fish,' said Sigtór, pointing at a cage that was especially messy: with small salmon jumping out of the water as if trying to say hello to us.

'Very playful,' Sigtór observed. 'We inject them with vitamins and eventually they can reach ten kilos each. This cage alone gains five kilos of weight a day.'

213

'How do you . . . er . . . dispose of them then?'

'We pump them into a special tank with carbon monoxide which makes the fish groggy, then we cut their gills out and throw the fish into another tank where they swim and bleed for about ten minutes. Blood gets out of their bodies quickly. Besides, we starve them for two weeks before killing to clean their stomachs.'

'I don't envy the fish their plight,' I mumbled.

Sigtór grinned: he had obviously heard this before.

'The fish feel no pain, that's what we think.'

I was somehow sure the fish themselves thought differently. If they could think at all.

'I seldom eat salmon myself,' Sigtór added almost apologetically.

'Don't worry. I eat it for you,' I hurried to console him.

'We only kill fish on Tuesdays, Wednesdays and Thursdays.' He was clearly uneasy about the whole business of fish killing and was trying to soften the issue.

It was Friday afternoon. The fish on Vestsalmon farm were enjoying a long carefree weekend before dying.

Professor Poulsen

Professor Jóhan Hendrik W. Poulsen, the Faroe Islands' leading linguist, was a typical Oxonian-type academic – grey-haired, bespectacled and soft-spoken. Yet his small cubicle of an office at the Faroes University was highly unusual and could best be compared to a fish farm. Only, instead of fish, be bred new Faroese words there.

The ancient Faroese language, a derivative from old Norse and West Norwegian, is now recognised as the main language of the Faroe Islands – quite an achievement, if we remember that until 1938 it was forbidden to teach it at schools, and that Danish had been the only official tongue in the Faroes since 1400.

'Faroese is the sister language of Icelandic,' said Professor Poulsen. 'It has got some Celtic words, too. Don't forget that the Shetlanders and the Faroese are basically the same people: the Shetlands were simply donated by the Danish king to Scotland as a dowry for his daughter's wedding.'

The Danes treated Faroese as a dialect of ignorant country bumpkins. For centuries Faroese remained just a popular spoken tongue, there was no literature in it until 1890. (Even William Heinesen, the Faroes' most famous author, who died in 1991, wrote in Danish, which prompted him to refuse the nomination for the Nobel Prize for Literature, suggesting that a Faroese-language writer should be nominated instead.)

This is no longer the case. One of the most amazing sides of modern Faroese culture is the number of books (150 titles a year!) written and published in the native language. Shakespeare, Dostoyevsky and even Homer have been translated into Faroese by local enthusiasts.

'Yes, Faroese can even accommodate hexameters,' smiled Professor Poulsen, who is also a member of the Committee for the Protection of the Language.

'Two years ago we introduced a parliamentary bill to protect our personal names. Unless the Committee decides otherwise, any child born on the islands has to be given a Faroese name to be registered and baptised.'

This might sound a bit too harsh, but the Faroese do have a point: their language has to be revived after five centuries of Danish domination, and this sometimes requires tough measures.

It is interesting that the Faroese, just like the Icelandic, do not have last names – only first names and patronymics. Example? Had I been a Faroeman, my full name would be Vitali Vladimirsen, since my father's first name was Vladimir; similarly, my son's name would be Dmitri Vitalisen (the son of Vitali) – a bit of a tongue twister, but nice and simple to remember.

The biggest problem the Faroese faced when trying to recreate their old tongue and turn it into a written language was the absence of words for such modern notions as 'television', 'video', 'computer', 'compact disc' and so on. And that was where Professor Poulsen came into the picture, or rather into the dictionary.

Instead of using foreign borrowings, he decided to come up with some genuine Faroese neologisms. 'Words are like bubbles of air resting at the bottom of the ocean. One day they can pop back up to the surface,' he told me poetically. Thus a computer became *telda* – from *tal* (number); a computer screen – *skiggi*, from the sheep's stomach stretched across the smoke-holes in the roofs of traditional Faroese houses to keep out the rain and let in light (predecessors of windows); the compact disc was baptised *flöga* – from round wooden pancakes put under haystacks.

'It took me a lot of time to find a proper Faroese word for a CD,' Professor Poulsen confessed. 'You see, creating new words is like spreading seeds: some fall on good soil, some on rock.'

Most of Professor Poulsen's linguistic creations fell on fertile ground: they are widely used in the Faroes and are going to be included in the first monolingual Faroese dictionary, which is to be published soon.

'My work is like that of a poet, only my poems consist of one word only,' he told me.

He looked a totally happy man, and I couldn't help envying him his job a little: had I not been a writer, I would have probably become a linguist myself.

At the end of our meeting, Professor Poulsen's secretary brought in some tea and milk in a plastic packet. I noticed that one side of the milk (*mjólk*) carton carried a tightly printed Faroese text that looked like a short article.

'What's that? Nutritional information?' I asked the professor.

'No, it's linguistic information,' he said. 'Some time ago, we decided to print language advice on milk packets. This one, for example, explains the difference in usage between the Faroese equivalents of the words "terrible" and "terrific".'

Unable to read Faroese, I thought I could still see the difference: the Faroe Islands were not a *terrible* – gloomy and whale-slaughtering – place, as most of the English-language publications and newspaper articles, in line with old clichés and stereotypes, characterised it. It was *terrific*.

216

7. GIBANMAMORGA

Gibraltar, Andorra, Malta, Monaco, Seborga

Gibanmamorga is a country not to be found on maps. It may sound as if it comes straight from *Gulliver's Travels*, but in fact, it is an acronym standing for five European mini-states – Gibraltar, Andorra, Malta, Monaco and Seborga – that I visited in one trip. So, for me, and for my son Mitya who accompanied me on this journey, they all merged into Gibanmamorga, a country that we crisscrossed in search of black trousers.

Why black trousers? Because, by the age of thirteen, Mitya had turned into a fashion-conscious Western kid, and it had become hard to satisfy his increasing appetite for 'smart' clothes. At the time of our journey he was preoccupied with getting himself a new pair of 'cool' trousers. Having discarded all imaginable trousers available in London – from Leather Lane street market to John Lewis's – as 'girlish', 'scruffy', or both, he was hoping to lay his hands on a decent (in his view) pair in one of the four European mini-states we were due to visit

(Seborga was not on our itinerary initially). This was how our trip had turned into a three-week-long hunt for black trousers.

This sudden consumerism was natural in a boy who, after four odd years in the West, could still remember the word *dostat*, a peculiar Soviet colloquialism meaning 'to buy with difficulty', as well as our daily wanderings around a vicious circle of several permanently bare shops in our Moscow neighbourhood in search of cheese, meat, fruit or mayonnaise, to say nothing of trousers or shoes. For two years I tried to buy myself a decent pair of shoes, the kind that could only be acquired with hard currency or special coupons given to shock workers (exemplary workers) at Moscow factories. I could not qualify as a shock worker, whose hard-working feet were worthy of wearing comfy shoes, though I was in a state of continuous shock caused by the Soviet reality. Being a shocked journalist was not good enough to get shoes.

My son's other passion at the time was writing short stories. Here's the beginning of the story he typed on my antediluvian Amstrad word processor one day before our departure:

> This was another typical day for Mr Amstrad. Having got up pretty early, he could find nothing better to do but to hurl the neighbours' cat by the tail all the way to the post office. Mr Amstrad walked to the post office every day as he was too scared to have a letter box, in case someone would want to steal his mail. But that could never happen as Mr Amstrad had never got any mail. Not one single postcard . . .

No Samuel Pepys, I nevertheless chose to write this chapter as a diary. The reasons? Firstly, a diary is a traditional travel genre that cannot fail to give the reader the illusion of spontaneity and keep him on the edge of his chair with excitement: 'Monday – Shaved my cactus. Tuesday – Found an empty beer can,' and so on. Secondly, travel writing as a genre has no rules whatsoever, and I am free to do whatever I like anyway.

* * *

10 April, London – Gibraltar

I like leaving London from Gatwick, so much quieter and cleaner than Heathrow. There are fewer people, no queues and they serve good coffee at the buffet, as opposed to Heathrow where coffee is weak, soapy and tastes of kitchen sink water. Even the immigration officers are nicer at Gatwick: they smile at you, whereas at Heathrow their 'smile' can be best described as a curved stiff upper lip.

On board the small Gibraltar Airlines plane we are surrounded by a bunch of cheerful Al Pacino types – suntanned, broad-shouldered and sporting crew cuts. They are probably 'Winston Boys' – the notorious Gibraltar smugglers, specialising in Moroccan hashish and Winston cigarettes – coming back home after a successful drug-trafficking holiday in Britain. I intrigue Mitya by saying that most of them use 'the Kid' as their nickname, or rather *nom de conrabande*. As to the Spanish customs patrols whom they never fail to outwit, the smugglers' code name for them is *'La señora mala'* – 'the bad lady'.

Meanwhile the unsuspecting 'smugglers' borrow a baby from a female passenger and play with it: toss it up in the air, put it on a trolley, as if trying to smuggle it through to the Business Class. The baby remains unperturbed, and Mitya assumes insightly that a) the baby is a dummy; and b) they are hiding drugs in its nappies. Thus, our journey has a thriller-like, if not a particularly thrilling, start.

From the 'GB Airways' magazine in the seat pocket in front of me, I learn that the airport in Gibraltar is 'within ten minutes walk from the centre' and that 'taxis to Spain are available from a taxi rank just across the Spanish frontier, a hundred yards away.'

This is a good introduction to the idiosyncratic nature of Gibraltar – six kilometres of largely self-governing British protectorate, sandwiched between the Mediterranean and Spain, the territory that became part of the British Empire in 1713 under the Treaty of Utrecht. Spain has never recognised the legitimacy of this treaty, and tiny Gibraltar has been a source of discord between Britain and Spain ever since.

219

'Are we going to fly over Spain?' Mitya enquires. 'No, we are not,' I reply. I am well aware of the fact that, due to an ongoing dispute, arriving aircraft from Britain are not allowed to fly over Spain: to reach Gibraltar they have to fly towards Morocco, then land from seaward. (Which is like going from London to Oxford via Glasgow.) In this age-long squabble, Britain and Spain behave like two hostile cats living in the same back yard and marking their respective territories and spheres of influence with their own urine.

Soon we get our first glimpse of the famous Rock of Gibraltar, a huge Jurassic limestone, formed 150 million years ago, a home for 30,000 Gibraltarians and eighty-nine Barbary apes, Europe's only wild simians.

The plane lands straight into the blue sea. We close our eyes, waiting for a loud splash, when a narrow airstrip materialises from under the plane's wing. It looks like a two-lane highway, and, in fact, it is a highway, doubling as a runway. When a plane is about to land, they simply halt the traffic. I recall the sign I once saw on the airfield of the extremely congested Hong Kong airport. 'Give way to planes', it read.

In a striking contrast to London, Gibraltar is basking in bright sunlight. 'Welcome to Gibraltar!' they stamp in our passports at the airport's immigration control. This gigantic saucer-size stamp takes half a page in my treasured Australian passport, with an emu and a kangaroo on its dark-blue cover. I can almost hear the poor Australian animals squeal with pain on being stamped upon with such elephantine force.

Why are immigration officials all over the world so eager to spoil a blank page in your passport by stamping it in the middle? Maybe they simply want to irritate you. Or do they think that their precious stamp is so important that it must enjoy proud solitude on a passport page?

I have also noticed another strange correlation: the smaller the country, the bigger the stamp. The largest one in my passport comes from Macau. It occupies only slightly less space than Macau itself (straight in the middle of the page, of course). It must be a manifestation of an inferiority complex, caused by the countries' minuscule size.

We are standing at a bus stop outside the air terminal. The border with Spain is indeed just a hundred yards away, and we can see Spanish customs officers in grey uniforms rummaging through the boots of the cars that form a long tailback on the Spanish side. The Spanish guard the frontier closely – almost to the point of Cold War paranoia, which has turned Gibraltar, a party to the European Union via the British connection (though not a signatory to the EU customs union), into an *enfant terrible* of unified Europe, a prisoner under house arrest in the 'new European home'.

'Buses do not work today because of Sunday,' a sympathetic passerby informs us in broken English, so we have to flag down a cab. 'Ambassador of the Rock' is written on the driver's nametag, next to the glove compartment. I remember that a similar tag in a Sydney cab said 'Public Passenger Vehicle Driver'. The simple words 'taxi driver' are clearly not acceptable in our age of political correctness.

A friend of mine recently received a letter announcing that his lawyer is to undergo a sex change and live as a woman. Nothing extraordinary by modern standards, you might think. The most curious thing about the letter was its title: 'GENDER REASSIGNMENT'. The formerly male lawyer must have thought that 'sex change' would sound too raunchy and decided instead on a tongue-twisting linguistic monster.

This was just another example of the extremely dangerous phenomenon of PC (political correctness), spreading throughout the Western world like a bushfire or plague. Reams have been written about PC of late, but there have been few attempts to define it. The Prince of Wales angrily described PC in one of his speeches as 'testing everything, every aspect of life, every aspect of society against a predetermined, preordained view.'

The doctrine of PC was born in left-wing American universities, its birth coinciding with the collapse of Communist ideology. A new dogma was necessary to pull together the shattered ranks of Communist sympathisers, and PC was chosen as the best available substitute. Similar to the Russian Bolsheviks who started their reign of terror by littering the Russian language with unpronounceable abbreviations and unpenable neologisms, the proponents of PC began with a massive linguistic assault.

Destruction of common human notions and values starts with their disappearance from the lexicon. 'If we change language, we change everything,' Henry Beard and Christopher Cerf wrote in the introduction to their witty *Official Politically Correct Dictionary*. Tongue in cheek, they suggested replacing the male-chauvinist word 'history' with 'herstory'.

Since then PC has stopped being just a joke, and the latest edition of the *Oxford Dictionary of the English Language* seriously lists 'herstory' among its entries. Newspapers are now wary of using 'sportsman', 'fireman' and 'policeman', preferring the more politically correct 'sports person', 'firefighter' and 'police officer'. Who knows how long it will be before we start saying 'hispes' instead of 'herpes', 'femstruate' instead of 'menstruate' and 'ovarimony' instead of 'testimony'?

The politically correct version of 'A short, bald, serial killer was imprisoned for his crimes' will soon read: 'A follicularly and vertically challenged person with difficult-to-meet needs became a client of the correctional system after displaying sexually dysfunctional behaviour.' 'Spouse equivalents' will replace 'lovers', 'unpaid sex workers' or 'acquaintance rape survivors' will be used instead of girlfriends, 'nonhuman beings' will swarm in zoos and forests instead of animals. How terrifyingly boring!

The manifestations of PC are not restricted to language. They are becoming more common in everyday life. A man opening the door for a woman runs a very real risk of getting if not a box on the ear then a murderous look. Smokers inadvertently lighting up in restaurants have to be prepared for a barrage of plates and glasses from neighbouring tables. There have been cases where smokers have been killed or severely beaten for lighting up in public. I can't understand why smoking and drinking are thought to be politically incorrect while taking soft drugs is socially acceptable in the so-called 'chattering classes'.

And what's wrong with the good old word 'girl', now increasingly avoided by the print media to be replaced with 'woman', or even 'womyn'?

It has become politically incorrect to speak out against political correctness itself. Yet, similar to the Communist dogma, PC is certainly doomed. It contradicts human nature and natural desires of flesh-and-blood human beings (not genderless 'persons') to love, to be loved and to be able to say, write and do whatever they want.

Luckily, Mitua is as yet unaware of political correctness. During our five-minute ride to the hotel, he keeps craning his neck to stare at every passing young girl (he has just started taking interest in the opposite sex). 'Girl', not 'woman', I stress. To get to the town, we take the runway-cum-highway again, this time in a car, and I am genuinely scared we might take off by mistake.

Having checked into a nondescript and colonial hotel, we go out to explore the town.

At first glance, Gibraltar looks unmistakably British, with its Wimpy snack bar, Marks & Spencer store (the only sort of Marxism that seems to work), red pillar-boxes and a branch of a familiar building society. The Angry Friar pub in the Main Street has a fat rosy-cheeked (and not at all angry) monk in faded brown (formerly black) robe painted on the sign above the door. Inside, several English peasant types are feasting on ale and steak and kidney pies and staring moodily into the fireplace.

'We are like an English village forty years ago, especially on Sundays,' an English porter in our hotel said. Born in London, he lives in the Spanish town of La Linea across the border and works in Gibraltar (he can't afford to live there). He has to undergo long and humiliating Spanish customs checks every time he goes to work in the morning. He told us that it is impossible to buy a Spanish newspaper in any of Gibraltar's newsagents, and that almost all foodstuffs – even bread – are brought to the colony not from neighbouring Spain but from Britain, nearly 2,000 kilometres away.

Yet Gibraltar is definitely the place where, contrary to Kipling's predictions, East and West meet. Its little narrow lanes, revolving around the Main Street hub, with their Regency houses and Moorish courtyards, its gardens and ancient churches, its clay and mudbrick huts, its colourful togs, put out to dry on tiny colonial balconies, add up to an exciting blend of cultures and traditions, all held together by the Rock. Gibraltar is simultaneously African and European, Spanish and Arabic, Jewish and Moroccan. With people of forty-four nationalities living here, it is cosmopolitan to the extreme. Gibraltar has no clear-cut identity. It reminds me of myself . . .

The early history of Gibraltar resembles the layers of a puff-pastry pie, or the strips of a zebra. It was the Moors (Arabs) who first settled on the Rock after invading Spain in the eighth century under the command of Tarik Ibn Zeyad. The name 'Gibraltar' is a corruption of the Arabic words '*Jebel Tarik*' – Tarik's mountain (corruption – lexical and social – was evidently widespread under Tarik: just imagine calling a mountain after yourself). From then the Rock was constantly under siege: the Spanish besieging the Moors, the Moors besieging the Spanish, the British besieging the Spanish and the Spanish besieging the British. Gibraltar was under Moorish control until 1309, then under Spanish control until 1333; once again Moorish until 1462 and once again Spanish until 1704. In 1704 the Rock was captured by a joint Anglo-Dutch force, and the territory was ceded to Britain in 1713 by the Treaty of Utrecht. In all Gibraltar survived fourteen sieges, the last and longest being the Great Siege of 1779–1783. It was changing hands like a relay baton in a two-team marathon until it reached its present-day dubious status – caught between the Rock and the hard place in the dispute between Britain and Spain. At present, passions in this childish brawl are running high. One Spanish columnist went so far as to call Bienvenida Sokolow, a stunning Spanish courtesan who made headlines in Britain after her clandestine affair with Sir Peter Harding, a top British Defence Ministry official, 'our revenge for Gibraltar'. It only takes a quick look at Bienvenida's photo to understand why revenge can sometimes be so sweet.

Modern Gibraltar suffers from congestion. It is seriously overpopulated, and its high-rise human beehives in the airport area give it the air of South East Asia (Hong Kong or Macau). Or of a Moscow suburb.

The Rock itself adds to the colony's claustrophobia. Its sinister presence is felt everywhere, hanging above your head day and night like the Sword of Damocles. There is no place where you can hide from it.

The locals, whose travel outside the protectorate is severely restricted by the Mediterranean from one side and by the Spanish frontier from the other, seem to find a temporary escape in careering along the town's steep and narrow lanes in their cars, with powerful ghetto blasters turned to full volume. This explains the large number of people with their limbs in plaster in the streets of Gibraltar, a country which can be crossed in a car in ten minutes — the duration of a couple of rock songs, so to speak.

Even though almost all British troops have been withdrawn from Gibraltar, its spirit remains jingoistic to the extreme. Rusty cannon balls seem to be the most popular interior decoration in shops, pubs and hotels. Piles of them are scattered in the streets next to monuments to obscure military commanders and the gates of the Trafalgar military cemetery. 'Here lie the remains of soldiers who died of wounds in Gibraltar after Nelson's great Victory in October 1805, those killed during the battle having been buried at sea,' the memorial plaque at the cemetery gates runs. The Rock seems to have cost dearly for both defenders and attackers who swapped roles regularly but invariably ended up either in the cemetery or 'buried at sea' which, for them, was not that much of a difference.

Mitya insists we have dinner at Burger King. I don't know why all teenagers of all countries are so fond of Burger Kings and McDonald's, these smelly ice-breakers of Western civilisation. Reforms in Moscow started with the first McDonald's which opened on our last day in the Soviet Union. I went to have a look. A snaking line of several thousand people was cordoned by numerous policemen and separated from the rest of the world by metallic turnstiles. It was freezing, and I calculated that it would take those at the end of the queue five to seven hours to get inside. The happy ones came out clutching paper flags, plastic plates and glasses, the rubbish which people in the West throw out without thinking.

There is no queue at Burger King in Gibraltar. To lure customers, they give you a free plastic bum bag with every Whopper Meal. 'Is it a free bum bag or a free baggy bum?' Mitya asks mischievously. He ignores his bum bag, and I nearly swallow mine instead of my Whopper. I don't think the difference in taste would have been that great. Mitya doesn't allow me to take my free bum bag with me. 'I won't walk next to you if you wear it on your belt,' he threatens. With a sigh I leave the bum bag on my tray. I know that I am going to regret it for days.

There is nothing much to do in Gibraltar on a Sunday evening. The Queen's Cinema – the only entertainment in town – is showing *Free Willy*, a film that Mitya has seen three times and I have no desire to see even once. The 'Things to Do' section of the locally published illustrated guide to Gibraltar suggests a dozen or so exciting pastimes – from 'Have a flutter on the Gibraltar Government Lottery' to 'Go fishing . . .' The last one sounds pretty much like 'Go to hell . . .' It also lists bird-watching at Jew's Gate which, to me, sounds much less thrilling than Jew-watching at Bird's Gate, say.

We end up walking up and down Main Street and gaping at shop windows, stuffed with electronic toys and extremely cheap, almost free, cigarettes and alcohol – a bonanza for the Winston Boys. There is nothing much else to do but buy a bottle of cheap whisky, stick a cheap cigarette in your mouth and drive around with your car windows wide open, deafening the world with your ghetto blaster.

We bump into a number of Russians hanging around corners in their regulation Adidas tracksuits and cursing loudly. They must be sailors from a Russian ship in the port. Or maybe they are eye surgeons from the floating Russian eye clinic, moored to a Gibraltar pier. Whoever they are, they look as bored as the locals.

Finally, we retire to our hotel room, where I read and Mitya continues his Mr Amstrad epic:

> After returning from the post office, Mr Amstrad had breakfast and then decided to hurl the neighbours' cat by the tail, this time all the way to the tube. He liked hurling cats by the tail. 'I like hurling cats by the tail!' thought Mr Amstrad . . .

The silence of the velvety Gibraltar night is occasionally broken by loud Russian obscenities reaching us from the street.

11 April, Gibraltar

After a lousy breakfast at our hotel (no wonder, with all the foodstuffs brought from England) we start our day by browsing through the shops in search of black trousers for Mitya. It looks like all the trousers they have on sale were brought from England too: Mitya quickly discards them as 'old-fashioned'.

In a bookshop he is tempted by a locally published volume *The Governor's Cat*, probably describing the Governor's passion for hurling his cat by the tail, but I object. *Anecdotes and Stories about the Gibraltar Post Office* is the title of another book on sale in this bookshop. Mitya is not interested in it. I wonder who would be . . .

In one of the shops we are approached by a scruffy unshaven type who offers us a guided tour of the Rock for just twenty pounds. Now it's Mitya's turn to object, but I use the authority of a father, and after a short argument we board a battered Toyota mini-bus.

Our guide's name is Luis. He is Spanish by birth, but calls himself a Gibraltarian. Driving us up the Rock, he pours scorn on Spain and the

Spaniards. 'The Spanish come here and litter our Rock. They have no respect for authority, they cannot even feed themselves,' he says. 'Gibraltar has been British for hundreds of years, and it should remain British forever. In the 1977 referendum only forty-four Gibraltarians voted against staying with Britain, and they were all myopic old ladies putting the cross in the wrong box. Even Hitler never captured Gibraltar. He tried human torpedoes, but we had a net in the sea, so they couldn't get in . . .'

If Germans are human torpedoes, then Italians are human tornadoes, I think all of a sudden, without any connection to what Luis is saying.

He shows us rusty water-pipes running down from the very top of the Rock. 'Gibraltar still uses rain water,' he explains.

We soon reach the top and climb out of the van. 'From here you can see Spain across the bay,' Luis says with sudden nostalgia. It is clear he suffers from a severe mixed identity problem. Like Gibraltar itself.

The Rock's summit is 412 metres above the sea level. The high-rise buildings of La Linea and the outlines of the Moroccan coast thirteen miles away are clearly visible in the distance. The sea gulls bark like dogs above our heads.

We can also see the abandoned old docks and the brand-new ones, also abandoned. The latter are called Europort. It is lined with Europa Towers – Gibraltar's answer to London's Canary Wharf. Luis tells us that out of several hundred luxury flats and offices in Europa Towers, only ten have been rented out so far.

There is also a good view of Gibraltar airport and of the traffic jam, caused by a landing plane.

We don't notice a family of Barbary apes appearing behind our backs, looking as content and self-important as a family of middle-class shoppers in Brent Cross on a Saturday morning. Luis produces a banana and gives it to the father. 'I hope the banana is included in the price of the tour,' Mitya grumbles.

Like Manx cats, the apes are tailless, but, unlike Manx cats, they are very active and lively.

'No one knows how the apes came here in the first place,' Luis says. 'Maybe they came from Morocco through a natural tunnel underneath the Strait. When they grow old, they simply disappear, and no one knows where and how they die: not a single skeleton has been found yet. A legend goes that should the apes leave the Rock, the British will leave Gibraltar, so we hope they will stay here forever.'

He tells us how, during the last war, when natural causes had diminished the apes' numbers alarmingly, Winston Churchill ordered some additional animals to be imported from Morocco. He tried to cheat the legend, and that's probably why the British troops had to leave Gibraltar by 1992. But the apes, which used to be officially part of the British garrison, remain and are taken care of by tourists and soldiers of the Gibraltar regiment. So, the British military presence in Gibraltar is now reduced to three flocks of apes. (I wonder whether they can qualify for British citizenship).

Isn't it here that the solution to the mystery of the old apes' disappearance lies? Can it be that, like so many retired military officers, they are appointed governors of remote British dominions and never return to the Rock?

Whatever the truth, we are intrigued by the memorial plaque we spot near the Apes' den: 'On this site HM Queen Elizabeth II and the Duke of Edinburgh, together with their Royal Highnesses Prince Charles and Princess Anne, made friends with the apes on 10 May, 1954'.

As an old Russian proverb goes, 'Tell me who your friend is, and I will tell you who you are'.

I am just in time to stop Mitya from crossing out the word 'friends' from the plaque and writing 'love' instead. How come modern teenagers are so sexually advanced?

Not far from St Michael's cave, a natural amphitheatre where the pop group Boney M once performed, we see another memorial plaque, attached to an antediluvian mortar: 'Cut into solid Rock in 1771, Healey's mortar was intended to hurl over a 1000 stones weighing over 1 lb each onto any attacking forces, but it proved unsuccessful as most stones fell inside the fortress.'

Another example of 'friendly fire' . . .

Back in town I give Luis his honestly earned twenty pounds, and he promptly vanishes without a trace – like an old Barbary ape.

We have a couple of official meetings to attend. The first one is with Joe Bossano, chief minister of Gibraltar's Labour government. My press file on this former trade union officer listed 'thinking' as one of his recreations. It also said that he used to keep a Dobermann pinscher in his office (Mitya thinks it was because the Governor used to have a cat).

To Mitya's considerable disappointment, there is no Dobermann pinscher to greet us.

'My government's main problem is employment,' Mr Bossano says, switching on his dictaphone, a precaution probably resulting from his previous sad experiences with the press (or is it just a substitute for the Dobermann pinscher to keep nosey journalists at bay?). This makes me feel uncomfortable and puzzled as to who is interviewing whom.

'After the British army withdrew from Gibraltar, unemployment reached six per cent.'

One doesn't have to go far to see that employment (or rather lack of it) is a burning issue in the colony (one doesn't have to go far for anything in Gibraltar). Outside Mr Bossano's offices, a group of unemployed Moroccans hold a peaceful sit-in (or rather drink-in) rally. They sit at the tables of an open-air café and drink coffee under posters declaring: 'The only dectator [sic] in Europe: the government of Gibraltar' and 'Animal have rights in Great Britain. Are we less than an animal?'

'These Moroccans are the British responsibility,' Mr Bossano says to his dictaphone. 'They have brought them here for the sake of their military establishment, so they should now provide for them.'

My file contains Mr Bossano's recent statement, in which he indicated that every Moroccan immigrant worker was likely to bring

with him four wives and ten children. He was clearly unaware of the
fact that Moroccans are monogamous.

During my brief interview with Mr Bossano (or was it his brief
interview with me?), he spoke strongly in support of Gibraltar's
complete independence from Britain. This view is not shared by the
British Governor General, Sir John Chapple, whose residence, guarded
by the constantly goose-stepping Gibraltar regiment soldiers, is situated
across Main Street from Mr Bossano's offices.

We are met by Captain Tom Owen, the Governor's aide-de-camp,
a young man in civilian clothes with a military bearing. He shows us
through ornate gardens and plush banquet halls with paintings of battle
scenes on the walls, through long dark corridors, decorated with
ubiquitous cannon balls.

'Gibraltar, this most fought-for place in the world, is British,' smiles
the Governor, a retired admiral himself. 'There is a good deal of
affection towards Her Majesty, if not towards Her Majesty's
government, here. The Gibraltarians don't want to be just Gibraltarians. They want to be British.'

At this point, I remember Joe Bossano's words: 'There's a good
chance of the conflict over Gibraltar lasting another 300 years.' It
looks as if in this particular instance the Chief Minister was right.

As we are escorted out of the residence, Mitya asks the Governor's
aide-de-camp about the Governor's cat. 'Oh, that was a long time ago,
when Sir William Jackson was the Governor,' Captain Owen replies.
'His cat's name was Solo.' I am worried Mitya might ask whether Sir
William Jackson was in the habit of hurling Solo by the tail and hurry
to change the subject. 'Was it Sir William Jackson who called Gibraltar
a British bureaucracy, complicated by *mañana*?' I intervene. 'I am not
sure,' Captain Owen frowns. From the expression on his face, I can see
he didn't like my question.

On the way back to the hotel I have to restrain Mitya from turning his
head too obviously as he gapes at flocks of sun-tanned Gibraltarian

school girls in British-made uniforms returning to their Spanish-speaking homes from their English-language schools.

In the evening we have a little argument. Mitya wants to eat at Burger King, or, if the worst comes to the worst, at Pizza Hut, whereas I fancy something with a touch of local flavour. Arguing, we walk up and down the crooked hilly streets of the old town, where curly-headed Moroccan children, supervised by old Moroccan *babushkas* in long dresses, play on the cobbles.

I manage to drag Mitya into The Leanse, a Jewish kosher restaurant 'under the supervision of the Rabbi of the Jewish community of Gibraltar'. It is situated in a shabby old building, also housing the local Jewish club, next to the synagogue. There is no one inside, except for two young Orthodox Jews studying Talmud at one of the tables and a waiter wearing a skullcap. 'See? There's nobody here!' Mitya hisses, trying to drag me back into the street. But I am already ordering my favourite aubergine salad with African hot sauce, to be followed by the pea soup. Yummy!

'Yak!' grimaces Mitya asking for a hamburger (I am glad he didn't ask for a pork chop). Soon he gets quieter, stuffing down his kosher burger with real gusto. 'It is not such a bad place after all,' he mumbles. Why are modern children so conservative? (Forgive me if I sound like an old fogey, although probably I *am* one).

The waiter puts on a Spanish 'kuku-ruku-ku' record and brings me a bottle of Lanjaron mineral water – the first Spanish product I see in Gibraltar (not counting Luis, of course).

This lovely 'kosher quality control' restaurant – with wonderful Jewish-Moroccan food, with posters of Barcelona Football Club and the Queen Mother on the wall, with Orthodox Jews praying noisily in the neighbouring room as we eat (or were they just quarrelling?) – is the most Gibraltarian place in the whole of Gibraltar.

'Right! Tomorrow we'll go to your beloved Burger King!' I say decisively while we wait for the bill. 'No, let's come to this restaurant again!' Mitya begs. And adds imploringly: 'Please, Dad!'

* * *

It is cold tonight. The wind is dragging an empty Coke can along the dark empty lanes of the old town. The can is rattling against the street cobbles like a cargo train car that has come uncoupled.

12 April, Gibraltar

I like starting my mornings with a good newspaper. The only fresh one available in Gibraltar is *Gibraltar Chronicle*, a tabloid that advertises itself as 'The Paper without Political Bias'. It is without any real news either (today's issue features a 'Chronicle/Wimpy prize draw worth £10' on the front page), and I have to wait for the afternoon when the British newspapers arrive.

Today we are visiting the Russian floating eye clinic that, together with the Rock, has become another permanent, though not at all ominous, presence in Gibraltar. It is conveniently situated on board *Piotr Perviy*, an Odessa-registered ship, with a human eye painted on her starboard, which has been moored in Gibraltar for more than one year. She can be seen from our hotel window.

The first of its kind, the clinic is an offshoot of the Moscow Institute of Eye Microsurgery. In the ship's operating theatre, Russian eye surgeons operate on patients from all over Europe, for myopia, astigmatism and cataracts. Prices are reasonable and results encouraging. A number of blind people were able to regain their sight on board *Pyotr Perviy*, and one fifty-one-year-old British woman from Wiltshire was able to see her twenty-nine-year-old daughter for the first time in her life.

To get on board, we have to obtain passes from the clinic's booking office at Caleta Palace Hotel. I assure a tired receptionist that there is nothing wrong with our eyesight (Mitya is worried they might operate on us by mistake or as a punishment for our defection from the Soviet Union) and that I am a *columnist* from London who wants to write about the clinic.

She gives us name tags. 'Vitali Vitaliev. Communist', says mine (to Mitya's considerable delight).

'Here you go. Your father has become a Communist at last,' I say to my son as we climb up the gangplank. A moment later we step on to Russian territory – for the first time in four and a half years.

On board the *Pyotr Perviy* we find an ordinary hospital. Not an ordinary Soviet hospital, but an ordinary Western hospital, mind you. What's the difference? To give you an idea, here's a brief description of the ordinary Soviet hospital in Kharkov, where I was treated for my stomach ulcer in 1976.

My hospital ward had peeling stucco on the walls and dirty streaks all over the ceiling. There were at least forty patients there. Some, I felt, were dying, while others looked perfectly healthy, even robust, and were playing dominoes, drinking vodka and hurling empty bottles – made from heavy glass – at each other. The one and only toilet for the whole building, which housed about 200 patients of both sexes, was in the courtyard. It was just a hole in the ground.

The doctors and nurses were generally good, but they had a nasty habit of lavaging patients' stomachs on a massive scale, with all 200 of us receiving the procedure almost simultaneously. You can imagine what kind of corridor races started after that, and how violently the door of the only toilet was pounded. There was no water – hot or cold – let alone a shower. Almost all patients, including me, had infiltrates (skin lumps) caused by dirty syringes. Thank heavens AIDS did not exist at that time, otherwise you probably wouldn't be reading these lines now . . .

I am slightly taken aback by the pile of old Soviet propaganda albums on the table in the reception room. On such a table in a London hospital reception one can find a stack of yellowish dog-eared copies of *Punch*, a three-year-old *Vogue* without its front cover and a tattered brochure on *How to Lose Weight without Eating*. Here, on board the *Pyotr Perviy*, a patient, while waiting for his eyes to be fixed, can while away the time leafing through the *Heroic Sights of Kiev* (mainly statues of Lenin in different postures) and *The Soviet Moldavia* photo albums. The latter is supplied with captions in English (or rather in 'Englavian' – a mixture of English and Moldavian) with such linguistic pearls as 'stingy landscapes of Moldavia' and 'the tomorrow of our land will be even more nice'. Looking at these albums might easily discourage a would-be patient from having an operation to improve his eyesight.

Oleg Savinkov, the clinic's medical director, shows us around the ship.

'We have been here for almost a year. It is psychologically very hard for the staff to be confined to the same place all the time. Even on holidays we can't leave Gibraltar, Spanish authorities snub us, and we are not allowed to travel outside the colony. They do not want us to enter into competition with Spanish eye surgeons, since our results are better and our prices are cheaper. That's why we get lots of negative coverage in Spanish newspapers. We feel claustrophobic here.'

Having discovered that there are two Russians visiting the ship, nurses and surgeons flock around us. They are especially warm towards Mitya, who reminds them of their children in Russia. They show him computers, electronic microscopes, and even allow him to fiddle with a laser apparatus, used for treating myopia. 'You must write something nice about these wonderful people,' Mitya whispers to me. His fear of a forced eye operation is gone.

In the middle of the operating theatre is a star-shaped operating table, capable of accommodating five patients simultaneously. The table rotates slowly, and each of five operating surgeons performs one little procedure on the patient's eye before another patient is delivered by this unique opthalmological conveyer.

The operating theatre is equipped with a special shock-absorber, so no sea turbulence can be felt here.

The conveyer method of eye operations was invented by the famous Russian eye surgeon Professor Fyodorov. His techniques were first discovered during World War II, when some Japanese kamikaze pilots who survived air-crashes reported a dramatic improvement in their eyesight. It was established that this improvement was somehow due to tiny fragments of glass embedded in their eye. By making non-penetrating incisions in the cornea with a laser ray, the surgeons are now able to produce the same effect.

Several years ago Professor Fyodorov took his clinic on the road – in a train, then in a bus, and now on board the ship. His Moscow-based Institute of Eye Microsurgery became the Soviet Union's first fully privatised enterprise – the icebreaker of free-market reforms. No wonder Professor Fyodorov's portraits can be seen everywhere on *Pyotr Perviy* – like those of Lenin in every Soviet establishment.

'We are not gods or magicians,' says eye surgeon Tamara Kliuvayeva. 'Twenty-five per cent of our patients simply cannot be helped. But with myopia we have a ninety-seven per cent success rate.' I almost regret that my eyesight is perfect; it would have been fun to have a minor (a very minor – like a speck of dust in the eye or conjunctivitis) problem and put myself into the caring hands of these hard-working doctors, capable of bringing their patients back to the real world, with its beautiful palette of colours, tints and shades.

I ask Dr Kliuvayeva what patients are the most difficult to deal with.

'The English,' she smiles. 'They like things concrete and require lots of persuasion. The Spanish are the easiest – they are so trusting.'

The surgeons seem to be fed up with Gibraltar. 'It's an abnormal country. Too small and idiosyncratic,' they keep saying. I don't blame them. In fact, this morning I faxed my travel agent to change our flight from Malaga to Barcelona (on the way to Andorra) to tomorrow, instead of the day after.

We are getting fed up with Gibraltar ourselves. I come to realise why the marriage of the Prince and the Princess of Wales has ended in dispute: they had their honeymoon in Gibraltar and were probably infected with its atmosphere of all-permeating quarrel. Disputes are not just unsettling: they are also contagious. Gibraltar is like a packed Moscow tram, which carries a never-ending argument: the passengers who started it got off a long time ago, but the passions keep running high, and the newcomers get unwillingly involved in the row on wheels, the initial causes of which have been irretrievably lost.

The centuries-long squabble over Gibraltar continues, and the vision of both the British and the Spanish governments appears to be seriously impaired by anachronistic cataracts. Russian eye surgeons are helpless here, and the cataracts remain stubbornly inoperable.

We are invited for dinner at the ship's restaurant to be followed by a glimpse at post-Communist Russian television, which can be received on board. We decide to sacrifice The Leanse for the sake of this impromptu Russian evening in Gibraltar.

My 'Communist' nametag must have alerted our hosts. That's probably why we have a companion for dinner – a young Spanish girl from the clinic's PR department – to keep an eye on us. Her name is Maite.

The ship's restaurant strikes me as very Soviet. Five buxom Russian waitresses in the corner are involved in a lively conversation about their latest acquisitions in Gibraltar and pay little heed to us, their only clients. They don't know that we (me and Mitya) can understand their every word.

'I bought a nice camcorder today,' one is saying. 'It was such a good bargain.' 'You are telling me!' the other one waves her plump hand. 'I've bought four!'

'This journalist from London, how much do you think he earns?' she continues pointing at me. 'Go and ask him!' 'What are you talking about? It is not polite to ask questions like this in the West, don't you know?'

We start with the salad (which is called Russian salad in the West and Olivier salad in Russia), followed by stiff unedible pork which is impossible to cut with our 'Soviet' knives – blunt as the Communist dogma itself. I have always thought that a good restaurant starts with sharp knives.

I feel as if I am back in the Soviet Union. This feeling is enhanced by delicious and slightly raw bread which they bake on the ship – the best thing on the menu.

Unlike myself. Mitya rather enjoys the food, saying that it reminds him of McDonald's.

'One day you will come to Barcelona, and I will cook paella for you,' Maite says in an attempt to smooth things over. I have heard this before. A Spanish female friend in London once promised to make a paella for me and never did. Is promising you paella a peculiar quality of Spanish women? Or does cooking paella mean something more than just cooking paella? Or something less than just cooking a paella (like *not* cooking a paella, say)? I hope one day I will know the answer.

After dinner we move over to the ship's lounge, where an old TV set stands on a podium − like a monument to an unknown Soviet TV viewer. A handful of Adidas-clad artificial blondes from the crew are sitting there, staring at the screen.

Advertisements appear every few minutes, mercilessly interrupting every programme, even children's cartoons. It is like Chinese water torture: a drop falls on your head every few minutes. After a couple of days the victim goes mad.

'Organisation sells wholesale: Soviet champagne and stainless steel,' a cold male voice behind the screen is saying, as if itself made of stainless steel.

'Ivanovets cranes and high boots for women − direct from the warehouse!' an equally sombre voice echoes.

'Soyuz-chicken firm has just acquired fresh chicken fillets! Good for you, Soyuz-chicken!'

'Ladies and gentlemen! You are invited to take a cruise to the Canary Islands!'

Lots of commercials advertise curtains. They probably need many now to replace one huge common Curtain, made of Iron.

In-between the commercials I try to follow *The Field of Miracles*, a quiz show just like Western ones, with the startling exception of the flamboyant presenter, who is showering the audience with such witticisms as 'Take these pants and I'll stay in mine!' 'Are you some Tajic Indians, or what?'

Next comes a concert by Russian variety stars. The stars are all familiar, only somewhat older. A dishevelled singer and composer is performing one of his pop songs with a heartrending refrain: 'I can't leave my country, and I can't stay in Russia either, so the only solution is to put a bullet through my forehead.' He seems in no hurry to shoot himself, though, and writhes enthusiastically to the strangely optimistic up-beat tune.

Lulled by this cheerful song, Mitya falls asleep. As to Maite, she has been asleep for a long while. They both miss the programme on people with extrasensory perception. One Alexander Ilyin is explaining how he managed to cure a woman invalid who had been walking on crutches for fifteen years, simply by staring at her for half an hour. 'Then she threw away her crutches and walked away,' he says. I wonder what would have happened had he stared at her for a whole hour.

Another man, Magician Longo, seriously tells viewers that he has made an offer to the authorities to revive Lenin, but (understandably) was not allowed to do so. Listening to him, I suddenly think that it would probably be much easier to galvanise Lenin's mummy than to breathe new life into Russian television, still dominated by the same — though differently slanted — old clichés and stereotypes.

I wake Mitya up and we go back to our hotel.

13 April, Gibraltar – Barcelona

We are standing outside the hotel with our suitcases. Our flight to Barcelona leaves at two forty-five p.m. from Malaga. My travel itinerary suggested we took a bus from La Linea to Malaga airport (about three hours). 'Why should you bother bumping along in that bus? My wife will drive you there in comfort in just a couple of hours for twenty-five pounds only,' the hotel porter had said to me yesterday. The offer was too good to refuse.

The porter's wife, who lives in La Linea, was supposed to pick us up from the hotel at nine a.m. It is ten o'clock already and there's no sign of her. At ten-thirty she calls the reception and says she is stuck at the border. We grab a taxi, and an 'Ambassador of the Rock' drives us to the Spanish frontier in just three minutes. Unlike normal ambassadors, 'Ambassadors of the Rock' (read Gibraltar taxi drivers) are not allowed to cross the Spanish border, so we have to carry all our luggage through the frontier post. Our progress is slow. It looks like the Rock, hanging sinisterly above our heads, does not want to let go of us and drags us towards itself like a magnet.

We are lucky: the unpredictable Spanish border guards have probably decided to focus their attention on those travelling from Spain to Gibraltar today, so we cross Europe's last Cold War frontier unhindered. On the other side of the border post, there's a huge line of cars waiting to be checked on their way to Gibraltar.

What a relief it is to be in Spain! I can finally stretch my legs properly, without my left leg hitting the Rock and my right leg getting stuck between the turnstiles of the Spanish border. It is wonderful to see wide expanses of land, unrestricted by rocks and frontiers. We are free again. Goodbye, claustrophobia! Goodbye, Gibraltar!

Soon we find our driver, the porter's wife. Her name is Helga. She is a tall, elderly Swedish woman, speaking heavily accented English.

'Yesterday someone tried to smuggle fifty million pesetas into Gibraltar, that's why the border guards have gone berserk today,' she explains. Her breath reeks of alcohol, and I express my concern as to her ability to drive us to Malaga. 'Don't be nervous!' Helga chuckles. 'I have only had a glass of brandy to wake me up in the morning. I don't start drinking seriously before lunchtime.'

We drive through Andalucia, along Costa del Sol. Spain looks shabbier than Gibraltar, yet somehow much more cheerful.

Helga keeps chattering non-stop behind the wheel. 'You look very much like a young Peter Ustinov,' she says to me. 'Do you really know him? How nice! Tell him next time that a mad Swedish woman fancies him. Don't tell him how old I am, ha-ha. Don't be nervous. I am just trying to be funny . . .' Despite her frequent pleas, I find it increasingly hard not to be nervous: she drives her car erratically, in fits and starts. I begin to regret that we didn't take a bus.

'You are going to Andorra, aren't you?' she prattles on. 'I used to live there myself a long time ago. Terrible place, and the people are nasty. But, don't be nervous: I have good contacts there. I'll give you their telephone numbers. Nice people, but a bit capricious, if you know what I mean. They can easily turn you down. They did it to me. If they do, don't get nervous, just show them this,' she makes an indecent gesture, letting go of the wheel with both her hands, and we nearly hit a tree.

I decide to stay away from her 'good contacts'. It is not hard to predict what reaction her recommendation would trigger: they would probably get extremely 'nervous' the moment you say: 'Helga gave me your number', and I don't blame them.

Malaga airport is spectacular: it looks like a modernised Roman temple, with pillars and marble floors.

We have some time left before the flight, and Helga insists on having lunch with us at the airport's cafeteria. While paying for our lunch, I spot a sign above the cash desk: 'This establishment has a claim and complaint book at your disposition [sic] if you so request it'.

My 'disposal' leaves much to be desired. Helga has had a bottle of red wine with her lunch. 'If I don't drink wine for two days, I lose three kilos of weight,' she informs us. From the way she disposed of the bottle, it was plain she was not in danger of losing much weight in the near future.

She picks up leftovers from our plates and puts them into her handbag: 'I'll eat them on my way back . . .' Finally, red-eyed and red-faced, she stumbles to her feet. 'D-don't be n-nervous!' she stutters as we part. I sincerely hope she makes it back to La Linea in one piece.

On the plane to Barcelona, while I savour every moment of Helga's absence, Mitya goes on with his story:

The phone rang. Mr Amstrad picked it up and soon realised it was his mum, Mrs Macintosh. A cranky old hag of a woman. She loved watching videos where people were suffocating. After watching, she would rewind them and watch again. As usual, she just wanted Mr Amstrad to come over – to have another look at his ugly face, as she always said. He agreed. This time Mr Amstrad installed a nuclear time bomb under her sink . . .

I wonder whether this bit was somehow inspired by Helga . . .

We spend a relaxing evening in Barcelona – mixing with a cheerful Catalan-speaking crowd, having coffee (me) and Coke (Mitya) in street cafés, basking in the hubbub of a large bustling city and window-shopping for black trousers. I finally get my long-awaited paella at a restaurant in Via Napoleone. Made by a male cook, it tastes great – as if prepared by a loving Spanish woman.

14 April, Barcelona – Andorra

At nine a.m. we are at the Plaza Catalonia station in Barcelona, waiting for a train to the French village of La Tour de Carol, from where we are supposed to take a bus to Andorra. One of our suitcases is covered with foam like a tired horse – the result of yesterday's shampoo bottle leakage and Helga's hectic driving. It smells like a portable Body Shop.

It is probably the smell that attracts the beggars: in just twenty minutes we are approached by three. 'I don't speak Catalan, and even if I did I wouldn't give you any small change, because I don't have any. Please convey this to all your colleagues, queueing behind your back!' I tell off the fourth scrounger – a shabbily dressed little fellow with a backpack. 'I am not a beggar,' he says in perfect English. 'I just wanted to ask you when the next train is due.' 'Where are you going to?' I ask him. He shrugs: 'I have no idea. I am a violinist from Göteborg. My symphony orchestra is touring Spain with a Brahms concerto, for which they do not need my violin. So they told me to get lost for ten days . . .'

'My God, not another mad Swede,' I think.

'Would you like to visit Andorra?' I say aloud.

'Why not? It makes no difference to me. What is Andorra, by the way?'

242

'Well, there are actually two Andorras. One is a fictional Fascist state from the play by Max Frisch. The other is a tiny principality in the heart of the Pyrenees between Spain and France. Which one would you prefer?

'I would opt for the latter,' says the musician. 'I don't like fascists.'

The train journey to La Tour de Carol takes us four hours, instead of the scheduled hour and a half. Unhurried Spanish peasants with aquiline noses, boarding the train at countless whistle-stops, speak in a gurgling aquiline language. The slow-moving train itself has the character of a Spanish peasant, and rattles its wheels with a guttural Catalan sound.

Lars, the musician, tells us about his life. A first violin in the Göteborg symphony orchestra (they have several first violins there, as he says), he has been 'trying to play the violin' for fifty years. He is fifty-seven, yet, being the same height as Mitya, he looks much, much younger. 'A small dog is always a puppy' as they say in Russia.

Lars claims that once, on a tour of Japan, he was persuaded to sell his old violin to a local collector for one million yen. 'Excuse me, but why are you so modestly dressed, if you are a millionaire? And where is your luggage?' Mitya asks him. 'Oh, I simply like travelling light,' smiles Lars. 'Tonight I am going to chuck out the shoes and the clothes I am wearing. Tomorrow morning I'll buy myself a new outfit.'

I can see that Mitya is impressed by his answer. I am sure he wouldn't mind being a millionaire (even a yen millionaire) himself, just for the sake of not having to arrange his clothes neatly on a chair before going to bed.

The train climbs puffingly towards the clouds. Patches of snow start appearing along the track, and after Seo de Urge the snow-capped Pyrenees come into view.

'You know, you look exactly like the Russian conductor Aronovich,' Lars tells me. 'Thank you, but one of your compatriots yesterday said I had the looks of Peter Ustinov.' He studies my face for a moment: 'That's right. I think Ustinov looks very much like Aronovich, too . . .'

At La Tour de Carol we quickly find out that we have just missed the only daily bus to Andorra, and that the next one is not due until tomorrow. The alternative is a taxi which will cost us an equivalent of a hundred dollars in either pesetas or French francs.

La Tour de Carol is a one-house French village, and this house is the station building. We settle for *la plat du jour* at the tiny station restaurant, packed with French railway workers, hastily consuming their lunchtime doses of Stella Artois. The prospect of spending the night in this god-forsaken place does not look attractive to me.

'We can split the cab fare to Andorra between us,' I suggest to Lars. 'I am afraid I can't afford it,' he says with a sigh. 'I think I will stay here and do some hiking around.'

'Where do you think he is going to buy his daily change of clothes?' Mitya asks me in the cab. 'He'll probably get a taxi to the nearest hypermarket. Only for that he will have to cross the Pyrenees,' I reply.

Andorra leaps into view after the umpteenth turn of a winding mountain road. The effect is similar to that of St Isaac's Cathedral, in St Petersburg, which is hidden by surrounding buildings until suddenly, the moment you step into the square in front, it emerges in all its splendour. The country does somewhat resemble a huge cathedral, with snow-capped peaks as spires, and ski slopes merging into a giant white dome. Andorra's towns and villages are scattered on its surface like mountain climbers frozen to the spot in mid-ascent.

No one stops us at the border, and we drive past the shops of Pas de la Casa, the first Andorran village, on our way to Andorra la Vella, the capital. 'Andorra, the country of the Pyrenees,' the road signs say in Catalan, French and Spanish, the mini-state's official languages. Our ears get clogged as we pass the peak mark of 2407 metres above the sea level, and start descending into the valley.

'Too little history and too much geography,' they say about

Australia. Andorra has plenty of both for its minuscule size: 453 square kilometres. 'A big country crammed into a small space', as one tourist brochure calls it, Andorra was founded in the year 784 by the Roman Emperor Charlemagne and was a joint feudal posession of the Bishops of Urgel, the nearest big Spanish town, and the Counts of Foix from 1278 to 14 March 1993, when its voters chose to end 715 years of feudal rule and adopt a parliamentary system of government. The co-princes, one of whom is now President François Mitterand, sealed Andorra's future with a friendly handshake at the second ever meeting of the co-sovereigns on Andorran territory.

Situated in a no man's Alpine land between France and Spain, the Andorran valleys (that's what the country is officially called – 'Andorra' is a Moorish word that means 'a thickly wooded place') were always disputed and yet, unlike Gibraltar, they haven't seen any wars for more than 800 years. This was due to the fact that France and Spain, rather than squabbling over Andorra, wisely chose to agree on joint rule, leaving the Alpine country alone. For all these years (until 1993), the Andorrans dutifully paid *questia* (tax) to the co-princes. In years ending in even numbers, the Bishop of Urgel would get 460 pesetas (now the equivalent of three dollars), twelve cheeses, twelve capons, six chickens and twelve partridges. In years ending in odd numbers, the Count of Foix, and later the French President as his heir, would receive 960 francs on the condition that he bought all his food himself (with 296 different sorts of cheese made in France, the French President could easily do without the extra twelve).

It's interesting that after the revolutionary government in Paris renounced co-suzerainty over Andorra in 1793, the Andorran people wrote a petition to Napoleon asking him to restore the dual rule over their country. Napoleon, who didn't often get petitions like that, could not help obliging the tame (or were they just peace-loving?) Andorrans, and the joint suzerainty was restored in 1806.

This idyllic existence, summed up in the words of the national anthem – 'Faithful and free I wish to live, with my princes as my protectors', was briefly disrupted only once, in 1933, when a group of

245

young Andorrans broke into the building of the Council General (Andorra's parliament, democratically elected since 1419) and demanded universal suffrage. This mild revolution was quickly ended by a unit of *gendarmes*, sent by France. Not a drop of blood was shed.

After the Second World War, the Andorrans survived by smuggling goods to Franco's Spain where everything – from cigarettes to buttons – was in short supply. The Spanish customs didn't have a big problem with the cowardly Andorran smugglers, who would usually drop their goods and flee back to Andorra after the first warning shot was fired in the air. Playing smugglers and customs officers remains Andorran children's favourite game.

Now, with twelve million tourists (read shoppers) a year and a staggering £13,900 annual per capita income, Andorra, this duty-free haven of a country, thriving upon the economic imbalances of its neighbours, boasts the world's highest rate of personal income growth. A feudal possession until 1993, it has become Europe's newest sovereign state.

Eighty-five per cent of Andorra's 60,000 population are foreigners (mainly Spanish): it takes thirty years of permanent residence in the country to be eligible to apply for Andorran citizenship. So if I decided to move to Andorra tomorrow, I would have a good chance of becoming its citizen and getting the right to vote by the age of seventy-five.

Andorra la Vella resembles an international airport duty-free area. One London journalist aptly called it 'a vast Tottenham Court Road plonked down between high mountains'. Apart from the mountains, everything here is new and artificial: gleaming shop windows, high-rise banks, offices and hotels. There are seventy hotels and forty-five restaurants in Andorra la Vella, a small town of 15,000 people.

In December 1994, Andorra made headlines throughout the world when a truck went out of control in Avinguda Meritxell and crashed into a restaurant. It is hard to avoid a collision with a restaurant in Andorra. Especially if you run out of control . . .

Traffic policemen in bright-red uniforms, which make them look like

Australian rosella parrots, find it hard to cope with a permanent traffic jam in the narrow canyon of Avinguda Meritxell, the one-kilometre-long main shopping street, and keep waving their hands helplessly, like rosellas with their wings cut. Having parked their cars at the curb, the drivers leave the keys in the ignition and go shopping.

Mitya spots a McDonald's and comes to the conclusion that Andorra is a civilised place, after all.

The view of the Pyrenees from our hotel window is blocked by a couple of modern office blocks. I can see a man jogging on the roof of one of them: it is not easy to find a flat spot for jogging in Andorra.

At Andorra's tourist office in the centre of the town we are greeted by an attractive middle-aged woman. 'Do you speak English?' I ask her. 'Yes, I do. And you?' She is the tourist office director and her name is Roser Jordana. 'Last names in Andorra are made up of a father's and a mother's names. In my case, I decided to skip my mother's,' she smiles. In no time she supplies us with piles of books and pamphlets on Andorra, books us on a bus tour of the country, fixes appointments with the Prime Minister and the Subsindic General, one of the two presiding officers of Andorra's parliament. In addition, she gives Mitya a stack of Andorra posters and invites us for dinner at her house, where 'one interesting Russian lady is going to be present'. Amazing efficiency. She must be favourably impressed by the visitors who came to have a look at Andorra, not just to browse through its duty-free shops in search of bargains.

As we realise later, the little nation's tax-free trade is largely a booby trap, so outrageously expensive are most of the goods displayed in the windows of countless Lancome, Nike, Christian Dior, Sony, Rolex, Tubleron and all other imaginable shops. We don't dare go inside them, just stop and ogle huge bottles of French perfume that would last a lifetime for the most smell-conscious of fashion models; at the latest electronic miracles; at crab-like penknives stirring their multiple blades threateningly; at luxury watches and batteries of Chanel.

With Andorra's main shopping specialities being cosmetics, clothes, electronic goods and small arms, the perfect shopper here is presumably a classy criminal who sprays himself with high-priced scent to the strains of hi-fi music, then puts on a chic designer suit and murders his rival with an expensive custom-made pistol.

We feel alien at this feast of extravagance, and Mitya even selflessly decides to forget about his black trousers for a while.

I do have a purchase to make, though. Unpacking my shampoo-soaked suitcase earlier, I discovered the absence of my beloved Australian Koala-painted pyjamas, probably left behind at the hotel in Barcelona where we stayed overnight. Trying to liberate my faithful sleeping partner, I called the hotel, and asked them to kindly send my pyjamas to Andorra. 'Do you have a reservation?' the receptionist asked after a long pause. I was then transferred to a woman, probably the hotel's greatest expert in spoken English, and repeated my pyjamas query. 'Do you have a reservation?' she asked me eventually. Her English was indeed slightly better than that of the receptionist. I slammed down the phone.

The pyjamas section of 'The Pyrenees', Andorra la Vella's main department store, offers pyjamas for millionaires of every build – stout, plump or skinny. The most expensive ones – probably self-washing, self-ironing and hole-proof – are priced close to a Ferrari car. The medium-priced pyjamas – electronically tested and bed-bug repellant-saturated – are available for the cost of a Caribbean weekend for two (a man and his pyjamas). I go for the cheapest available, called 'Traveller by Night' – a flimsy, almost transparent (and clearly bed-bug friendly) set of blue satin shorts and a short-sleeved top, and it costs me 3,500 pesetas, almost thirty dollars. The section attendant gives me a special sort of a look, the one you are likely to get if you ask for a pound of used nails at Harrods, and I can see that her respect for me is not going to be redeemed, even if one day I win the Nobel Peace Prize.

(Needless to say, I found my old pyjamas several days later, in Malta: I packed them at the bottom of Mitya's suitcase by mistake.)

In the evening, when day-shoppers go back to France and Spain,

Andorra La Vella becomes empty and windswept. We are the only customers at a pizzeria in Avinguda Meritxell where waiters and cooks are busy having a meal. They treat us as an unwelcome distraction. To irritate them even further, we both order paella, an extremely hard to cook dish.

On the way to our hotel, we bump into Roser Jordana walking back home after a late meeting at her tourist office. It is always nice to see a familiar face in an unknown town – a clear indication that you are getting adjusted to it. It is equally nice to know that there are still places in the world where people can walk to their office in the morning and walk back home after work.

Back at the hotel, Mitya installs himself in front of a TV set and starts channel-flicking. News, dramas, documentaries and weather forecasts in French, Catalan, Spanish and German burst into our small hotel room in the heart of the Pyrenees at the press of a remote-control button. My son has the whole of Europe literally at his fingertips. Or is it just another TV-inspired illusion?

The magic of the small screen. I will never forget the day in 1958 when, at the age of four, I was first introduced to it. The screen, in the centre of a huge black box that my parents proudly installed on a chair in our one-room flat in Kharkov, was small indeed, the size of a packet of Belomorkanal cardboard-filter cigarettes – the brand my father was smoking at the time.

The name of this first mass-produced Soviet TV set was KVN, though no one knew exactly what this mysterious abbreviation stood for. Some wits deciphered it as *Kupil, vkliuchil, nye rabotayet* – 'Bought, switched on, doesn't work.' It could easily have meant Kit of Visual Nonsense, or something of that sort.

The box was proudly plugged in, and the screen unexpectedly came to life with a blurred and twisted image of a woman's head. '*Dobriy vecher, tovarishchi!*' (Good evening, comrades!) said the squeaky head. 'Good evening!' I replied groping the box's surface in search of a trapdoor to release the poor little woman. This was how my first TV-inspired illusion was broken.

When the BBC phoned me in 1988 and suggested that I become a regular on the *Saturday Night Clive* show, I was flattered. My segments were to be broadcast by satellite.

I was sitting in a studio in front of a tattered, fly-blown picture of Red Square (to create an illusion of being in Moscow, when in fact I *was* in Moscow), with a prickly little earphone like a hearing aid. The helpfulness of the device was minimal: the technicians on both sides had lots of problems with sound and kept losing the satellite (or maybe it was the satellite that was losing them, I am not sure).

Unable to hear much, apart from crackling noises, I frantically tried to guess what the presenter in London was asking me. 'Is it true that people are constantly watched in the Soviet Union?' — 'I am not so sure about the Soviet Union, but dead sure I am being watched in Britain at the moment.' (This joke was later edited out.)

The sensation of being watched by millions of eyes, when the only thing you could see was the gaping muzzle of a hostile TV camera, was unsettling. But it was not until my next visit to Britain that I realised the full power of the small screen. The first person to recognise me was a Customs officer at Heathrow. 'Ha! I've seen you on telly!' he said triumphantly. This didn't stop him ransacking my suitcase, by the way. He was probably just curious as to what the guys from the telly carried in their luggage.

Viewers kept approaching me in the streets, in shops, in public lavatories, as if having been on 'telly' made me common property. 'We know you!' they would exclaim, instead of introducing themselves or just saying hello. They thought that basic etiquette could be ignored when dealing with someone from the box.

Television is like a thermonuclear chain reaction: one appearance triggers more of the same. I started getting invitations to other shows in Britain and abroad. At the German ZDF TV Channel, in Mainz, they insisted I spoke Russian, since their German viewers 'liked the sound of the Russian voice'. Their insistence was quite superfluous as I couldn't speak German anyway.

Soon I was invited to write and present a documentary for the BBC.

The film unleashed a flow of reviews by TV critics with double-barrelled names, as if they were all suffering from split personalities (a normal thing for someone who watches too much television).

A flamboyant female reviewer for a tabloid wrote that I had an 'incredibly sexy accent'. 'Give him his own series!' she demanded. I fled to Australia.

'Can I have this nice-looking loaf of bread?' I asked in a small Jewish bakery in Melbourne. The buxom saleswoman was staring at me like the steam engine at Anna Karenina. 'Syoma!' she screamed suddenly. 'Syoma! Come quick! This guy from the telly is here!' Her elderly husband was already limping out of the box-room, pointing at me menacingly with his walking stick. I didn't realise that *Saturday Night Clive* was broadcast in Australia.

Australian TV took hold of me. I was interviewed in the bush wearing a silly Australian army hat. I was forced to drink a bottle of vodka with the presenter of a popular evening show in front of the camera (the presenter was drinking water, of course). And good old *Saturday Night Clive* found me there, too: 'Is it true that fifty per cent of Australian males are gay?' 'Yes, it is. In fact, they are all gay. Females and children, too. Gay and merry. They enjoy life.' At least the quality of sound was better.

Television turns you into a non-person, a walking face from the screen. It also creates an illusion of fame. This is transitory and fragile. Like television itself, it is just make-believe. 'Fame is not a wife, but a widow,' one Russian poet rightly observed. He must have been on TV a lot.

Once I was asked to appear on a BBC comedy quiz show. It was fun taking part, and I was falling over myself to jest in competition with the show's regulars – professional comedians. The shock came when the show went on air. Eighty per cent of what I had said was edited out. More than once my jokes were cut in the middle as if I was being gagged. Watching, I had the feeling that it was not me, but my dumb sheepish lookalike, with the black box of the antediluvian KVN TV set stuck into his mouth. What could I do? You can't explain the subtleties of TV editing to every person in the street, can you?

'Vitali Vitaliev said nothing,' a suitably double-named TV critic of a London newspaper wrote. I wonder whether he would be able to say much with a KVN gag in his mouth.

Why do I keep appearing on TV? Because television is like smoking: it is addictive. Without qualified medical help (like a couple of anti-TV patches to cover your eyes, say), you simply cannot give it up.

So next time you see me on TV, remember: it's not me, but my dwarfish TV lookalike who, placed in the box against his will, is looking for a trapdoor to escape from a heavily made-up, electronic make-believe world into the real one – with its uncensored smells and sounds, its life-size people and its wonderfully unedited unpredictabilities.

15 April, Andorra

In the morning, the mountains are covered with fresh snow. 'Too showy. Weird kind of beauty. An idiot's imagination,' Ostap Bender, the protagonist of a famous Soviet satirical novel, said about mountains.

A former London journalist who lives in Andorra tells me over the phone that the mountain pass could be closed, and we might have difficulty leaving the country. Pristine life. No trains, no planes – just buses and mountain passes . . .

They give you two packets of sugar with a glass of orange juice in Andorra. Each hotel and restaurant has its own sugar packet design. Our hotel aptly promotes its own fitness centre – 'swimming pool, tennis, Finnish sauna, gym, massage'. The message (to say nothing of the massage) is clear.

At breakfast I keep wondering how to address a Sindic. One of the books, given to us by Roser, says it should be 'Your Lordship'. Mitya suggests a less formal 'Sindie'. Since it is not the Sindic, but the Subsindic General whom we are going to meet, I play with 'Your

Sublordship', but quickly dismiss it as tongue-twisting.

We have a couple of hours to spare before our official appointments, and Roser sends us on a tour of the Casa la Vall (House of the Valley), the seat of the Council General, Andorra's ancient parliament. She asks Cuca, a young woman who works at the House, to show us around. 'Cuca is not her real name, it's her childish nickname,' Roser explains. 'We call nice-looking babies Cuca in Andorra.'

Everything is tiny in Andorra la Vella, the minuscule capital of the minuscule state. Even monuments to prominent Andorrans (mainly clergymen) in the town square are teeny-weeny, almost pocket-size. Mitya wonders whether the Andorrans have to water the toy-monuments, like flowers, for them to grow taller.

Cuca, indeed a nice-looking babe, produces a huge key out of her pocket and unlocks the heavy wooden door of the House of the Valley. 'This is the original Key to the House. It weighs one kilo,' she explains.

At the entrance, we see several round pigeon holes in the wall. These used to house specially trained carrier-pigeons – Andorra's only 'postmen' until not so long ago. The pigeons provided a first-class mail service between the parishes with minimum expense involved. Maybe this is why, even now, all mail is delivered free within Andorra: if the customers are not happy with the state post, they can always switch back to carrier-pigeons.

Built in 1580, the House of the Valley used to be a family home, a church and a prison before it was bought by the parliament in 1702. We enter the Council General Hall, a modest little room, where Andorra's main governing body of twenty-eight part-time MPs meets once a month under a coat of arms with the slogan 'Unity makes you stronger'. ('Unity' refers to the seven Andorran parishes.) The portraits of François Mitterand and the Bishop of Urgel, the present-day co-princes, whose role now is purely traditional, are on the wall. At the head of the long table with twenty-eight red benches around it, is a large armchair for the Sindic General. Next to it is a smaller one for the Subsindic General. This reminds me of the Russian folk-tale about three bears – Big, Medium and Small – each of whom had his own chair – big, small and tiny.

Eight black benches for seven ministers and the Prime Minister stand in the middle of the room. In the corner, there are three simple wooden benches for the public.

'Only citizens of Andorra are allowed to be present at the Council General sessions,' says Cuca. 'Do you check their passports?' I ask her. 'No,' she smiles. 'We know them all by their faces.'

This shouldn't be too hard, since out of Andorra's 60,000 residents, fewer than 10,000 have full citizenship.

Cuca shows us the 'Seven-Keyed Cupboard' containing Council documents which, by law, can only be opened by one of the seven councillors – one from each parish – provided the other six are present at the session.

From the Hall we proceed to the parliamentary kitchen, where, until recently, a local woman called Carmen used to cook for the hungry MPs from distant mountain parishes, who would spend the night in the building, sleeping on the kitchen floor near the fireplace. Near them was placed an old rusty wolf trap, in case a wild wolf wandered into the parliament house, attracted by the smells of freshly cooked meat.

Carmen can't have fed the MPs too well, since the Council General was extremely slow in certain matters. Andorran women were the last in Europe to win the right to vote, in 1974, and the death penalty, although 'prohibited' by the 1993 Constitution, is nominally still in force – quite ridiculous for a crime-free country where people do not lock their cars and houses and where the first robbery in its history was recorded in 1978. The last murderer was executed by rifle in front of all the residents of Andorra La Vella in 1943.

For a short period during the 1920s, the House of the Valley had an extraordinary Russian tenant. His name was Boris Skosirev. An Officer of the Tsar's army, he emigrated from Russia after the 1917 revolution, and, having lived in England and France, ended up in Andorra. Skosirev liked the country so much that he decided not just to settle in Andorra, but to become its ruler. He proclaimed himself Prince Boris I of Andorra and moved into the House of the Valley, where he used to receive the locals, settling their arguments and hearing complaints.

The self-appointed monarch quickly gained popularity among the law-abiding Andorrans. He penned down his version of the first Andorran 'constitution' and printed 10,000 copies of it. He called for creating banks and insurance companies on Andorra's soil 'to drag the country out of the Middle Ages'. The Bishop of Urgel got very alarmed by the revolutionary innovations of this Russian impostor and sent four Spanish soldiers to arrest him. One fine morning, Prince Boris I was frogmarched from the House of the Valley and out of Andorra. He died 'in exile' in Portugal several years after.

'From here there's a passage to the prison,' says Cuca, pointing at a dark corridor in one of the wings of the House. 'Our prison can accommodate thirty inmates. Now there are eight of them there. They stay for a maximum of six months and are then transferred to prisons in Spain or France.'

Among the recent inmates there were Antoni Ubach, the former director of Andorra's social security service and Isidro Baro, the former president of the country's Olympic committee, both imprisoned in 1993 over the embezzlement of eight billion pesetas of state funds — a huge sum for Andorra's government, whose annual budget is one third of that of the Barcelona Football Club. Their arrest became possible only due to the new constitution, adopted three months earlier. Prior to that, all judicial powers in Andorra were in the hands of the co-princes and *veguers* (the co-princes' representatives residing in Andorra) who always preferred covering up a scandal.

Imprisonment in Andorra is not too much of a punishment. Until recently, the 'senior prisoner' was entrusted with keys to all the cells. He could reward his fellow inmates for good behaviour by letting them out for a cup of coffee, or for a brief reunion with their families.

The Andorran criminal law remains archaic. Here's the bizarre procedure for starting a murder investigation, as described by two British visitors to Andorra in 1953: 'On the discovery of a corpse believed to be that of a murdered man, one of the bailiffs, accompanied by the usher of his court, a clerk, a doctor and the friends or relatives of the dead man, will . . . proceed to the scene of the crime. When the doctor has established that the corpse is, in fact, a corpse, the bailiff will tell the usher to cry three times:

"Dead man arise, as justice demands of thee!"

'If the dead man fails to do so, the usher now cries:

"Dead man, who killed thee? Say who killed thee!"

'If there is no answer to this too, the bailiff then announces:

"This dead man is indeed dead, since he neither arises nor replies."

'The corpse is then handed over to the friends of the deceased, who remove it for burial, while the Andorran police set about finding the assassin.'

Luckily, this cumbersome ritual now exists on paper only, since, as Cuca puts it, 'we have neither murders nor crime in Andorra'.

The sounds of a toilet being flushed behind the wall accompany our short meeting with Miguel Aleix Areny, the Subsindic General. I was expecting him to be dressed in the traditional ceremonial costume of Andorran councillors: silver buckled slippers, blue worsted stockings fastened below the knee with red garters, short grey trousers, red sash, long black coat with crimson collar and large black cocked hat. But he is sporting a modern, double-breasted brown suit, and his cocked hat is hanging on a coat-stand in the corner.

'Yes, in the Council we still wear our traditional uniform,' he says in French, having noticed my interest in his hat. (Toilet is flushed behind the wall.)

'We have achieved full sovereignty. Previously we had a political impasse. The co-princes had absolute power though they never came to Andorra. Now our main task is to adjust our old traditional institutions (he points at his cocked hat) to the new reality.' (Toilet flushed.)

'The co-princes now have the role of constitutional monarchs, like the Queen in Great Britain, and our state is now called a parliamentary co-principat.'

As a memento of our meeting, the Subsindic General presents us with the facsimile edition of the medieval Andorran code of laws in Catalan. (The volume, weighing at least five kilos, is to become our curse for the rest of the journey, until we finally decide to abandon it in our hotel room in Monte Carlo. Mitya will nickname this book 'Sindic').

As we shake hands, the toilet explodes again, as if flushing the whole of Andorra's feudal past down the drain.

Our conversation with Oscar Ribas Reig, Andorra's Prime Minister and the chairman of Argrupament Nacional Democratic, one of Andorra's thirty-two political parties, focuses on more up-to-date matters.

I ask him the reasons for the abnormally long and cumbersome procedure of getting Andorran citizenship, which means that the overwhelming majority of the population is denied the right to vote.

'We have to guard our national identity,' he says. 'Don't forget that eighty-five per cent of our population are foreigners, and forty per cent are Spanish. Just imagine them all getting citizenship and voting to join Spain.'

Frankly, I find this hard to imagine: had the Spanish migrants wanted to be part of Spain, they wouldn't have chosen to leave their country and settle in Andorra in the first place.

From our further conversation it transpires that the Prime Minister himself does not seriously believe in the prospect of Andorra joining Spain or any other country in the foreseeable future, since it is quite happy on its own.

'Historically, mini-states appeared before big states. Andorra is older than France, Germany or Spain. We have more legitimacy. In all the 800 years of our democracy, we have never been occupied, never took part in a war and never had an army. We didn't have a revolution in 1993, it was evolution. We are now a full member of the UN and can look to the future with optimism. Yes, we have a

budget deficit, but this can be corrected. Our new constitution allows
for income and turnover taxes for our citizens – for the first time in
Andorra's history. But even if we introduce them, they are going to be
very low,' he reassures me.

Having no immediate plans to become an Andorran citizen, I am
not particularly worried. I don't think income tax can work in Andorra
anyway. Imposing it on this famous tax-haven would be like sanction-
ing sex shops and strip joints on Mount Athos.

In the evening we are invited for dinner at Roser Jordana's flat. She lives in
a high-rise apartment block across the road from the House of the Valley.
The tenants' shoes are displayed outside the doors of every apartment
in the building, like at the entrance to a mosque. Is this an old Andorran
custom, or just a reflection of an affluent crime-free society?

Roser introduces us to her husband Carlos, a delightful extrovert of a
businessman and an unparalleled erudite, with a slight propensity
towards exaggeration and name-dropping. He speaks English with a
thick American accent and seems to know everything about everything
– from the last Russian tsar's pedigree to the exact number of
second-hand bookshops in the Welsh village of Hay-on-Wye. He
claims to have met every bearer of a title of nobility in the world.
'Baron Falz-Fein? Of course I know him! He is quite a character, I can
tell you!' 'Have I heard of Count Tolstoy? What do you mean? We are
old friends. I correspond with him! An amazing character!'

His special interest is little countries, and he claims to have visited all
of them. 'Whenever I am in San Marino, I go to the university and eat
with the students there. They tell me everything. That's what you
should do wherever you travel – go to the university and eat with the
students!'

I try to object meekly that there is no university in San Marino.
'They have just opened one there!' Carlos assures me. 'Where are you
going next? To Malta? Go to the Maltese university – and make sure
you have a long meal with the students!'

He tells me that his wife Roser is an extraordinary and

258

plenipotentiary ambassador of Seborga in Andorra. 'What is Seborga?' I ask. 'It is a new independent republic on the border of Italy and France run by Prince Giorgio I. I know him well. You must go and visit him. He is such a character!'

To my great surprise, he demonstrates his wife's ambassadorial credentials – complete with the Principality of Seborga stamp and the curly signature of Prince Giorgio I himself. He gives me the phone number of the Prince's secretary. 'He is a great chap! Speaks all the languages! What a character!'

Other dinner guests arrive, an elderly Turkish businessman and his wife, a fifty-three year old Russian lady called Marguerita (five minutes before Carlos referred to her as 'the Russian girl'). 'Do you know how old he is?' Carlos shouts introducing the businessman. 'Eighty-three! Can you believe it? His father used to own all newspapers in Turkey!' 'Come on, Carlos, it was only one little newspaper in Izmir,' the businessman objects.

His wife left Russia before the last war, and can hardly speak the language any longer. ('She speaks perfect Russian!' Carlos had assured me.) 'We go shopping to London,' she tells me in English. 'It is cheaper than Andorra . . .'

Her husband suddenly plunges into a long pro-Communist, even pro-Stalinist, diatribe – the last thing one expects from a millionaire (at least, Carlos told me he was a millionaire). 'What a great man Stalin was,' he sighs. 'It was he who won the Second World War!'

'Yeah, he was quite a character!' Carlos echoes without much enthusiasm. I wouldn't be surprised to hear that Carlos knew Stalin very well, corresponded with him, maybe even ate with him when Stalin was a student.

It's time to go. I drag Mitya out of the neighbouring room where he has been playing computer games with Tom, Carlos and Jordana's sixteen-year-old son.

We go out into the street, stumbling across the shoes outside the doors. I tell Mitya about Seborga, and we decide to visit it when we are in Monaco.

We both agree we have just had a very nice evening.

16 April, Andorra

We go on a bus tour of Andorra. First we head east of the capital, to Pas de la Casa. We are the only non-Spanish people on the bus, and the driver-cum-guide, who provides on-the-route commentary in Spanish has to repeat it in French, exclusively for my sake. After a while, I tell him not to bother, since his microphone doesn't work anyway.

We drive past old Romanesque churches, modern cottages and *bordes* – typical Andorran sheds made of stone and wood, where straw, farming tools and livestock are kept. We rattle across ancient Roman bridges. On leaving the capital, we pass by the Church of Our Lady of Meritxell, the patroness of the Valleys of Andorra. Or rather we pass by the place where the church used to stand until 1972, when it was completely destroyed by fire. In its place, Ricard Boffil, an architect from Barcelona, erected something which could pass for a cross between an Islamic minaret and Charles de Gaulle airport in Paris. The centre of this modernistic structure with huge windows, pillars and a rectangular bell-tower is open to the sky. It is freezing inside, and the mass has to be broadcast through loudspeakers. But the patroness herself doesn't seem to mind.

The higher we climb up the mountain road, the more snow is piled up at the curb. After the town of Canillo, standing at an altitude of 1,530 metres above sea level, snow lies everywhere in a thick crusty carpet.

The main (and only) sight of Canillo is the Ice Palace of Andorra – another nondescript modern structure. Its purpose escapes me: there's plenty of ice around, even without the Ice Palace. Mitya spots a woman handling a long and thick icicle. 'An ideal disposable vibrator,' he says. I tell him to shut up.

We are overtaken by cars with skis tied to their roofs. Hardly surprising when you remember that Andorran wealth has always rested three 's's – skiing, shopping and smuggling.

We are getting further and further into winter. The visibility gets poorer with every mile, because of the blizzard. It is then that our driver suggests we should get out to take some photos. 'Normally there's a wonderful view of Pas de la Casa from this spot,' he apologizes.

Normally the view might be wonderful indeed, but now we can hardly see our own outstretched hands. It is so cold that our noses feel as if they have shrimps stuck into them. This 'photo opportunity', as they say in tourist brochures, has to be called off in a couple of minutes.

Without reaching Pas de la Casa, we have to start cautiously driving back towards Andorra la Vella. As we crawl down, we are unable to see a thing and have to rely on our driver, who can't see a thing either. He tries to compensate with a verbose commentary in Spanish, which Mitya and I don't understand. And the microphone doesn't work anyway.

After lunch in the capital, we board the same bus again, this time to explore the Three Valleys (or the Silent Valleys) area in the north. We have a different driver, a much more engaging character, who seems to know everyone in Andorra and greets each policeman and every other passing car with a friendly honk.

Our first stop is at the village of Ordino where we have a quick look at the main (and only) square, in which, according to my Andorran guidebook, the only thing worth seeing is 'an iron ring, attached to the wall, that was formerly used to fasten offenders for public exposure'. The ring does not look particularly impressive. Maybe because there are no 'offenders' fastened to it at the moment.

At the parish church of Sant Corneli i Sant Cebria I learn a new word – 'comunidor'. I am tempted to think that it denotes a painfully familiar Soviet communal flat corridor, where the tenants have to queue for the flat's only bathroom in the company of dogs and children. My Andorran guidebook, however, disappointingly describes comunidor as 'a structure used for religious ceremonies intended to invoke protection against storms'. You live and learn.

This trip begins to look more and more like a useful lexicologic experience. At the church of Sant Roc in the slate-roofed town of Sornas. I learn another new word – '*retable*'. This time, my guidebook does not provide an explanation, and I leave the church convinced that a screenlike structure behind its altar is 'a table bought to replace the stolen one' (my own definition).

The Romanesque church of Sant Mari in the village of La Cortinada has one curious feature, according to my guidebook: 'the graveyard is located in front of its doorway'. To be frank, I've never seen a church with a graveyard *behind* its doorway. But to have a graveyard at the front of the church, rather than at its rear, is an obvious convenience: you can bury the parishioners who die of boredom during the service quickly and quietly without having to carry their bodies all the way round to the back.

As soon as we arrive at El Serrat, where 'the sights include panoramic view of the valley', it starts snowing again, and we have to seek shelter in one of the village's five restaurants, all situated in one tiny square, no larger than an average restaurant table (or a *retable*, if you wish). I imagine how severely they must be competing for customers. We are unlucky with 'panoramic views' today.

A couple of miles from El Serrat, at Coma del Forat, the paved road ends. This is the end of the line, and we have no other choice but to return to Andorra la Vella.

Our last evening in Andorra passes quietly, without incident.

17 April, Andorra–Barcelona

It is Sunday today, yet all the shops in Andorra are open.

After lunch, we board an oblong green bus for a three-hour drive back to Barcelona. Why didn't we take the bus *from* Barcelona in the first place, instead of going by train to La Tour de Carol? A good question, which should be addressed to the travel agent that had planned our trip. (Someone told me later that travel agents do not take commission from bus companies and always try to make you avoid travelling by bus, even if it is much shorter and cheaper than a train alternative. No pain – no train, as some bad travel agents might say.)

From Barcelona we are to fly across half of Europe to Malta, and then back to Monaco, which doesn't make a lot of sense either: Monaco is literally round the corner from Andorra.

Mitya is delighted to see that our green bus is equipped with a TV set. To my satisfaction, it doesn't work, and we drive to Barcelona to the accompaniment of classical music, of which our glum elderly driver seems to be a fan. Mitya tries to persuade him to put on one of his rock cassettes, but, fortunately for me (and for everyone else on the bus, apart from my son), the driver speaks no English and cannot understand what this foreign boy wants of him.

The road we take is the only escape route from the shopping paradise of Andorra, and on this Sunday afternoon it is heavily packed with cars carrying duty-free loot back to Spain.

Having nothing better to do, Mitya decides to carry on with his story, writing it in a notebook on his lap:

> On the way to the bus stop, Mr Amstrad hurled a cat by the tail and only let go when a policeman came by. When the policeman left, he chased the cat, caught it and dragged it to the bus stop. The bus was nearby. Suddenly Mr Amstrad felt a real urge to step forward in front of it. Something tickling inside him told him to do so. His legs moved by themselves, and he stepped in front of the seven-tonne moving bus. No one noticed anything: the bus was red anyway. Only the cat sitting nearby was laughing his ass off.

We must have been travelling on too many buses of late . . .

We leave Andorra, the country whose very name sounds like that of a distant little planet, with the knowledge that we are unlikely to come back again (unless one day Mitya decides to write his own book on mini-states of Europe). I think we both liked it – for its mountains, for its friendliness, for its history. The miniature state in the Pyrenees has shown the world that it is possible to achieve lasting peace and prosperity without shedding a single drop of human blood, through evolution alone. Where are all those bishops, counts, feudal lords and emperors who tried — jointly or single-handed — to dictate their will to Andorra? All gone without a trace, as if flushed down the Subsindic General's toilet. And the sovereign state of Andorra, recognised by all the powers of the world, thrives and looks to the future with a glittering snow-white smile. Napoleon was a wise man, after all. 'It is too extraordinary a place to be invaded,' he is supposed to have said about Andorra. 'Let it stand here forever as a museum piece.'

Goodbye, the planet of Andorra!

Spanish customs officers check the luggage compartment of our bus at the border (I was hoping they would confiscate the bulky volume of Andorra's medieval laws, presented to us by the Subsindic). The Pyrenees soon disappear behind our backs, giving way to a boring plain where it mainly rains in Spain, if we believe *Pygmalion*. After the winding mountainous road in Andorra, the driver of our bus is so pleased to be steering along the flat wide highway that he starts speeding and gets stopped and fined by the vigilant Spanish traffic policemen in green uniforms.

The Catalan villages we are passing through look like old fortified castles, with satellite dishes instead of cannons, on their turrets. One of the hamlets is appositely called Martinet.

We enter a four-kilometre long tunnel and drive through pitch darkness for what feels like eternity, until a tiny sparkle of light appears ahead. This sparkle keeps growing and soon turns into blinding daylight, that envelops our bus and makes us screw up our eyes. I think suddenly that all our life is, in a way, a journey into the unknown through a long dark tunnel, and there must be some light at the end of it, no matter how little.

Little is the light.

18 April, Barcelona–Malta

We have an early breakfast at our Alfa Aeropuerto Hotel restaurant surrounded by loudly chatting Spaniards. Listening to them, I come to understand why Spanish (and Catalan) punctuation rules require question and exclamation marks at the beginning of a sentence as well as at the end. Too impatient and emotional to wait for a sentence to end, the Spaniards hurry to add emphatic intonations to its very first words.

We are flying Iberia to Rome, from where we will take an Air Malta flight to Valetta, the Maltese capital.

At Rome's Fiumicino airport we unexpectedly get upgraded to Business Class. I've only flown Business Class a couple of times in Australia, and the real difference was they kept calling me 'Sir' and obsessively offering me free champagne at crazy hours of the morning. The sympathetic check-in lady at Fiumicino must have entered something special into her computer, since from this time on we'll be flying Business Class until the end of our journey. She probably just made a mistake.

We spend two hours at Fiumicino, watching grey-clad *carabinieri* patrolling the airport with snarling Alsatians on leashes.

'Good evening!' the Air Malta hostess welcomes us on board. It is two p.m. Perhaps it is already evening in Malta.

As part of our new Business Class perks, we get free copies of yesterday's *Sunday Times* and *Daily Mail*. The Economy Class passengers passing by our seats throw peculiar furtive glances at us, as if to say: 'Look at these Business Class fat cats. They don't know what to do with their money and pay through their noses just to get a free copy of a British rag!' This is how class hatred is born. Hopefully, it won't grow into a class struggle or a class war during the flight, with the Economy Class passengers hurling their plastic food trays at us.

Mitya, still unaware of the complexities of class distinction, is pleased as punch.

'This meal does not contain pork,' cardboard tags, attached to our lunch trays, say in four languages. Mitya crosses out the word 'pork' on his tag and writes 'food' in its place.

A passenger behind us complains he didn't get 'the Muslim meal' he ordered. The hostess explains they have run out of Muslim meals. What is a Muslim meal then? A smoked minaret? Or perhaps an empty tray?

We are flying over Sicily. From the sky it resembles a giant octopus, stretched out in the middle of the sea. The island's shape agrees with its Mafia reputation. I can almost hear gun shots reaching us from below.

We are given British landing cards to fill in. Haven't they got their own ones in Malta? Or has it re-joined Great Britain in the last hour or so?

My only encounter with Malta in the past was a huge consignment of Maltese blue jeans that suddenly hit the shops in the Soviet Union in the late seventies. Muscovites were killing each other for a pair. How come a Lilliputian state like that was capable of flooding the whole of the vast and populous Soviet empire with its trousers? I kept wondering then. A pair cost a hundred roubles (my monthly salary), half as much as on the black market.

As we land, we can clearly see the outlines of the three islands of the Maltese archipelago — Malta (153 square kilometres), Gozo (forty-two square kilometres) and in-between them Comino, the smallest populated island in Europe, with an area of 1.6 square kilometres and the population of three.

A moustachioed Maltese soldier with a submachine-gun on his shoulder meets us near the gangway at Luqa airport, the former RAF base. Welcome to Malta!

Our British landing cards prove to be a mistake and we have to fill in the Maltese ones. They also give us health forms which we are supposed to complete in case we have 'communicable diseases'. I am not sure whether they include inferiority complex, from which I suffered while flying Business Class.

Our unplanned hundred-dollar cab ride from La Tour de Carol to Andorra has all but exhausted our taxi travel budget, and we decide to take a bus to Valetta. Standing at the airport bus stop, we bask in sunshine and warmth — a welcome change from the crisp mountain air of Andorra. In the distance we can see thick clusters of towers, domes and minarets resembling bunches of pale toadstools growing sporadically from the ground.

The airport's parking lot contains a collection of old, very old and vintage cars in different stages of disrepair. Mysteriously, the jalopies keep coming and going with grumbling noises. Can it be that a meeting of the local vintage car collectors club is underway at the airport?

After almost an hour of waiting, we hear a sneezing and coughing sound. A green something – a cross between a motorised iron and a turn-of-the-century Singer sewing machine – rolls up to the stop jauntily. Its ramshackle cracked doors, resembling a dumped concertina, fold in with the squeak of fifty defective violins being tuned simultaneously, and we realise that this is our bus to Valetta.

The pre-historic mechanical monster is at least forty years old. The driver is a shaking octogenarian, suffering from St Vitus's Dance. He has a helper, also an octogenarian, presumably to assist him with changing gears and to replace him behind the wheel if he starts nodding off or dies of old age while driving.

The only redeeming feature of our forthcoming bus ride is the fare – eleven pence per head (despite the fact that local currency is the Maltese lira, divided into one hundred cents, the Maltese prefer to operate in the roughly equal pounds sterling and pence – a hangover from 170 years of British occupation). It is the standard fare for travelling by bus anywhere in Malta which should not be so surprising, if we remember that the whole archipelago is one quarter the size of Greater London, and the longest beeline distance you can cover without plunging into the Mediterranean is twenty-seven kilometres.

We crawl along the left side of the dusty road (another British hangover – the left side, not the dust, I mean) past endless stone fences, cacti and rows of low-built decrepit houses with tainted, peeling facades. One town grows into another with no countryside in-between. With its 380,000 people and little space, Malta is almost as overpopulated as Gibraltar. In fact, it does remind us of Gibraltar – the

267

same narrow lanes with laundry on the balconies, the same mixture of East and West in architecture and in the locals' clearly Mediterranean appearance. There are several things that are different, though: the guttural Semitic language (the only Arabic tongue to use the Latin alphabet), the abundance of old cars (or rather near absence of new ones), and . . . the women, all of whom seem to be beautiful, just like in Italy. We both quickly come to the conclusion that Maltese women and girls (Mitya is now inclined to call them 'Cucas') are much better looking than their sisters in both Gibraltar and Andorra. It is good to have a grown-up son with whom you can share such profound observations.

There seems to be plenty of mystery and immediate charm about these countless churches and temples; these statues of thoughtful saints at roadside; these winding cobbled streets without a trace of vegetation: these ancient cars and buses (my 1978 Volvo would look like the latest Porsche in Malta); these nice-looking people with kind dark eyes and crosses on their necks; these pot-holed lizard-friendly roads covered with the dirt of history and waded through by the legions, cohorts, regiments and squadrons of numerous colonisers.

Successively under Phoenician, Carthaginian, Greek and Roman rule, Malta later fell to the Arabs, was conquered by Roger the Norman, Count of Sicily in 1090, and then by Spain in 1282. In 1530 the Hapsburg Emperor, Charles V granted the islands to the Knights of St John (or the Knights Hospitallers), driven out of Jerusalem and Rhodes. They were expelled from Malta by Napoleon who, in his turn, was ousted by the British forces a year later, in 1800. The British military remained in Malta until 1979 (actual independence was achieved in 1964), having withstood Mussolini's claim to the islands and heavy bombing by Axis powers during World War II.

At one of the road turns our bus comes to a stop, and we are told to change. No explantion is provided, but I suspect that both the drivers and the vehicle are having simultaneous attacks of gout. We board a twin jalopy of a bus (our eleven pence tickets remain valid) and continue our long and bumpy journey. I try to make notes bouncing on the seat, which is covered with holes, with sharp springs sticking out of them like fractured bones, but instead of calligraphic letters, my notebook records the erratic cardiogram of the road – Malta's jumpy heartbeat.

More castles, cacti and cockroach-size black dogs barking at the bus from dark gaping gateways – and we are disgorged in the central square of Valetta.

We stand there for a while with our heavy suitcases, made even heavier by the Andorran laws folio. We have no idea which way to go and look around helplessly. An ancient mongrel of a taxi of indefinite make pulls over, and a fat, red-faced driver peeps out of the window: 'Where to?' 'Osborne Hotel,' I reply automatically. He is already putting our luggage into the boot. 'It is a good hotel,' he says. 'Very new.'

'When was your car made?' I ask him as we climb inside. '1960!' he answers proudly.

A taxi is not only a vehicle, but a means of communication, especially in a foreign country. My observations show that, just as dogs usually look like their owners, taxis have a certain resemblance to the native. Marvellous London black cabs are like the English themselves, only instead of the stiff upper lips they use stiff glass partitions to keep privacy by separating the driver from the passenger and potential interlocutor. New York yellow taxis, with bullet-proof glass and f-words scratched everywhere inside, resemble a street bully hanging around the city with a joint in his hand. Australian cabs are amicable and gregarious 'mates', and the driver gets seriously offended if you don't sit next to him. 'Am I smelly or what, mate?' he would ask you.

Moscow taxis, as far as I can remember, were as vicious, corrupt and misleading as the Communist system itself. A green light on the windscreen of a Soviet cab did not mean that it was free. In fact, it did not mean anything at all. In the late eighties, you could not flag down a cab in Moscow unless you had a packet of Marlboro or a ten dollar note clutched in your hand. The trouble was that Marlboros were not on sale, and Soviet citizens were not allowed to possess dollars. So unless you were a foreigner or a hard-currency prostitute (which most of the people were not), you had very little chance of stopping a cab in Moscow. I once tried to book a taxi by telephone. I spent two days trying to get through to the dispatcher, and, despite the fact that the booking was made two weeks in advance of the journey, the cab was still forty minutes late.

Our hotel proves to be 500 metres away from the square, and the ride takes us no more than two minutes. Yet the driver charges us three pounds (or liras) – thirty times more than our combined bus fare from the airport. 'You know what you should call your taxi company? Booby Trap Cabs!' I advise him.

The 'very new' hotel is a decrepit ancient structure, with an unshaven male receptionist and a fly-blown portrait of the owner in the lobby. There is a strong smell of dung in the air. The hotel leaflet says that all the rooms 'are equipped with central heating, telephone and pipe-music'. It doesn't say that they are also equipped with dirty blankets and windows; with wisps of someone's hair in the bathrooms and beds; with TV sets suspended so high under the ceiling that, unless you are a basketball player, you need a ladder to watch them (the rooms are not 'equipped' with ladders); and with an antediluvian telephone switchboard: you have to call the reception first to get the line for an outgoing call.

An hour later we sit outside a church converted into a café in Republic Street, and watch Valetta go by. There is no better way of getting the feel of a new place than sitting in an open-air café and imbibing the smells, faces and sounds.

Known as Kingsway under the British, Republic Street is the Covent Garden of the Maltese. They come here to shop and to stroll past the Presidential Palace and the ruins of the old Opera House; past cathedrals with two clocks – real and fake, to confuse the devil – on their facades; and past disorderly parked old cars, whose makes reflect the whole history of the world's car-building industry. (Maltese old cars are considered property of the State and are not allowed to be exported, just like old Russian icons.) Beautiful dark-skinned and black-eyed girls, young men looking threatening when they talk and affable when they smile . . . The city seems to be in the throes of a never-ending Mediterranean fiesta.

I can also feel a hidden mystery about the place, a mystery that escapes me so far.

The café has a set menu which includes 'free glass of wine'. 'Can I have a glass of water instead?' I ask a young waiter. 'No, you can't. Whatever is in the menu cannot be changed.' 'Well, don't bother bringing me the wine then!' I say to him. 'It is impossible,' he insists. 'Whatever is in the menu I must bring you.' He pronounces the word 'menu' with a truly religious respect. I am sure he writes the word with a capital 'M'. He probably worships the Menu, prays to the Menu and swears by the Menu too. In short, he lives by the Menu and will keep doing so until he reaches his *menu*pause.

Positively affected by Valetta's festive mood, Mitya quickly chooses himself a pair of trousers in a little shop off the main street. You might think it is the end of our hunt for black trousers, but it is not: after trying the trousers on at the hotel, he rejects them as too baggy. Tomorrow we'll have to take them back to the shop.

19 April, Malta

'What other prince, prime minister or sindic are we seeing today?' Mitya asks me in the morning. He seems to have developed a taste for meeting dignitaries. There are no princes or sindics in Malta, but there is the president, elected only a couple of weeks ago. I haven't made an appointment, but we can try . . .

For sixteen years, until 1987, Malta was ruled by an extreme left-wing Labour government, which stood for state-ownership and concluded pacts of friendship with Lybia, Iraq, North Korea, China and

271

the Soviet Union. The country's economy was in tatters, and food rationing had to be introduced. Why is it that socialism can only be attempted in a country with bare shop shelves?

In May 1987 the Nationalist Party came to power, and the process of economic liberalisation began. Malta was one of the few European states not to suffer from economic recession of the early nineties. The country is now back to normal. As an old joke goes, if they tried socialism in the Sahara desert, it would soon result in drastic shortages of sand.

At the entrance to the President's Palace I show my press card to the guard and he lets us in. We look strange for people hoping to meet the Head of State (even if he is the head of a mini-state) — both dressed in blue jeans and loose T-shirts (Mitya adamantly refused to tuck his T-shirt into his trousers). To make it worse, I carry a plastic bag with my son's discarded black trousers in it. Quite a delegation!

I learnt to ignore dress codes after my first visit to a well-known Pall Mall club in London in October, 1988. A guest of one of the members, I was thoroughly unprepared for the plushness of the place — I wasn't even wearing a tie. To let me inside, a sympathetic doorman had to lend me a tattered piece of silk which was probably used as a tie in Dickens' time. Having put it round my neck, on top of my sweater, I stepped into a dining room where the lucky members were enjoying their steak and kidney pies and sherries. I was shocked to see among them one youngish fellow sporting a stylish collarless shirt under his jacket. He was not wearing a tie!

I was insulted. Why was someone else allowed to be tieless? 'Look,' I said to my host angrily. 'This guy is not wearing a tie either, yet no one seems to mind . . .' 'Yes,' my friend answered, 'but he is a bishop.'

To get to the President's office, we have to pass through a suite of long empty corridors, lined with statues of bottomless medieval knights: heavily armoured on top, they wear nothing but silly black tights on the lower parts of their bodies, which makes them look like cancan dancers

(I wouldn't be surprised if they suddenly started kicking up their waxen legs in unison). Blows below the belt must have been strictly taboo in the Middle Ages.

Captain John Schembri, the President's aide-de-camp, sits in a huge circular office resembling an Irish football pitch. 'The President is very busy, but I might surprise you,' he smiles and disappears behind the heavy wooden doors of the President's study.

In less than a minute he reappears. 'The President is ready to see you,' he announces, holding the door open for us. 'You've got ten minutes.' Mitya hastily tucks his T-shirt into his jeans.

Ugo Misfud Bonnici, the President-elect of Malta, greets us warmly. 'I was only elected a fortnight ago, and you are the first international journalist who has come to see me,' he says. 'And you are my youngest visitor yet,' he smiles at Mitya.

'You must have heard that for 260 years Malta was under the domination of the Knights of St John,' the President continues. 'This Palace used to be the Palace of the Grand Masters. I am their successor, in a way.'

The walls of the office are decorated with portraits of the Grand Masters, all wearing wigs and stockings, which make them look like transvestites at Sydney's Mardi Gras festival.

'My position is like that of the Queen of England. Since Malta is not a presidential republic. I have no executive power. Nor do I have a personal opinion. I am just a symbol of unity.'

Despite the absence of a personal opinion, the President (who looks perfectly real, not just a symbol at all) shares with us his thoughts on Malta's desire to join the European Union. I ask him about the role of small countries in modern politics.

'Small countries can make themselves heard in the UN and other international forums without causing suspicion. For example, Malta proposed a Freedom of the Seas Convention in the UN. Just imagine something like this coming from the United States, or Britain . . . We have a good image of being an independent-minded country. Malta has never been a stooge of big powers. It has managed to retain its unique identity in the face of many cultural influences. We were never dominated by a European state, only by the Order of Knights which was itself independent.'

Like most of the Maltese, the President seems to be obsessed with the Knights of St John.

'What would you want to become?' he asks Mitya. 'A journalist and a writer, like my dad,' he replies to my great surprise (and delight). He has never said this before, asserting that freebies were the only thing that attracted him to journalism.

'That's a good boy!' says the President, patting Mitya on the shoulder. 'I've got two sons and they are both lawyers, like myself. And my daughter is studying to be a lawyer too.'

A worried aide-de-campe peeps into the office: we have exceeded our ten-minute limit.

As we leave the office, a dozen angry, important-looking men, probably ministers or ambassadors, rush in. None of them is wearing jeans.

We pop into the National Tourism Organisation across the road. Miraculously, the news of our impromptu meeting with the President has reached them already, and we are received with a certain pomp. We have to listen to a range of tourism officials complaining of the difficulties in trying to keep the number of tourists in Malta under one million a year. I ask one of the officials about the archeological excavations in the Republic Square. He explains that these are not excavations, but a new car park being built.

During one of the meetings, a fat, green-robed priest waddles into the room and, without any warning, matter-of-factly sprays the room with incense. They explain that this is just a tradition: after Easter, every Maltese office receives a daily spray (like an aircraft about to land in Australia). An interesting method of pest (or heresy?) control.

Our visit to the tourism organisation proves useful in the end: they volunteer to send us on a tour of Gozo and Comino tomorrow. For today, we plan to have a closer look at Valetta, 'the city built by gentlemen for gentlemen', as Sir Walter Scott once called it, and to visit Mdina, 'the silent city' and the country's ancient capital, built by Arabs.

What I really like about Valetta are its street signs and graffiti. 'You don't have to look for me, I'm here', is written on the door of a public toilet. 'I wanted a Lambourghini but I couldn't pronounce it (I couldn't even write it)', says a plate attached to the windscreen of an archaic Bedford mini-bus. 'Designed by computer. Built by robots. Driven by a maniac', a sticker on the bumper of an elderly Lada reads. 'Silent Place & No Problems', runs a graffito outside the 'Ale Bar', where the locals sit and chat incessantly. 'Bad Boy Cleaners' is inscribed on the side of a mini-bus. Humour is always at its best when self-deprecating.

One laconic sign in Republic Street looks pretty ominous though – 'Aeroflot. The Soviet Airlines'. Less than two weeks ago a Hong Kong-bound Aeroflot airbus crashed in Siberia killing all seventy-five people on board – another tragic episode in the chain of recent Aeroflot disasters. This particular crash had no parallel in the history of civil aviation: the captain left his fifteen-year-old son and twelve-year-old daughter to pilot the plane, while he chatted up some female passengers in the salon. The kids quickly sent the jet into a nosedive, and there was no time for the captain to intervene.

This incident might sound bizarre to a Westerner, but it didn't particularly surprise me. I still remember working as a part-time sleeper-car attendant, when a student in the Soviet Union in the early seventies. One fine night my car, number thirteen, was suddenly visited by the engine driver of our train which was, by the way, running ahead at a hundred kilometres per hour. The engine driver was drunk out of his mind. He said he felt like stretching his legs a little and had left the train to be driven by an 'auto-pilot'. 'Don't you w-worry, there are no stations on our way for a w-while,' he reassured me drunkenly. It took considerable effort (mental and physical) to persuade him to return to his cabin.

'Do you think they will allow me to fiddle with the plane's controls during our next flight to Monaco?' asks Mitya looking at the bleak Aeroflot sign in the centre of Valetta. 'They might, but I won't!' I reply thinking that, instead of their sacramental old logo 'Fly planes', Aeroflot might now use a new one − 'Fly Aeroflot − the world's first DIY airline!'

Inside the Aeroflot office, we find a nervous Russian artificial blonde, a deputy Aeroflot representative. She says that the boss is away. He probably went to meet the Resident: Aeroflot offices in the West have always been used as a cover for Soviet (and later Russian) spies. Should I pose as his KGB link?

'We were badly hit by the latest accident,' the blonde complains. 'There are lots and lots of cancellations.' No wonder: the Maltese are an extremely life-loving people.

I ask her whether children should be encouraged to pilot passenger jets.

'This is all dirty propaganda!!' she explodes. 'Our pilots are good professionals!'

'And good fathers too,' I remark.

'This is my paternal bequest to you, son: never fly Aeroflot!' I tell Mitya solemnly as we leave the Aeroflot office. It occurs to me suddenly that modern Russia herself is increasingly like a nosediving jet, piloted by kids.

Wherever you go in Valetta, you are constantly reminded of the mysterious Knights of St John and of their 268-year-long presence on Malta. They are treated with the same reverence as the Founding Fathers in the US or the First Fleet settlers in Australia. The adoration of the Knights is close to a cult. It was they who founded Valetta; it was they who saved Europe from the Turks and protected Christianity; it was they who erected Malta's most impressive buildings, including Auberge de Provence, Mdina Cathedral and St John's Co-Cathedral in Valetta, dedicated to St John the Baptist, the Knights' patron saint − all designed by Gerolamo Cassar, chief engineer of the Order. The Knights also patronised the arts and culture. They employed the famous

Caravaggio to paint their portraits. They constructed the 'Sacra Infermeria', the most advanced hospital of its time, which boasted close to 1,000 beds and a school of anatomy. A conference centre today, this sixteenth-century hospital, overlooking the Grand Harbour (also built by the Knights), still features the longest corridor in Europe – nearly two city blocks long.

Who were they, the Knights of St John? Warriors? Crusaders? Religious fanatics? Selfless educators?

Their history began in the middle of the eleventh century in the Holy Land of Palestine. The Order's original duties were to care for the sick and wounded pilgrims in Jerusalem (that's why they were called Knights Hospitallers) and to help the poor. But, as often happens, with time their duties expanded. They decided that, apart from treating patients, they could do a bit of infidel-hunting on the side. Gradually, the Knights became 'Soldiers of Christ' and started spreading Christian faith with fire and sword. No longer did they cure people, they killed, robbed and pocketed the loot, which allowed them to maintain huge estates and castles in the Holy Land and to own a large fleet.

With the advance of the Muslims at the end of the thirteenth century, the Knights withdrew to Rhodes and stayed there until ousted by Suleiman the Magnificent in 1522. They needed a new homeland and chose Malta, to which they were given tenure by Emperor Charles, who wore the crown of the Holy Roman Empire.

The Knights had their magnificent revenge on Suleiman the Magnificent in 1565 when, assisted by 7000 Maltese, they defeated him after the four-month Great Siege, under the command of Grandmaster Jean de La Valette.

The fall of the Ottoman Empire marked the beginning of the end for the Order. Without a serious military threat, the Knights basked in wealth, arrogance and debauchery. In modern terms, they became morally bankrupt. And when, in 1798, Napoleon, on his way to Egypt, dropped anchor in Grand Harbour, allegedly to replenish his water supplies, he found the Order weakened and demoralised and didn't have to fire a single shot to secure their surrender. He spent six days in Malta, a newly annexed *départemente* of France, before continuing his journey to Egypt. (The French didn't last long in Malta: two years later they were driven out by Admiral Nelson.)

The Knights were dispersed around the world. The last Grand Master, as the President of Malta told us, now lives in Rome.

The Order of the Knights of St John was like an exclusive gentlemen's club. Its members, the sons of the richest and the most noble families in Europe, originated from eight European countries and mini-states – Aragon, Auverge, Castile, England, France, Germany, Italy and Provence. They were divided into five strictly hierarchical groups – The Military Knights of Justice, the Chaplains of Obedience, the Serving Brothers, the Honorary Knights and the Knights of Grace. To join the Order was no easier than to join the Garrick Club these days (or the Soviet Communist Party several years ago): you had to be of noble birth from both parents for at least four generations.

And here's the procedure of initiation, as described by Joseph Attard in his book *The Knights of Malta*:

Accompanied by the Grand Cross who would have just dubbed them, they [the successful applicants] would walk bareheaded in the armour and robe worn at the investiture. Their comrades would receive them in the hall of the Auberge, where they would be made to sit on a carpet laid on the ground, and be offered bread, salt and a glass of water. The Knight presiding at the ceremony however, would later on that day give a banquet to the new Knights and his friends, as if to make up for the sense of austerity conveyed by the ceremony. The new aspirant Knight had then to undergo a novitiate of one year before they could join the Convent (as the central body of the Order was called) for military service, and with each year of duty being termed a 'caravan'. Then, after three such 'caravans', a Knight would have to reside for at least two years in the Convent. After completing duties with the Order, Knights would be free to return to their home in Europe, but they would always be subject to recall by the Grand Master in case of need.

The history of the Knights of Malta has lots of parallels with that of the Soviet Communist Party. Starting as a clandestine organisation of revolutionaries to protect the rights of the poor, it too had developed into an excusive 'Order', wallowing in corruption and self-importance, and began physically annihilating the 'heretics', those who didn't share the Communist faith, until, blood-stained, compromised and 'morally bankrupt', the Knights of Bolshevism were swept away by the Russian Napoleon – Yeltsin, whom they had nurtured in their own ranks.

As opposed to the Knights, however, one thing the Bolsheviks failed to deliver was a 'golden age' for Russia. Their rule was but a seventy-five-year-long dark age.

After lunch, we take a green coffin of a bus to Mdina, the ancient capital of Malta. The bus moves forward slowly (and not too surely) giving out piercing honks from time to time, like an old dying mule screaming with pain. It looks like all the power of its asthmatic engine goes into these loud shrieks.

I use the opportunity to do some more Maltese-watching and come to the conclusion that they speak English, look Arabic, have Italian temperament, Spanish mentality and French driving habits – an explosive mixture which can be best described as a Molotov cocktail or, in this case, a Malta cocktail.

Having coughed us out in Mdina, the bus chugs off, and suddenly we are alone, face to face with Malta's chequered history. There are very few people around, only churches and stone walls, and I start to understand the Knights, who described the thirteenth-century Mdina as an 'ancient and deserted city' (they described the whole of Malta as an 'empty rock with a few poor and terrified humans,' by the way). Nothing much has changed in Mdina since then.

At different times, Mdina (which roughly translates as 'the city surrounded by walls') was known as 'Rabat' (suburb), the Old City, the Noble City, the 'uncrowned Queen of Malta', and the Silent City. It remains old, silent and suburban.

279

Through the Main Gate, where the newly elected Grand Masters were presented with the keys to the town, we come to the Cathedral, built on the spot where St Paul (who was allegedly shipwrecked in Malta in 60 AD) allegedly converted the Roman Governor Publius to Christianity. Publius only agreed to be converted after St Paul (allegedly) managed temporarily to cure his ageing father of an unknown deadly disease which was probably called old age. By the time the old man died, his son had already been converted and became the first Bishop of Malta, so there was no going back.

In accordance with the old Maltese tradition, one of the two clocks on the Cathedral's ornate facade is painted. It takes us a while to establish which. I am not sure whether these faked Maltese clocks are really effective in confusing the devil, when he starts dealing with the souls of the dead, but they can't fail to dupe unwary tourists into missing their flights back home.

'Men in short trousers and women with bare shoulders are not allowed inside', warns the sign nailed to the Cathedral's heavy doors. There are neither men in short trousers and women with bare shoulders, nor women in short trousers and men with bare shoulders around, and the Cathedral, like everything else in Mdina, is shut. I suggest one more name for Mdina – the Dead City.

The only place open is Mdina Dungeons, the museum of medieval torture with a welcoming sign above the entrance: 'Not all will leave, ye who enter here'. Having once visited the London Dungeons, where corpses, skeletons and drowned men join you for a snack in the buffet, I don't feel like repeating the experience. But Mitya insists (kids have a strange fascination with torture), and we enter the dark cellar, from where recorded screams of the tortured can be heard.

The Dungeon captivates me from the start. It gives a final touch to the collective portrait of the Knights of St John which has already been more or less formed in my mind.

The darkest page in the history of the Soviet Communist party was Gulag, where sixty to ninety million people were murdered and tortured. The Knights of St John had their own smaller-scale Gulag –

the Inquisition, in which they took a very active part.

(Warning for the readers: the following four paragraphs contain descriptions which you might find distressing.)

The Mdina Dungeon documents numerous rebellions against the Order: the Conspiracy of the Slaves of 1749 (151 slaves arrested and 'torture in all its hideous forms . . . applied to thirty-eight of the presumed [sic] ringleaders'); the Vassalli revolt; the Priests' Uprising. Each time the Knights, these educators and patrons of the arts, were quick to react. The conspirators were tied to a cross, thrown into open carts drawn by mules and slowly driven to the execution ground in Floriana, a suburb of Valetta. At intervals, the executioner tore bits of flesh from the limbs of the culprits (or 'presumed' culprits, as the case may be) with red-hot-pliers, and poured boiling pitch on the open wounds.

Some of the rebels were taken to the middle of the harbour and their limbs were tied to eight boats which, at a given signal, were rowed with great force in different directions. The shattered corpses were then quartered and beheaded, and their dripping heads were placed on spikes on the nearby bastions.

The Dungeon displays the Knights' crime and punishment code. Those found guilty of blasphemy, say, had their tongues pierced with a needle or cut off altogether (depending on how serious the offence was), or were simply hanged. Slaves who refused to work had their ears cut off. Anyone found guilty of stealing wood from the Order's stores was condemned to the gallows. And so on.

Having dealt with 'criminals' and rebels, the Knights, similar to the Soviet Bolsheviks in the thirties, grew paranoid and started looking for 'internal enemies' within their own ranks. They imprisoned the famous Caravaggio, also a member of the Order, after he quarelled with one of the Knights. They tortured Gerolamo Cassar, their chief engineer and the architect of Valetta, on a 'Cumbo's Horse' (a sort of wooden horse on which they sat him with weights attached to his feet) for having allegedly misappropriated some gold items belonging to the Order. They even temporarily locked up their great Grandmasters La Valette and La Cassiere. As to the prominent Knight Jean Francois de St Clement, who was blamed for one of the Order's navy defeats, he was strangled in prison, and his body, enclosed in a sack filled with stones, was thrown into the sea outside the Grand Harbour.

Without realising it (hopefully), the Knights gradually built a totalitarian state, resting on unpredictability and fear, a state where no one was guaranteed against arrest and repression. This model was later emulated by a number of tyrants and dictators, including Joseph Stalin, who must have studied the history of the Knights of St John at the Theological Seminary in Tiflis – the only educational course he completed.

I think I have solved the evasive mystery of Malta. The wounds inflicted by totalitarianism take a long time to heal. In Malta, where the Order of St John was in power for almost 270 years, they are still bleeding. This explains the ongoing adulation the Knights, those sophisticated and noble medieval murderers, enjoy in this small and insecure European nation, so eager to join the European Union. This explains its fairly recent friendship pacts with the world's greatest tyrannies – Libya, North Korea, Iraq, China and the Soviet Union. Old habits die hard. Old fears die even harder. 'We must squeeze slavery out of ourselves drop by drop,' Chekhov once said. Drop by drop – that's how it happens. It is hard to imagine how long it will take Russia to allay all her fears and inferiority complexes, caused by the Communists of the Order of St Joseph ('Stalin Joseph'), the Knights of Malta of the twentieth century.

We spend the evening in Valetta, rubbing shoulders with old cars, and have dinner at the Bon Appetit café in Floriana, recommended by my guidebook as 'featuring simple Maltese dishes at absurdly low prices'. The dishes are simple indeed, and the prices are low, although not absurdly. The owner's two sons of about Mitya's age are sitting at the next table doing their homework. It is probably they who encourage

Mitya to revive his Mr Amstrad and to continue writing his story Hemingway-style – on the café table, covered with a soiled oil-cloth.

Mr Amstrad was a jolly good fellow when it came to work. He was a decent man with a good attitude, he always wore clean and ironed black pants [sic] and a blue or a grey shirt. He hardly had any hair left but he used to style it well. He had a shower every day and always washed behind his ears . . .

Mitya says it is Mr Amstrad's obituary. RIP, Mr Amstrad!

Three boys – two Maltese and one Russian – are scribbling their tongues out in a little café in Floriana.

20 April, Malta

In the morning, we are picked up by a tourism office car. It is a six-year-old Volvo, and it looks like a technological miracle in Malta, where a twenty-five-year-old car is regarded as brand-new. Patrick, the moustachioed elderly driver, speaks good, yet curiously intoned English, ending every statement with a question, like the Jews in Odessa do. He is taking us to Sliema, where we are to catch a ferry to Gozo.

We drive past hotels, marinas and churches draped with red damask and decorated with flowers. 'Is it some sort of a holiday today?' I ask Patrick, pointing at one of the decorated churches. 'We have festivals here every week, eh?' he explains. 'Every town and village has its own patron saint and celebrates its own *festa* with noisy processions. Every day I wake up and hear another "boom boom-boom!" in the street. Horrible, eh?'

We pass through the lovely seaside resort of Msida. Lots of people stand on the embankment, fishing in the bay. 'See those fishermen?' Patrick asks. 'Two weeks ago a storm destroyed a fish farm not far from Msida, and lots of big fish escaped into the sea. Now these people are trying to catch them. Stupid, eh?'

In Sliema, we find a long queue of people and cars to board the ferry. Using his tourism office card, Patrick manages to squeeze us on board. 'Otherwise you will stand here all day. Terrible, eh?' He says he will wait for us at Cirkewwa Harbour at five p.m. to take us back to Valetta along a different route.

The ferry is packed to the brim. It reminds me of *Fernanda F*, the 'sheep ship' I once saw in the port of Fremantle in Western Australia. Hundreds of bleating animals were placed in tiny pigeon holes on the deck — one for each sheep. They were supposed to cross the Indian Ocean in this floating beehive (or sheephive, to be more exact).

Here, instead of the sheep there are tourists from Manchester and Newcastle, whose northern accent sounds somewhat bleating to me.

In Mgarr, Gozo's main port, we are met by a taciturn old driver in an appropriately old black Mercedes. (I was beginning to believe that the minimum driving age in Malta is sixty.) First, he takes us to Victoria, the island's capital — a village of 3,500 people.

Gozo is known as 'the undiscovered paradise' or 'the island of calm and relaxation' which are basically synonymous. It is thirty-two miles long and is populated by 22,000 people living in fourteen villages. The locals, called the Gozitans, are the butt of jokes in Malta, like Newfoundlanders (Newffies) in Canada, Tasmanians and Queenslanders in Australia, and the Irish all over the English-speaking world. The Maltese claim that the Gozitans are 'simple peasants' (or country bumpkins) who should incorporate *gbejniet*, Gozo's home-made goat cheese, into their coat of arms. The Gozitans, in their turn, retort that it takes only one Gozitan to put ten Maltese in his pocket. They seem to have good reason for that: many of the leading personalities in Malta, such as the Archbishop and the Chief Justice, come from Gozo. Malta's President-elect Ugo Misfud Bonnici, whom we met the day before, is a Gozitan, too. As to *gbejniet*, the Maltese consume more of it than the Gozitans. This shows again how irrelevant all ethnic and regional jokes are.

The countryside in Gozo is pretty boring: cacti, road crosses, dirt tracks and locals carrying barrels of wine on carts dragged by mini-tractors. Our car is not equipped with seatbelts, and the driver steers it lazily from left to right and back, which allows me to conclude that in Gozo they drive on both sides of the road simultaneously.

Our first stop is the fifteenth-century 'Gran Castello', Gozo's main temple, built by the Knights. An interesting feature of this building is that, at the time it was constructed, money was short and would not run to a dome. This lack was brilliantly overcome by the Italian painter Antonio Manuele who produced a magnificent *tromp l'oeil*. He painted the flat roof in such a way that it gave the impression of the dome. A brilliant example of throwing dust (or rather paint) into the public eye, and a Maltese answer to the eighteenth-century Russian 'Potemkin villages' – brightly painted cardboard decorations built by Prince Grigory Potemkin on the banks of the Dnieper to mislead the short-sighted Empress Catherine the Great when she sailed down the river to inspect her dominions.

Victoria is a sleepy village (real, not Potemkin), with a market place as its only attraction. Mitya wants to try some black trousers there, but our serious driver hurries us up with an angry honk. In front of some of the houses we notice little statues of kangaroos. The families who live in them have relatives in Australia – a favoured destination for Maltese emigrants. In fact, there are 350,000 Maltese now living in Oz, only a wee bit fewer than in Malta itself. There are several Maltese newspapers and a couple of radio stations down under.

Next on our list is the Fungus Rock, where *fungus gaulitanus*, a rare plant, which was supposed to possess strong healing powers, used to grow. The Knights valued this plant (and their own precious health) so much that they kept the Rock under constant guard. They treasured the Rock as the Soviet leaders treasured their exclusive Kremlin drug store, the only place in the Soviet Union that had patent Western medicines on sale. Any actual or potential (!) thief of the miraculous fungi was instantly put to death by the enlightened Knights. (At least they didn't hit upon the idea of throwing sane people into psychiatric asylums, as the Communists did.)

The Rock itself looks unimpressive these days: the healing plant does not grow there any longer. The Knights must have used it all – they needed to be in good health to carry on their tortures and murders.

While on Gozo, we can't miss the famous Calypso cave, where the beautiful nymph Calypso kept Odysseus as a 'prisoner of love' for seven long years, while his faithful wife Penelope was crying her eyes out on Ithaca. The cave itself is smelly and dirty, with empty beer cans and cigarette ends littering the floor. It doesn't look like a cosy love-nest at all. Odysseus must have been really taken with Calypso to have spent seven years here (a modern extra-marital love affair lasts three nights on the average). On the other hand, I now understand why he chose to leave the nymph in the end, despite her immoral promises of immortality (or rather of immortal immorality), if he stayed with her for good. The conclusion is obvious: a woman must keep her cave (or house) clean if she wants to keep her man for more than seven years. (No male chauvinist, I hurry to add that the same is true of a man who wants to keep a woman at his place, of course.)

In the best traditions of the Great Leader Kim Il Sung, I give Mitya a little on-the-spot lecture on the importance of cleanliness.

Hordes of tourists besiege the cave, basking in the spirit of this classical case of adultery. For some reason, they are mainly French. '*Voyez! Il y a des fleurs ici!*' they scream, pointing at the flowers growing at the cave's entrance. '*Très romantique!*'

Next to the cave, there are ruins of the megalithic temple of Ggantija. It is built of gigantic stones, some of them up to six metres high. It is still a mystery how the people of those days were able to move them with their primitive tools. A legend goes that a giantess called Sunsuna carried the rocks on her head. A thought strikes me: what if it was Sunsuna, not Calypso with her messy cave, that kept Odysseus here for seven years? Who can resist a woman body-builder (and a temple-builder, too) capable of carrying huge rocks on her head? Or, maybe Odysseus, who was a notorious womaniser, shared his attention between two young ladies – the anaemic capricious nymph and the robust unpretentious giantess. Sunsuna . . . What a powerful name!

'What's next?' I ask our driver. 'Nothing. We have already been everywhere in Gozo,' he shrugs. The surprise of hearing his voice is similar to the effect of bumping into Sunsuna strutting along Republic Street with a six-metre stone in her handbag.

We have a leisurely lunch at the Oleander restaurant in the village of Xaghra. From the window we have a view of the Nativity of the Virgin church with a painted clock, of the building of Xaghra United Football Club and of two butchers' shops – 'Jimmy the Butcher' and 'Sam the Butcher'.

We start with stuffed squid, followed by bean soup and *fenek* – rabbit casseroled in red wine and garlic – a Maltese speciality. The restaurant is full of local beer louts. At one point, a big fat man enters and orders himself a cake. He starts eating it standing at the bar and drops it on the floor. The cake explodes like a fragmentation bomb. Undeterred, the man picks up the creamy fragments and stuffs them greedily into his Calypso cave of a mouth. Maybe the Maltese do have a point when they crack jokes about the Gozitans?

The boat to Comino leaves from Mgarr Harbour. It is a traditional Maltese fishing boat – small, narrow and snub-nosed. The island's only link with the world, it carries a couple of crates of beer and a carton of Nescafé for Comino's shop. We are the only passengers.

Comino is the smallest of the three Maltese islands. About two and a half square kilometres in size, it has a permanent population of five – three humans and two donkeys. There are no roads on the island, which nevertheless boasts its own priest and . . . police station.

The first thing we see as we approach Comino is the seventeeth-century tower, built by the Grand Master Alof de Wignacourt (there's nowhere you can hide from the Knights of St John in Malta). The second thing we see is the modern oblong building of Comino Hotel, overlooking the lagoon. There is nothing ese on the island to attract the eye.

* * *

Gordon Muscat, the assistant manager of Comino Hotel, greets us on the pier. 'Welcome to Comino, Europe's smallest populated island!' he chants.

Comino Hotel is a perfect hideaway. It was built ten years ago, when the island still had a population of fifty — an impressive figure. The hotel was expected to attract more people to live on Comino, but the effect was polarly opposite: Comino's population kept dwindling, from fifty to fourteen, then to eight, and finally to three. The locals were probably afraid that the four-star hotel would bring hordes of noisy holidaymakers to their quiet haven. It didn't.

'Our goal is to keep Comino as it is,' says Gordon Muscat as we sit on the hotel's terrace. 'Our staff do not live here, they come and go. We don't disturb the locals or make any noise, and our only two vehicles are a service truck and a Land Rover.'

We have to hurry to meet the remaining islanders before they all leave Comino for good, so we board the Land Rover and drive towards the village, scaring away lizards from under the wheels.

After about three minutes of a rough cross-country ride, we see a windowless clay hut with the sign 'Comino Police Station' above the door.

Inside, the police station looks as if it has just been raided by pirates. Or by the Knights of St John. Pens, walkie-talkies, details of police uniform, registers and a kettle are scattered all over the duty room. What's going on? Where are the policemen? Have they all been killed and dumped in the sea?

From the adjoining room we hear sounds of commotion. A scantily dressed and red-faced man emerges in the doorway. 'I am the policeman,' he says, pulling on his trousers. He is all creased, rumpled and sweaty, as if he has spent an hour inside a washing machine. 'Sorry, I was asleep,' he yawns. It is two p.m. They seem to have late mornings in Comino.

We enter the room from which the policeman has just emerged. It smells of army barracks. A couple of blankets are spread on the floor. 'We sleep here,' the policeman explains.

'And what is in there?' I ask, pointing to a little door in the corner. With unexpected dexterity, the policeman jumps in front of me, blocking my view. 'It is a bathroom,' he says. Too late. I notice a frightened human shadow hiding in the bathroom, before the policeman slams the door shut. I have no time to establish whether it was a man or a woman.

'Have you got loads of work here?' I ask the clearly embarrassed guardian of Comino's law and order. 'We have some accidents in summer,' he mumbles, throwing furtive looks at the bathroom door. 'How about crime?' 'Only speeding boats,' he mutters. 'Have you got a police boat to chase them?' 'No, we haven't.' I find further conversation meaningless.

'We've got a mobile telephone!' the policeman exclaims suddenly. He takes a battered old motorolla out of his pocket and scrutinises it with the joy of a child who has just spotted a new colourful fish in his home aquarium.

We find two thirds of Comino's permanent population repairing a motorboat in the village. They are Father Hili, the priest, and a man called Salvu. The remaining one third, whom they call 'ante Maria', is nowhere to be seen. Maybe it was she who was hiding in the police station bathroom?

Father Hili reeks of home-made wine. Dressed in a threadbare sweater, turned inside out, he giggles and chain-smokes, fumbling two packets of Rothmans in his hand like rosaries.

'I have been living here for twenty-three years, ha-ha-ha,' he sniggers, puffing at his cigarette. 'My parish is small, hi-hi-hi . . . I will probably go to Gozo soon. They have twenty-six priests in Gozo. More fun, uh-hu-hu!'

It is sad to realize that Comino is about to lose a further one third of its population.

'And I will never leave Comino,' says Salvu. 'I like it.' He has rough, crab-like hands and wears an 'Admiral' baseball cap on his head.

Father Hili forces me to smoke one of his Rothmans. 'Smoking is pleasing to God, ho-ho-ho . . .'

On the way back to the pier, we pass by the toy-size parish church where Father Hili conducts his Sunday liturgies. The door of the police station is wide open: the policeman is probably out on the beat – chasing lizards and keeping an eye on 'ante Maria', Salvu and the priest, in case they decide to commit an offence.

Back on Malta, Patrick is waiting for us at Cirkewwa Harbour, as agreed. On the road to Valetta we stop in the village of Mosta. Its spectacular parish church of the Assumption of Our Lady, also known as the Rotunda of Mosta, has a dome that is supposed to be the third largest unsupported dome in the world, after St Peter's basilica in Rome and St Paul's Cathedral in London. An incredible, but true, story is associated with it.

On 9 April, 1942, at four-forty p.m., a German air-bomb was dropped onto the church, where a mass was in progress. The bomb pierced the dome, fell down amidst the congregation of about 300, rolled along the perimeter of the church, but didn't explode! No one was hurt. The defused bomb is now kept at the church's altar as an object of adoration, and the whole incident has come to be known as 'the miracle of the bomb'.

'God likes Malta, eh?' says Patrick, steering his Volvo towards Valetta.

It is wonderful to know that there is a place in the world where miracles still occur. The mystery-clouded living museum of old cars, unexploded bombs and painted clocks. The long-suffering islands of make-believe.

I am not sure whether God likes Malta (I am not sure He exists, to be honest), but I certainly do.

21 April, Malta–Monaco

From the window of our plane we get a last glimpse of the three

Maltese Islands – Malta, Gozo and in-between them, the tiny Comino, where Father Hili and Salvu are still repairing their boat. And although we can't see them from the sky, it feels almost as if we can.

Having changed planes in Rome, we arrive in Nice half an hour before our Monaco-bound helicopter is due to take off. We are in a hurry, and that's probably why a burly French Customs official finds us suspicious.

'Where do you lads come from?' he asks. 'From Malta now,' I reply.

'Maltanau? *Q'est-ce que c'est?* You mean Yugoslavia?'

They have our suitcases x-rayed. The Andorran laws volume is ferreted out to be examined. Our Australian passports and my Russian accent (Mitya hasn't got one; he has a slight Aussie accent when he speaks Russian, though) puzzle them to the extreme. They don't know what to do with us, Russian Australians coming from Maltanau, and finally let us go.

We run to the Heli Air Monaco terminal, check in our luggage and step out onto the tarmac. I expect to see a chopper there, but, instead, there's a mini-bus waiting for us. We drive outside the airport, pass through a long tunnel and through a bit of countryside. 'When are we going to take off?' Mitya asks. This is the first helicopter flight in his life (in my life as well), yet so far it looks pretty much like a mini-bus ride.

Ten minutes later, we stop next to a red circle painted on the ground. The moment we get off the bus, thinking that we are already in Monaco, a chattering sound reaches us from above. A bright-red dragonfly of a helicopter falls down from the sky and lands exactly in the middle of the red circle. We jump in, the only two passengers in this toy-size four-seater (the seat next to the pilot – Business Class, three seats behind – Economy Class?), and before we realize it, we are airborne.

A vertical take-off gives you the sensation of a bungee jump in reverse. Not that I have experienced the sensation of a proper bungee jump. Well, I almost have . . .

It was in Australia, during one of those promotional journalistic trips, when I was supposed to familiarise myself with Australian fun-making. And to participate in it, too.

When I spotted the forty-four metre high jumping tower, I felt dizzy. I looked up and saw a man falling down towards me, like a huge screaming bat.

I closed my eyes. A fraction of a second before the bungee jumper was due to hit the ground and turn into scrambled eggs, he was stopped by the elastic rope tied to his ankles and started dangling in the sky like Foucault's pendulum, proving that the globe rotates. Having never had any doubts about the rotation of the Earth, I didn't feel much like bungee jumping myself. But they coaxed me into it.

They made me sign a form with my name, address, age, nationality, etc – almost like the questionnaire one had to fill in to go from the Soviet Union to the comradely Mongolia in the eighties. 'Why do you need all these details? For the obituary?' I asked sullenly. Then they weighed me and painted the figure (I am not going to tell you what it was) on the back of my hand, with a smiling face instead of a zero.

I was not smiling while I half-heartedly (one step forward, two steps back – as Lenin would say) climbed the steps to the top of the tower, which I reached in no more than an hour.

The tower was swinging with every gust of wind. I tried hard not to look down, where the figures of onlookers, no bigger than ants, could be seen. The girl who was to jump before me stood at the edge, trembling like an aspen leaf in a storm. Then with a guttural shout: 'I am crazy!!!' down she went, head first.

Three cheerful lads, staffing the tower's top, were stealing up to me with their hands outstretched. 'Come on, don't think! We'll tie you up!'

'Thank you, I am pretty tied up already, and actually I have to go, I've got a meeting downstairs . . .' I mumbled, but it was too late. Despite their order not to think, I couldn't help it. And the only thought on my mind was: in what part of South America will I emerge, having pierced the Earth like a chunk of hot metal pierces a rain-cloud? São

Paulo? Acapulco? Or the piranha-infested Amazon river . . .?

'Oh, you did a bungee-jump!' a receptionist at my hotel exclaimed with admiration an hour later. She was looking at my hand with the jolly dead-weight figure imprinted on it like an unwashable brand of cowardice. 'No, I didn't,' I said honestly and added: 'By the way, can you give me a room in the basement?'

For seven minutes only we hover above the blue bay, lined with villas and *belle époque* apartment blocks of the Cote d'Azur. The flight is over before we have time to savour it properly.

The first thing we see outside the little air terminal is a board advertising private jet hire and Rolls-Royce weddings. We are in Monaco.

A special Monaco Heli Air car (not a Rolls Royce) takes us to our hotel. We feel like millionaires, who have just arrived here by their own private jet (or indeed helicopter).

At a first glance, Monte Carlo looks familiar – a bit of Paris, a bit of Brighton, a bit of Sochi (a tacky Soviet seaside resort), a bit of Cairns. I feel like I've been here before. Perhaps this is due to the fact that I was once compared to Monte Carlo: 'You are like Monte Carlo: you have no taste,' a London lady-friend told me, criticising my style of dress.

The spotlessly clean streets are named after the dead and the living members of Monaco's royal family – Boulevard Albert 1er, Boulevard Rainier III, Princess Grace Avenue, Rue Grimaldi. The kerbs are lined with palm trees, laid out with pebbles. 'The cleanest, most polished place I've ever seen. Real Hell!' Katherine Mansfield wrote about Monte Carlo.

The principality of Monaco is the smallest fully independent state of Europe after the Vatican. Its size is close to that of Hyde Park. Out of 30,000 residents, only 5,000 are native Monégasques, and almost fifty per cent are French.

Apart from gambling, Monaco's most distinctive feature is the cult of the royal family. All its modest achievements are attributed to the genius of the ruling Prince Rainier III. The rhetoric of official guidebooks and media information booklets are reminiscent of those of Brezhnev's *Pravda* (or of the glossy [North] *Korea Today* magazine):

> In 1989, the Principality celebrated with *great enthusiasm* the 40th anniversary of the reign of H.S.H. Prince Rainier III . . . Throughout his reign, Prince Rainier has *skilfully* combined economic and cultural development and the growth of the tourist trade with *great* respect for the traditions which have allowed the country to remain independent for 500 years.
> (*Principality of Monaco: the Official Guide-Book* — the italics are mine, the style is not.)

On the day of the 'glorious' anniversary, each Monégasque household received a free memorial plaque and a special commemorative stamp with the portrait of the Prince.

The media info pack, released by Monaco's state press centre, is also full of eulogies to the ruling dynasty of Grimaldi: 'Among the families of the Genoese aristocracy . . . one of the most *brilliant* was the Grimaldi family,' states the booklet in its outline of Monaco's history. (It also puts forward the rather bizarre and historically unsound idea that Monaco was founded by Heracles, no less, and 'Monoikos', of which 'Monaco' is a derivative, rather than being the name of an ancient Ligurian tribe, meaning 'Heracles on his own'.) It is interesting that throughout the booklet He and She are printed with capitals whenever the members of the royal family are concerned.

Monaco's royals have special red-carpeted entrances to theatres and public buildings, not to be used by anyone else. Not just the streets, but libraries, conference halls, gymnasiums and schools are named after them. Here I can't escape associations with Saparmurat Niyazov, the former Soviet Communist Party *apparatchik* and the President of Turkmenistan, one of the former Soviet republics of Central Asia, who has established one of the most ridiculous personality cults of modern times. Popularly known as 'Turkmenbashi', the father of all Turkmen, not only did he award himself the title of 'The First Hero of

Turkmenistan' and have himself nominated for the Nobel Peace Prize, he even named a pig-breeding farm after his own mother!

Any open criticism of the royals is not tolerated in Monaco, and the details of their income remain a state secret. Close circuit video-cameras and bugging devices are scattered all over the place to monitor potential dissenters, who are likely to get a summons from the authorities and be asked to explain their behaviour. The punishment for an excessively talkative visitor is deportation or a lifetime ban from entering. It is duly exercised by the principality's massive police force of 4,000 agents (one for every ten residents!) making Monaco Europe's largest police state. Hearses are not allowed to enter the main streets (probably not to spoil 'the festive mood of the citizens', as they would say in North Korea). Suicides, of which there are plenty in the principality, are not reported. Yes, Monaco is safe. Safe to the point where a naked woman wearing nothing but jewellery can walk quietly from the Casino to her hotel in the middle of the night. But so was Moscow under Stalin. Totalitarian rulers think that they have the monopoly on everything, including crime, and do not tolerate competition.

Politically, Monaco is a dictatorship. Prince Rainier III, who holds all executive power in the country, suspended the National Council (parliament) in 1959. Later it was revived under complete domination of the pro-Rainier party – National and Democratic Union – that won all eighteen seats in the parliament in the 1978, 1983 and 1988 elections, effectively turning Monaco into a one-party state, à la China, North Korea and the former USSR.

The Prince is the main shareholder of the Société des Bains de Mer, the company that owns almost everything in Monaco, including the Casino and the famous Hotel de Paris. So it wouldn't be an exaggeration to say that Monaco is not simply ruled but also owned by the Prince.

I sympathise with Monaco's royals. There seems to be a long-time curse, similar to that of the Kennedy clan, hanging above the Grimaldi family. 'Never will a Grimaldi find true happiness in marriage,' a

Flemish beauty, betrayed by one of Monaco's womanising rulers, proclaimed in the beginning of our century. She was probably a clairvoyant. Or a witch. Rainier's marriage to the Hollywood film star Grace Kelly ended in a tragedy, when Princess Grace's car plunged off a mountain road in 1982, killing her and injuring Princess Stephanie, one of the couple's three children.

Three versions of the accident were subsequently put forward: 1. The Princess was a lousy driver and had been drinking before the accident. 2. She was upset after a family row, caused by the seventeen-year-old Princess Stephanie's desire to go and live with her boyfriend at a car-racing school. 3. She was the victim of the Mafia, upset by her growing reluctance to influence her husband to provide lucrative investment opportunities for foreigners in Monaco.

A proper police investigation into her death was never conducted.

The marriage of Princess Caroline, the royals' elder daughter, came to a no less tragic end in 1991: her husband Stefano Casiraghi perished when his yacht crashed during a race. After his death, Caroline left Monaco and now lives in Provence.

Princess Stephanie always behaved like a spoilt brat (she probably *was* a spoilt brat). An ardent opponent of bras and bikini tops and a connoisseur of four-letter words, she was once photographed by the *paparazzi* making love in a swimming pool and was eventually made pregnant by her bodyguard whom she subsequently married. Her face can now be seen on billboards advertising Stéphanie perfume all over Monte Carlo: *'Mon parfum est comme je suis'* – 'My perfume is like I am.' Does this imply that the perfume is topless or that it is foul-mouthed (if not foul-smelling)? In any case, I doubt that this ad serves its purpose properly.

With all this sad history in mind, no wonder Prince Albert Alexandre Marie Pierre, Marquis de Baux, the heir to the throne and the family's last hope (I am talking about one and the same person, of course), remains single, despite his notorious appetite for blondes. He comes across as a serious young businessman, whose biggest dream, as he said in one of the interviews, is to be able to do his own shopping.

Who knows, he might succeed one day . . .

All my attempts to secure an interview with a royal at Monaco's state press centre fail (I can't even secure an interview with the head of the press centre itself who is busy at the Monaco Open Tennis Tournament). They tell me one has to apply for such an interview in writing several months in advance.

Unable to talk to the royals, I am left to imagine what questions I would have asked them, had an interview been granted.

'Are there any chances of Monaco being renamed Rainierstan or Grimaldia in the near future?' I would ask Prince Rainier III.

'Is it the perfume you advertise that the light bulbs in the Avenue des Beaux Arts are sprayed with each morning?' I would question Princess Stephanie.

'How much pocket money will your father give you, when you first go shopping on your own?' I would enquire of Prince Albert, who would probably ask me in return what exactly the word 'money' means.

In the afternoon we sit at an outdoor table in the 'No Service' area of the famous Café de Paris in La Place du Casino. Why not in the 'Service' area? Because the cheapest item on the café's menu — a tomato salad — costs eighty francs (about ten pounds). In front of us is the American Bar, known to have the highest concentration of jewels per square metre on earth. Since we are wearing not jewels but jeans, we are not allowed inside.

The air exudes exquisite designer fragrances emanating from leisurely crowds that can be easily divided into two categories: the voyeurs who come here to do some star-spotting; and the exhibitionists, the so-called glitterati, who dress and behave as if they are stars, while in fact they are just wealthy crooks. Looking at this second category, I begin to understand Guy de Maupassant who once said that Monaco is populated with the scum of Europe.

It is hot and sunny (twenty-two degrees Centigrade), but a number of women are wearing furs (animal rights activists have not discovered

Monaco yet). We spot a ten-year-old girl in a mink coat getting out of a gleaming Porsche (Nabokov would call her a nymphette). Those women who are not dressed in furs are sporting tight glistening dresses which make them look either like self-important penguins or like no-less-self-important seals – depending on their size. Some of the women carry Gucci handbags, pressing them tightly to their chests, as if they were their pets; others carry fluffy shampooed mini-dogs, pressing them tightly to their chests as if they were their Gucci handbags.

Men are mostly Serge Diaghilev and Prince Rainier lookalikes – grey-haired, pot-bellied and cigar-puffing. They look bored and openly ogle mini-skirted Lolitas, whose heavily made-up little faces bear traces of all imaginable human vices, as they stroll hand-in-hand with their sugar daddies. These couples puzzle Mitya to the extreme. 'Is he her father, or what?' he keeps asking.

He tears a blank sheet of paper out of my notebook – to be ready to take an autograph in case he spots a star. He is proud of his collection of autographs that includes Pele, Rudolf Nureyev and Rowan Atkinson, all of whom I interviewed in the past. I think, Mitya is unlikely to increase his collection here, though: celebrities are few and far between in Monaco these days – Nureyev is dead. Rowan Atkinson (alias Mr Bean) was long ago banned from Monte Carlo for driving a shameful mini. As to Pele, he would probably agree with the bitter words of his fellow footballer Jurgen Klinsmann, who used to play for Monaco Football Club: 'Here [in Monaco] Titanic syndrome prevails – here they dance before dying.'

The scene in La Place du Casino is almost unreal. It is like watching a bad movie about life in Monte Carlo. Or perhaps life in Monte Carlo is a bad movie?

'This place reminds me of a spoilt child from a rich family showing his gifts to a poor friend,' says Mitya looking at this human zoo parading in front of us.

On the other side of the square, chauffeur-driven Bentleys and Ferraris keep arriving at the entrance of the neo-classical Casino building, which is surmounted by two pinnacles over a glass roof – a cross between a birthday cake and St Pancras railway station.

Why all this money? To stroll around La Place du Casino and to sit in state in the Café de Paris, looking around triumphantly? How boring! Mitya and I are doing exactly the same, without having much money in our pockets, even if we have to sit in the 'No Service' area. We can go round the corner, get some take-away coffee in plastic cups and drink it at our 'No Service' table, thus saving twenty pounds or more. We could buy a couple of books with the money instead.

I look down at my fingers: they are as blue as a corpse's, coloured by my brand-new blue T-shirt which I bought in Leather Lane street market in London a couple of weeks ago. I don't care. I am even slightly proud of my scruffy looks. For the first time in my life, I feel like staging a little revolution, to get rid of these dumb arrogant mugs.

After the warm informality of Malta, we feel alien and out-of-place in Monaco, as if we said hello to the place and it told us to sod off.

I know what Monaco's main quality is: in its politics, architecture and everyday life, it is *vulgar*.

22 April, Monaco

In the morning, I dial the number of the office of the Prince of Seborga given to me by Carlos in Andorra. I get through to the Prince's secretary, who, according to Carlos, speaks all existing languages, including Swahili, Malayalam, Amharic and Bambaric. This proves to be another overstatement: the secretary's only language is Italian, so he transfers me to the Prince himself, who speaks French. Giorgio I kindly agrees to receive us on Sunday and promises to send a car to pick us up: Seborga is just a forty-minute drive from Monte Carlo, across the Italian border.

'We haven't seen any presidents or princes for a couple of days,' I say to Mitya. 'So brace yourself for a bit of royal experience on Sunday.'

* * *

Meanwhile, we continue exploring Monaco.

It takes us about twenty minutes to walk from Monaco-ville, where our hotel is, to the centre of Monte Carlo. We walk past palm trees, fringed with pebbles and marble; past luxurious boutiques with no shoppers; past little printing shops where you can order yourself a stack of huge business cards with lacey vignettes and golden characters (Peter Ustinov once showed me a card like this saying simply, 'Sir Peter Ustinov, Membre de l'Institut'); past the ubiquitous portraits of Prince Rainier; past security video cameras staring at us blankly with their single Cyclops' eyes; past the yachts of the rich and the famous moored to the marina like floating white palaces, with wood panels and winter gardens inside: past currency exchange offices where sleepy female clerks adamantly refuse to accept our Abbey National travellers' cheques.

At the BNP bank, a tired Italian man, with black circles under his eyes, tries to explain to the clerk that he wants to invest some money. He obviously hit a jackpot last night.

'The Canine Society of Monaco', the sign on one of the buildings says. I try the doors: they are firmly shut. What a pity: Monaco's dogs could tell us lots of exciting stories.

Monte Carlo wakes up late. The only pedestrians in its streets at eleven a.m. are cleaners with brooms and hoses, and strikingly beautiful oriental women walking tiny dogs on leashes – the imported wives and mistresses of Monaco. 'Didi! Minoux! Fifi!' they call out their dogs' names. These diminutive Vietnamese, Thai and Philippino women look like expensive exotic doggies themselves.

Having not gone very far with the state press centre yesterday, I decide to try and organise our programme through the Société des Bains de Mer (SBM), a state within a state in Monaco.

The PR department of the SBM, the company with an annual turnover of one and a half billion francs, is at the Hermitage Hotel, second in plushness only to the Hotel de Paris. The department is staffed by stylish and efficient ladies who quickly arrange for us guided tours of the Casino and of the Hotel de Paris. 'The only problem is that you can only visit the Casino with a child under eighteen before the customers start arriving at around three p.m.,' they explain. Mitya tries to protest that he is not a child, but finds it hard to prove that he is over eighteen.

I am not particularly upset about not seeing the gamblers. Having been to a number of casinos in different countries of the globe (as a journalist, not as a punter), I came to the conclusion: seen one – seen them all. There are slight variations, of course. Burswood casino in Perth, until recently the largest gambling pit in the Southern hemisphere, has neither clocks, nor windows – probably to confuse the gamblers. If so, they have succeeded; I heard a story of an old woman who spent forty-eight hours on end there without realising it. She was found by the police, alerted by relatives who had reported her missing.

I will never forget my first ever visit to a casino. It was in Hobart, the capital of Tasmania, in 1990.

Wrest Point Hotel Casino is the loudest architectural statement in Hobart – a piercing scream in the placid symphony of the city. The tower-shaped building, dominating the local harbour, resembles a big candlestick without a candle. Gambling, in my mind, has always been associated with burning candles and an exposed card-shark being hit on the head with a heavy brass candlestick (or a candelabrum).

On the official Soviet scale of moral values, a casino has always occupied the last-but-one place, followed only by a bordello. They were illegal in the USSR, apart from at the best hotels for foreigners, who were exempt from the moral code of the builders of communism.

From reading Russian literary classics, I had come to associate gambling with bubbling passions, strokes of wild luck and terrible blows of fortune. 'A three, a seven and an ace' from Pushkin's *The Queen of Spades*, *The Gambler* by Dostoyevsky, who was an inveterate punter himself ('The roulette wheel has no memory and no conscience,' he used to say), and things like that. If gambling was able to inspire so many writers, there must be something about it, I thought. Wrest Point kept pulling me like a magnet, especially during the night, when it was brightly lit from inside. I felt like a moth attracted by a street lamp, but still scared to approach it lest its wings should be burnt. On my last night in Hobart I decided to risk my hypothetical wings and visit this den of passions.

The first revelation was that this finger-like eighteen-storey building had only seventeen floors. Floor number thirteen was missing, and in the lifts the 'twelve' button was followed by the 'fourteen'.

At the casino's main floor entrance was a curious banking machine with only one function – cash withdrawal. It accepted all types of credit cards. Next to the machine stood a burly guard (or rather a bouncer) who also performed only one withdrawal operation – removing drunks and people in jeans from the crowd and blocking their entry.

The dimly lit room was full of winking screens of poker machines. The people crouched around them were all smoking like chimneys, so one could be excused for thinking that non-smokers were not allowed to gamble, like drunks and people in jeans.

The players' faces were very serious. The machines were emitting short squeaking sounds like rubber toys when squeezed tightly. From time to time the clinking of coins falling out of the machines' bellies could be heard. The sound was excessively loud.

In the corner a game of keno was in progress. The jackpot was 149,637.61 Australian dollars. The sixty-one cents, for some reason, looked impressive.

But the main gambling was taking place in another big room, where more chain-smoking fortune-seekers were playing cards with croupiers. With quick and smooth movements the croupiers shoved banknotes into narrow slits in the green tables. The money disappeared down the slits like greased lightning, never to be seen again.

I started watching the punters. A middle-aged bespectacled man was counting tokens, paying no heed to the smoking cigarette stub protruding from his mouth. The filter was burning already, but he remained unperturbed, totally engrossed in his important business. Another man was mumbling to himself with his eyes fixed on the table, as if praying. A woman with her pregnant daughter, both smoking, were pulling alternately at their wine glasses and at stacks of tokens.

The most distinctive feature of the room's atmosphere, apart from clouds of smoke, was a complete lack of joy, grief or any other emotion that gambling should theoretically inspire. The gamblers reacted with equal nonchalance to wins and losses. Poker-face — now I knew exactly what it meant.

The croupiers acted automatically, like machines. A casino official whose position was 'pit boss' explained that croupiers, like doctors or lawyers, must have a licence. (*A Licence to Gamble* — a good name for a thriller.)

I couldn't leave my first casino without an attempt at gambling. The only game that was vaguely familiar was blackjack. I climbed on to a stool opposite the croupier and handed him a ten-dollar note. Before I could say 'Jack Robinson' or even 'Blackjack', the money disappeared down the slit.

I was cautious and tried to put on the cloth no more than two two-dollar tokens at a time. 'Twenty!' announced the croupier, giving me the third card. 'Enough!' I said, rubbing my hands (mentally, of course). The croupier started making his bid. In a flash, he threw three cards on the table. I couldn't believe my eyes: he had twenty-one!

Next time, I had twenty-one and was feeling triumphant. You won't believe it, but the croupier drew a ten and an ace — the blackjack! — for himself. He definitely had all the cards, that croupier!

I slid off the stool and started towards the exit. Strangely, I didn't feel sorry for the lost money. I did have a good time and temporarily forgot about my problems, big and small. I discovered that gambling (within reasonable limits, of course) was fun.

I went out. The waves of the Pacific Ocean were rustling softly against the sand like a croupier's fingers against the cloth. The half-moon was hanging above the casino like an ace of hearts on the black card of the night. The blurred evening lights of Hobart were blinking in the distance like a ten of diamonds.

'The blackjack! At last!' I cried out into the darkness.

* * *

Little is the Light

The history of the Monte Carlo Casino started in the middle of the nineteenth century, when the first uncertain lines of what was to become Modern Europe were appearing. The international *beau monde* of the period, rich, elegant and titled, always launched the fashions and dictated the conventions.

For the Cote d'Azur, the half-century was marked by huge development. Nice and Cannes welcomed thousands of rich foreigners, mostly British. Chateaux rose out of the ground. Hotels lined the avenues. Only Monaco, a straggling township of 1,200 inhabitants, remained poor and forgotten.

It was then that the future Prince Charles III decided to breathe some life into the moribund state. Gambling was forbidden in France, but the Principality of Monaco had been independent since 1489. Why not open a gaming room in the principality and turn it into another Baden-Baden, where gambling was bringing in more than 200,000 tourists a year, he thought.

The idea was launched. In 1856, the first gambling licence was issued to two Frenchman, Albert Aubert and Léon Langlois, who opened a roulette in Villa Bellevue, an isolated house in the Condamine, a God-forsaken suburb. To get there, the potential gamblers had to take a coach from Nice. The journey lasted for more than four hours. The road, which had no protecting parapet, ran along a precipice and the passengers arrived in Monaco more dead than alive. The only alternative route was by sea: the *Palmaria*, an old paddle-steamer could carry a few passengers along with sacks of flour and barrels of olive oil.

As to the citizens of Monaco (the Monégasques) themselves, access to the roulette was denied to them.

In these conditions, it is not surprising that only one player visited the casino in November, 1857. He won two francs. The journey by road cost him four francs, including tip.

A new page in the Casino's history was associated with Francois Blanc, an art-loving businessman, who invited Charles Garnier, the famous architect of the Paris Grand Opera, to build a new casino and to design the whole ensemble of La Place du Casino, which was to become the 'Golden Square' of the principality. Communications were improved and trains from Nice started running.

Charles III, who had become a full-scale Prince by that time, wanted to find a name for Monaco's new capital. A humble person by nature, he hesitated between Charleville and Albertville (his son was called Albert), but finally settled on Monte Carlo – Mount Charles.

In the years to come, the Casino was frequented by Alexandre Dumas, Baron Rothschild, Jacques Offenbach, Napoleon, Caruso, Sarah Bernhardt, Winston Churchill and many more. Mata Hari shot a fellow German spy there. Aristotle Onassis, on a gambling spree with Jackie, once remarked: 'Can you imagine it? The Monégasques are the people who run a Casino at a loss!' Indeed, for many years the grand Monte Carlo Casino was not making any profits and was regarded as a source of easy money. Even now, in contrast to what many might think, gambling accounts for only five per cent of Monaco's income.

Monsieur Pierre Dupont, the Casino's PR manager, is waiting for us in the Hermitage Hotel lobby. He is involved in a lively conversation with a stylish old gentleman wearing a bowtie.

'Do you know who this man is?' he asks me a moment later, instead of saying hello. 'A German Prince, one of the casino's old-timers and a good friend of mine!'

Monsieur Dupont is in his early sixties. He is dressed in a light-brown Armani suit, with a Rolex watch showing from under his left sleeve and a golden wrist chain from under his right one. He smells of exquisite perfume, and his manner is friendly, but his fast oily eyes remain cold and prickly as he talks.

He takes us on a short walk to the Casino. 'I used to be the manager of the Cannes Casino, and the manager of the Monte Carlo Casino. I also own a casino in Dieppe,' he says on the way. 'It was I who made the Monte Carlo Casino the first casino in France in turnover.' Two words: 'I' and 'casino' – seem to account for fifty per cent of his lexicon.

'Running a casino is like running a restaurant,' he carries on. 'People like to play, that's what a casino is for. Going to a casino is like going to a theatre, in both cases you are not sure whether you'll get the price of your money – you might lose and the play might be bad.'

As a good illustration of what he says, we can see the Monaco Opera Theatre, occupying the back wing of the Casino building. There is a special red-carpeted entrance for the royal family there, too.

At the Casino doors Monsieur Dupont is warmly greeted by the guards. 'They are all my friends,' he smiles. 'I often go to the airport to meet some big rollers from Japan or Thailand. I give them VIP treatment, because they are my friends. I look after them. If their wives do not gamble, I look after them, too. It is important that the wives want to come back. If your son doesn't play, I look after him. You are my friends now.'

'Friends' is clearly Monsieur Dupont's third favourite word.

'We have many players from Russia these days. Lots of money they have, I can tell you. All extremely nice and honest people, and all my very good friends . . .'

I know exactly what sort of people he is talking about – the Russian new rich, who have made millions by shamelessly robbing their fellow citizens, the former KGB and Communist Party *apparatchiks* turned '*businessmeni*' whose unwritten code of business conduct allows anything from chicanery to murder. The Russian mafia. I am not surprised they like Monte Carlo. Monte Carlo, I am sure, likes them, too.

'This is one of the oldest casinos in the world,' Monsieur Dupont informs us as we proceed inside the building. 'It was opened in 1883. When we say "Monaco", we mean "the Casino". When we say "the Casino", we mean "Monaco".'

This reminds me of a popular Soviet hooray-patriotic rhyme: 'When we say "Lenin", we mean "the party"; when we say "the party", we mean "Lenin".' It was always like that there: people said one thing and meant another. Do they play a similar game in Monaco?

'What? Las Vegas? It compares to Monte Carlo like a cheap

supermarket compares to an expensive designer shop. Monaco is safe. You can leave the Casino at three a.m. with a million dollars in your pocket and no one will bother you. Inside the Casino, we have video cameras above each table.'

So, they have video cameras in the Casinos as well. Nowhere to hide from Big Brother . . .

We pass through the atrium – a marble vestibule with twenty-eight columns; cross the Renaissance Hall, with frescoes on the ceiling – just like inside the Stalin Gothic railway station building in Kharkov, and reach the Salon of Europe, lit by eight Bohemian glass candelabra, each weighing 150 kilograms (no card-shark would survive a blow on the head with a candelabrum like this). The huge hall is now empty, not counting a couple of char women with buckets and several 'garçons des salles' cleaning roulette tables and slot machines – a tiny fraction of the Casino's 1,000-strong and almost exclusively Monégasque staff. The minimum slot-machine token you can use in this room is one franc – 'for the people not to say they can't afford it,' explains Monsieur Dupont.

A giant jackpot machine, which takes only 5,000-franc chips, stands in the corner. 'You can win 500,000 francs in one go here,' Monsieur Dupont assures us. I don't ask him how much one can lose on this machine, which had an arm the size of an early water-pump: it can clearly pump a fortune out of your pockets, provided the fortune is there, of course.

We enter the so-called 'salles privées' – the private rooms. To gamble here one has to pay another fifty francs on top of the fifty francs general entrance fee. It is funny how people are willing to pay for the doubtful privilege of losing their money among columns, frescoes and candelabra.

The 'private rooms' and the 'super-private rooms' down the corridor are not private at all, in the true sense of this word. The overhead cameras record every movement of the gamblers, and the hidden microphones follow every remark – allegedly, to settle any disputes that might arise between them. Here people play more serious games –

baccarat, blackjack, craps – under the video cameras' all-seeing eye. The minimum stake is 20,000 francs, the maximum – 300,000 francs. 'We are prepared to pay any sum to the winner: we've got plenty of cash in our safe,' Monsieur Dupont says complacently. 'But, mind you, we don't rob anyone – we simply take the money from the loser and give it to the winner. Both are our friends, since two centimes of every franc that comes to the Casino goes to the SBM, the corporation that owns us.'

'How do you make sure the cards are not marked?' Mitya asks.

'When we receive a box with stacks of cards, it is sealed. Each stack is numbered, and we store them in a fire-proof safe. When we open new stacks, we destroy an equal amount of the old ones in special shredding machines under police supervision. Each stack is used only once.'

The 4,000 Monaco policemen must have their hands full. They must also have sharp eyes to cope with all this watching and supervision.

'The roulette machines are under control as well. After one strong push each of them must rotate for two hours.'

He gives one of the roulette wheels, with 'neither memory nor conscience', a push with his sleek hand, and it starts rotating smoothly. How many keen tearing eyes, bloodshot and swollen after a sleepless night, had followed unblinkingly this merciless rotation, both blissful and lethal in its quiet unpredictability – and unstoppable as the rotation of the Earth itself. How many people put their lives and fortunes at the mercy of this soulless wheel!

We don't want to wait for two hours to expire. We feel uncomfortable and claustrophobic in the stuffy atmosphere of the empty casino, crammed with the ghosts of all its famous and infamous players of the past, the present and the future.

'You are my friends for life,' Monsieur Dupont tells us drily when we part. 'I am your father,' he informs Mitya. I have to restrain myself from reaching for the nearest candelabrum to voice my strong disagreement with his last statement.

· · ·

A long queue is snaking around the only McDonald's in Monaco. This is the second queue to a McDonald's (after Moscow) that I have ever seen.

We are in Fontvieille, the small principality's small industrial area. And next to it, is Monaco-ville – a graceful old town, hiding from the gamblers' view behind the Rock of Monaco, as if ashamed. We are here to attend the French Premier League football match – Monaco vs Nice. Mitya is a great soccer fan and a Manchester United supporter. He is also a cricket, rugby and Aussie rules football (or 'footie', as they call it in Australia) fan. He plays all these games, too.

As for me, I have all but lost my interest in football since coming to the West. In the Soviet Union a football stadium was the only place where one could get rid of the unbearable pressure of totalitarianism. It was the closest thing to freedom, where it was possible, at least for couple of hours, to behave like a normal uninhibited person. It was like a glass of vodka to provide you with momentary oblivion.

I used to support 'Metallist' – a team from my native Kharkov – nicknamed 'Scrap Metal', since it didn't perform well. I always waited impatiently for the sports news on TV, only to find that my team had lost again. Sometimes, though, it won. The very unpredictability of the result, in a country where almost everything else was predictable *ad nauseum*, was inspiring. Weather and sport were the only touches of objective information that one could get from the Soviet media. I used to discuss the matches with my Russian friends, and the fact that we could openly express contradictory opinions, that at least something was not affected by the iron grip of the party line, never failed to give us *kicks*, making us all into football players (or rather footballs) of Soviet life.

It was in Luzhniki stadium in Moscow that I had my first serious argument with Mitya, who was then seven. My Kharkov team was playing in the National Cup Final against the Moscow Torpedo. My son, a born Muscovite, was supporting the latter, of course. When my team won, he burst into tears and refused to look at the field, where the

Cup was presented to the sweaty but triumphant Kharkov boys. I was in the seventh heaven.

Living in Britain, I have often wondered what makes English football fans so wild and violent. The main reason, to my mind, is the unwritten code of conduct that forbids an Englishman to express his emotions freely. Like in the Soviet Union, it is only at the stadium that he can throw off the barriers and become his true self; to relax his stiff upper lip, bringing out the long-suppressed screams, shouts and four-letter words to the surface.

In Australia, on the other hand, football fans never grow violent, and the spirit of mateship and camaraderie prevails over passions. Maybe this is due to the fact that Australia, unlike Britain, is a vast and underpopulated country, and the Aussies still enjoy the feeling of togetherness, whereas the Brits, having to elbow their way around their small and overcrowded island, tend to secretly hate each other, as people in a thick pushing crowd always do. Thus, we may assume that a football stadium can serve more or less as an adequate model of society.

Louis II stadium in Fontvieille is an alternative model of Monaco. It accommodates 20,000 people, half of the principality's population. And the better half of it from what we can see. Gamblers and glitterati are few and far between here. On one of the terraces we spot the loser-friendly figure of Monsieur Dupont. He gives us, his 'friends for life', a half-hearted nod and turns away.

We sit next to an Israeli man, who came all the way from Tel Aviv to support his nephew playing for Nice. Monaco's most popular player is Petit (meaning 'little' in French), who is the tallest of the team. A six-year-old boy behind us, a real *enfant terrible* with a police-siren of a voice, keeps cheering him at the top of his lungs: 'Petit! Pe-e-tee-e!!!'

Both teams have a couple of Russian players in their ranks. Monaco scores. 'It is a Russian who scored!' Mitya says. 'No, son, it isn't!' 'Why?' 'Because the player who scored was black!' We are about to have another little argument.

Monaco scores four goals in no time. Nice players look totally demoralised. 'Monaco has probably bribed them all,' Mitya suggests. I share his irritation: my rule is always to support a loser (unless the Kharkov 'Scrap Metal' is playing, of course): a winner does not need much support. A family argument is avoided.

The waves of the Mediterranean are splashing indifferently behind the terraces, as if repeating after the fans: *'Allez, Nice! Allez, Monaco!'* As usual, the sea is reluctant to take sides and remains immune to earthly passions.

Until late at night, the happy fans of Monaco and the distressed supporters of Nice shout and chant behind our hotel windows. I find it hard to fall asleep: the piercing yells of the *enfant terrible* from the stadium resound in my ears: 'Petit! Pee-tee-ee!!!'

23 April, Monaco

After the Casino, the second best known institution in Monaco is undoubtedly the Hotel de Paris, with its glorious Le Louis XV restaurant, run by the world's most famous chef, Alain Ducasse. Built in 1864, together with the Casino and the pigeon-shooting stand (another popular attraction which allowed hapless punters to let off steam), it offered five-franc set dinners for its fifty guests paying twenty-five francs a day for full board. From its very first days, the Hotel has always been fully booked for months ahead, but both its building and the prices have undergone substantial enlargements since then. The cheapest room these days costs about 200 pounds per night, and the cheapest starter on Alain Ducasse's menu, *Cannelloni d'herbes et salades ameres juste gratinés, sauté minute d'artichant du pays*, is priced at 185 francs, or about sixteen pounds, the equivalent of a good value pair of trousers for Mitya, which we have failed to buy so far.

Now you will understand why, rather than staying at the Hotel de Paris and having a leisurely lunch at its restaurant, we choose to have a tour of the place in the morning, when the restaurant, that is open only for dinners, doesn't serve any food. Just to avoid the temptation.

Besides, we have left our tuxedoes in London, and they require evening dress at Le Louis XV (to be frank, we haven't got any tuxedoes, flannels or top coats in our wardrobe, although Mitya has got a T-shirt, inscribed 'Tuxedo' at the front).

I will spare you the description of the Hotel de Paris exterior and interior, kept in exactly the same plush and tacky style as the Casino (see above). One interesting thing is that during the First World War the Hotel was used as a hospital. I imagine how it must have felt to be dying (or recovering) among all these crystal chandeliers and marble columns. It probably was like being buried alive, since the hotel's interior has the distinctive look of an expensive funeral parlour.

The restaurant, however, is well worth describing. The decor of the comparatively small dining hall for sixty patrons is little short of grandiose – a brilliant example of the 'grand opera' Empire style, which in plain words means that everything is gilded and shining. The tables are covered with cloths of damask linen and set with the finest monogrammed porcelain one can picture, cutlery in authentic silver gilt and glasses of cut crystal on gilded trays.

The detail that strikes me most, though, is a special stand for ladies' handbags near each table.

This restaurant room remembers lots of grand feasts. The turn-of-the-century Russian Grand Dukes (of whom there were many), who rented whole floors of the hotel, drank gallons of champagne themselves and gave some to their horses, used to throw banquets for their friends there. Perhaps they had almost as many friends as Monsieur Dupont. One night the party of Grand Duke Dimitri (Mitya's namesake), having consumed heaps of caviar, *blinis* and salmon *pojarsky*, ordered sixty magnums of champagne of which the majority ended up broken to smithereens against the marble columns. What a waste . . .

I am sure that, if one scrutinised the carpet properly, tiny prickly fragments of these bottles could still be found, the fragments of the *belle époque* itself.

Its modern fame came to Le Louis XV in 1987, when a thirty-year-old Alain Ducasse was appointed its chef. With his 'new style of cooking' (whatever it means, I still think that there can be only two styles of cooking – good and bad), he won himself three Michelin Guide stars, thus becoming the world's youngest chef ever to be awarded such an honour. The 1994 list of the world's Top Tables places his restaurant as the third best in the world, after 'Joel Robuchon' in New York and 'Lai Ching Heen' in Hong Kong, making Le Louis XV officially the best restaurant in Europe.

The statistics of Le Louis XV are staggering: it employs ninety cooks (one and a half times more than the maximum number of customers); its kitchen is 1,100 square metres; its wine-cellars store 300,000 bottles of wine; it offers 500 varieties of cigar.

As for the food, I won't tire you with the original French names of the dishes, each occupying at least three lines in the giant menu, on to which a Monaco Heli Air chopper can easily land. To give you a better idea, here are some *poetic* English translations (they have to be translated like poems, these culinary hexameters): 'Provençal home-grown vegetables with oil from the mill beyond the water stewed with crushed black truffles' (starter); 'Breton lobster cooked over charcoal, juice from the press, spaghetti with truffles or tomato or basil' (first main course); 'young pigeon from the Alps of High Provence, cooked over charcoal, grilled fattened duck's liver, heads of boletus stuck with garlic and stewed' (second main course); and, to crown it all, 'wild strawberries in lukewarm juice, water-ice and mascarpone – a Lombardy cheese prepared as a dessert' (dessert).

Still hungry? Then how about a 'chump end of the loin of a free-range suckling calf cooked like an old-fashioned roast with real sauce, stewed carrots, new potatoes and small round onions'? I'd better stop here before you start salivating (I already have).

'What do you think Alain Ducasse would do if I came to his restaurant and ordered a Big Mac?' Mitya whispers.

'He would probably commit suicide on the spot,' I reply leading my son out of the dining room.

Shamefully, we do have lunch at McDonald's, the only eating place in Monaco that we can easily afford. After a couple of fat-oozing burgers (gobbling on them, I keep imagining they are something else – like 'thick pieces of hake cooked in the Basque country manner', say), our appetite for all young calves, suckling pigeons and strawberry lobsters in the world fades away. 'Just think how much money we have saved,' Mitya says cynically. 'And the result is the same: we have stuffed our bellies really well.'

What can I say? Within an hour we have experienced the cooking of the two most successful restauranteurs in the world – Alain Ducasse and Mr McDonald.

We walk in the narrow streets of Monaco-ville, the small and cosy old town on the Rock, free from the all-permeating kitsch of Monte Carlo, apart from huge public sculptures of fat female torsos, headless, armless and legless, with all remaining prominent parts of their anatomy meticulously preserved. They look like a good example of socialist realism, but in this case it is rather 'sexual realism'.

The sign near The Palace of the Prince warns against entering the Palace grounds 'bare-chested or barefooted' and threatens prosecution. What about Princess Stephanie who seldom seems to wear a bikini top? Would she be allowed into her father's palace bare-chested?

In the Museum inside the Palace one can gape at the wax sculptures of the royal family: glassy-eyed, as if heavily intoxicated, Princess Grace sitting in an armchair, with Stephanie, an innocent five-year-old, at her side. On one of the walls is the branchy Grimaldi family tree. I wouldn't be surprised to see a Grimaldi Mausoleum somewhere nearby.

We watch the changing of the blue-helmeted guards in the Palace Square, full of extremely expensive souvenir shops, and, having walked past the Albert I Grammar School and the Princess Grace Irish Library, reach the aquarium, which, although not named after a royal, has some royal memorabilia on display. 'This whale was harpooned by Prince Albert I on 26 May, 1896,' a brass plate on the poor whale's skeleton says. The skeleton is bare-chested, and Mitya wonders why it was allowed in.

The colourful tropical fish have blank expressionless eyes of hardened gamblers, and suddenly the aquarium starts resembling a silent underwater casino. I can even recognise Monsieur Dupont in a piranha stirring his stylish fins grandly, as if saying: 'I am your friend for life' — as a prelude to eating you up.

Mitya wants to go and see the Monte Carlo Tennis Open Tournament. I am not too enthusiastic about it. To me, tennis is like chess — fun to play, but boring to watch. Our first flat in Sydney overlooked the White City tennis courts, and we had to watch the tennis players from morning till night. They were totally immersed in the game, as if the rest of their existence depended on a lucky shot. Pok . . . Pok . . . Our whole new life was accompanied by this monotonous alien sound, and I entitled my first newspaper column written in Australia 'Tennis and Tears'.

It was largely to escape the tennis players that we eventually moved to Melbourne, only to find, yet again, tennis being constantly played under our windows. What a playful country Australia is . . .

The audience at the Monte Carlo Country Club, where the tennis tournament is held, is very different from that at the football stadium — much more *beau monde*-ish, if I can put it like that. The atmosphere is different, too. '*Silence, s'il vous plait, mesdames et messieurs!*' they announce before each serve. The announcement is quite superfluous: the terraces are silent anyway. There is not much emotion around. There are not many faces around either — just hats, sunglasses and stylish casual jackets.

At the Country Club, like in the Casino, they have '*tribunes privées*' (private boxes) permanently reserved in the names of 'Lancaster', 'Puma' and a mysterious, but obviously rich, 'Mr Fadhi'. They are all empty.

The tedious game of tennis is over, The players shake hands, pick up their gear and leave. The crowd gradually disperses, but we are still sitting on the terrace. Our trip to Gibanmamorga is coming to an end. Tomorrow we are visiting Seborga, the last mini-state on our list.

Our game is not finished yet.

24 April, Seborga

We are sitting in our hotel lobby, waiting to be picked up by the Secretary to the Prince of Seborga. The old leather armchairs are disarmingly soft: they sink under your weight with a heavy senile sigh.

The Secretary proves to be an athletic young man. His name is Francesco di Bisceglie, and he combines his duties as the Secretary with those of Seborga's Minister for Sport, Tourism and Spectacles, manager of the local souvenir shop, one of the five soldiers of Seborga's army, and a gardener. The latter is his main full-time occupation, by the way.

Disappointingly, Francesco drives not a black Mercedes, as promised by Carlos, but a modest battered Renault.

He doesn't speak any French (or English), and, with my basic Italian, we can hardly exchange a word during our thirty-kilometre drive to Seborga as we leave Monaco and cross the border into Italy. In fact, we pass through a couple of Italian hamlets on French territory, *before* the Italian border – a curious geographical twist.

The first view of Seborga, perched on top of a hill, opens from the village of Sasso, now a part of the Principality of Seborga. White-and-blue Seborgan flags flutter above the roofs. 'Gorgio I', a graffito on the fence says. To me, the graffiti looks slightly offensive: in Russia they mainly wrote f-words on the fences.

'*Mamma mia!*' Francesco exclaims loudly. At first, I think that he is cursing, but he is actually pointing at an old peasant woman standing in the doorway of one of the houses and waving to us. '*Mia mamma!*' he repeats.

After a quick drive up the hill, past the Italian sign 'Welcome to the ancient Principality of Seborga, 517m above sea level', we arrive at

Seborga's central square, empty, except for a couple of dishevelled village chickens chased by a lop-eared puppy, and a parked van, inscribed 'Seborga Fiori' (Seborga Flowers), probably belonging to the local flower cooperative, the Principality's only industrial enterprise. To the right of us is the two-storeyed Il Principe (the Prince) restaurant, to the left – Via Antico Principato (Ancient Principality Street) with a church and a couple of shabby country houses in it.

Having left us on the open verandah of the Il Principe restaurant, Francesco goes away to inform His Serene Highness that we have arrived. He comes back in a quarter of an hour with a French-speaking man (too young to be the Prince) who introduces himself as Marco, Seborga's Minister of Manifestations and Free Time. What a wonderful job – the Minister of Free Time! I'd like to be one myself, I can tell you!

So far, we have met two citizens of Seborga, and both of them are Ministers, which prompts Mitya to suppose that the waitress serving us on the restaurant's terrace is Seborga's Minister of Food. He might be right . . .

Marco explains that His Serene Highness Prince Giorgio I brings us his apologies: he is presently busy pruning flowers (after all, he has been a flower farmer all his life) and will be with us within half an hour. Meanwhile, he offers me a cup of coffee and Mitya a glass of Coke, and volunteers to brief us on the history of Seborga. He is a real master of free time, this Marco,

Seborga, now a village of 350 souls, first gained its sovereignty in the year 954 as one of the many post-Roman mini-states on the territory of the present-day Italy. Independence was bestowed on the village by Guido, the Count of Ventimiglia, the nearest coastal town.

Seborga became a principality in 1040. For several hundred years, prior to its incorporation into the Austro-Hungarian Empire, it had been under Vatican protection and even had its own mint until it was forced to close in 1686 for making too many counterfeit ecus.

After the defeat of Napoleon, when inter-European borders underwent considerable redrawing under the Treaty of Vienna, Seborga and the neighbouring Monaco were simply forgotten due to their insignificance and minuscule size. Monaco was soon remembered, but Seborga wasn't and automatically became part of Italy.

About twenty-five years ago, Giorgio Carbone, the son of a local flower farmer and a flower farmer himself, decided to revive Seborga's statehood. He proclaimed himself Prince Giorgio I and started campaigning for the village's separation from Italy and complete independence. By the early nineties, he had managed to lure into his camp (or rather into his self-proclaimed principality) not only all 350 residents of Seborga, but also about 2,000 people from several neighbouring village communes, who were obviously fed-up with the unending scandal and corruption of Italian politics, as well as the high Italian taxes.

Seborga's independence was officially announced in August, 1993, when three Seborgan soldiers (three fifths of its army) in Napoleonic uniforms sneaked unnoticed through the Passo del Bandito mountain pass and nailed Seborga's flag to the door of the church of San Michele, one of the three parish churches Giorgio I wanted to reclaim (together with the parishes, of course). They managed to get away with this. The Italian government stays mum, ignoring all developments in Seborga, or (which is more likely) is simply unaware of them. At the same time, about thirty countries of the world have already recognised Seborga's independence.

When I enquire which countries, Marco shrugs: 'I am not sure. You'd better ask the Prince.' I understand him; his responsibilities are free time and manifestations, not diplomatic affairs.

A small group of tourists, with their cameras ready, materialises out of nowhere and gathers in the centre of the square. 'The Prince is about to arrive,' Marco announces solemnly.

A black Mercedes, flying a white-and-blue flag, crawls into the square. A bulky bearded man, dressed in pitch-black gleaming shoes, black trousers, blue shirt with Seborga's crest on its pocket and white blazer (to match Seborga's flag colours?), gets out of the car, blowing air-kisses to the waiting crowd. This is the Prince. He is followed by another man in a plain black suit. 'He is the governor of San Remo's prison, the Prince's personal friend,' Marco whispers respectfully.

'Prince Giorgio I seems to have friends in the right places,' I say to Mitya in Russian.

The Prince, looking somewhat like a wood-goblin from a Russian fairy-tale, is surrounded by the tourists. For twenty minutes he is busy kissing women's hands and cheeks (he seems to be enjoying this immensely), patting children on their heads ('*Principe! Principe!*' they shout), posing for the cameras with his hands outstretched, and answering questions in a true royal fashion – quite extraordinary for a fifty-seven-year-old bachelor without a drop of blue blood. He chain-smokes all the while, clutching a fag between the thick soiled fingers of a flower farmer.

Eventually, having satisfied the tourists' curiosity, the Prince joins us on the terrace and immediately orders himself a scotch. 'I am the Prince!' are his first words to us (with the stress on 'I'). He utters them with a touch of hostility in his hoarse low voice, as if he regarded me and Mitya as potential contenders to his throne. We communicate in French, of which His Self-Proclaimed Highness has a good command.

'We are the oldest constitutional monarchy in the world, and Italy is only 133 years old!' he declares, downing his drink and lighting up an umpteenth Nazionali cigarette.

'Who wrote the constitution?' I ask the Prince.

'I did!' he replies. 'But don't think that I am a dictator. I am a democrat. My people support me. It won't be long before Seborga is recognised by the whole world and becomes a UN member. We have nothing to do with Italy, and there isn't a single archive document that proves otherwise. So why should we keep paying taxes to a foreign power? Our citizens want to work for the benefit of their native Seborga . . .'

'How are you going to survive on your own?'

'Easy! We already export our flowers to Germany, Sweden and the United States. We can declare ourselves a tax haven. Just look at San Marino – they are doing well. And we are older than they!'

319

I touch upon the delicate question of international recognition.

'We have already been recognised by forty countries: San Marino and . . . and . . . about twenty or thirty African states, I don't remember which. But I can tell you something, if you promise not to write about it . . .'

Without waiting for my promise, the Prince carries on: 'We have been recognised by Saddam Hussein!'

For the first time, I start doubting his sanity.

'We've got ambassadors in 151 countries of the world!'

Thinking that I have misheard him, I give him my notebook, and he scribbles '151' there.

'Yes. Most of our ambassadors hold more than one office, of course. For example, our special envoy to China, Eastern Europe, the Baltic republics and London is Sino Polo Pavlich Padolecchi, the Duke of Dalmatia.'

Again, I ask him to write down the name and he does.

The situation becomes terrifyingly clear: here we are sitting in a village-size lunatic asylum on top of a hill, talking to a mad Prince, surrounded by his mad lieutenants (or are they the hospital orderlies?). What if the Prince is dangerous and should not be approached? What if he starts biting? We'd better take to our heels before it's too late . . .

But, wait a second . . . What about the tourists? What about the two Ministers – Francesco and Marco, who sound perfectly normal, if somewhat confused? And the flags? And the Prince's latest printed decree on the wall: '*Noi, S.A.S. Giorgio Io, Principe di Seborga per grazia di Dio e per volonta del popolo sovrano, SCRIVIAMO . . .*' – 'We, HSH Giorgio I, the Prince of Seborga by the grace of God and by the will of the sovereign people, hereby DECLARE . . .'?

No, I shouldn't jump to conclusions. My journalistic self tells me to stay on and to find out more (my paternal self, on the other hand, urges me to take my unsuspecting child, who doesn't speak French and, bored out of his mind, is flattening the empty Coke can against the table, away from danger).

Biding my time, I ask the Prince to pose for a photo. He agrees willingly and, standing on the edge of the restaurant's terrace, spreads his hands as if trying to embrace the whole of Seborga, or perhaps the entire world. At this point I discover that I have run out of film. The Prince gives orders to Francesco to go and get me a new one.

'Now, I invite you for lunch,' announces Giorgio I, finishing his fifth Scotch. 'On the way, I'll make you Seborga's citizens, if you wish.'

Our progress through the village is slow. Dogs, chickens and children, screaming: 'Principe! Principe!' — run after us. A lanky young man approaches the Prince in Piazza Martiri Patrioti and starts a long conversation with him. 'This is our Minister of Agriculture,' Marco explains. 'The Prince is giving him instructions on where to send flowers.'

It looks like every male in Seborga is a member of the Prince's cabinet.

As soon as the monarch terminates his Kim Il Sung-style on-the-spot guidance for the Minister of Agriculture, his attention is distracted by a group of teenagers, one of whom has a toy penis, made of glass, in his hand. He shows the toy to the Prince who examines it with interest. 'Seborga's future,' he tells me gravely. I am not exactly sure what he means — the teenagers or the penis.

Giorgio I takes a long time to say goodbye to the teenagers: patting the boys on their shoulders and kissing the girls (with real gusto).

Our procession approaches the village post office, serving simultaneously as a souvenir shop, a passport office and the Prince's throne room. The choice of souvenirs on sale is reduced to one faded postcard with a view of Seborga's main square and one dirty, formerly white, T-shirt with the principality's coat of arms.

The monarch lowers his bulk onto a wobbly chair (his throne?), and, having asked for my and Mitya's dates of birth, scribbles something on two pieces of white-and-blue cardboard. From a squeaky drawer he produces a huge round seal, breathes at it lovingly and, having stamped the pieces of cardboard in the middle, gives them to us.

'Congratulations!' he says. 'You two have just been made Seborga citizens!'

I look in disbelief at my brand-new 'Principato di Seborga Passaporto' number 461: the Scotch-smelling stamp, the validity dates and the potentate's curved signature, resembling a cardiogram of a person on the verge of a heart attack — everything is in place.

'You will need to attach your photos on page two,' Marco explains. 'But you can do it later.'

It takes two years of permanent residence to become a citizen of Australia. In the US, one has to wait for five years, in Britain, for four. In Liechtenstein and Andorra naturalisation takes thirty years. It took us less than two hours to become the citizens of Seborga.

'Is it possible to travel with this passport?' I ask Marco.

'Yes, if you want to end up in prison,' he chuckles.

The Prince is clearly enjoying himself. He offers to make me a Cavaliero del'Academia (whatever that means). I politely refuse.

He then shows me the list of his fourteen cabinet Ministers, which includes the Minister of Urbanisation, and opens his mouth, probably to offer me the job of the Minister of the Posterior and to make Mitya the ambassador to Estonia, Brazil and Vanuatu, when a sad-looking Franscesco turns up. From his frantic gestures, I understand that he has ransacked the whole of Seborga, but failed to find a new Kodak film. The Prince is angry. He barks something out in Italian and dismisses Francesco with a quick wave of his royal hand. The Minister for Sport, Tourism and Spectacles walks away with his head down — not too cheerful a spectacle.

It looks increasingly like a dress rehearsal of a new production at the Theatre of the Absurd where we are both the audience and the cast.

We resume our unhurried walk through the narrow winding streets of the village.

'Ladies and gentlemen, the Prince of Seborga!' the owner of the L'Osteria del Coniglio restaurant announces in Italian as we enter. His tone is somewhat ironic, or maybe it is his uncertain Italian intonation that plays tricks on me.

The restaurant is full of customers who burst into applause at the sight of the Prince, bowing right and left and kissing women's hands as he makes his way to the table in the corner. *'Bon appetito, tutti!'* he roars amicably. We follow him, basking in the rays of his royal fame.

The table iis sagging under starters and bottles of red wine. The Prince pours himself a glass, downs it and plunges into a long monologue in Italian, addressing everyone in the restaurant except for us. He drinks and talks, drinks and talks and eats, drinks and talks – louder and louder, faster and faster. I can only catch occasional words: 'Napoleon', 'Japan', 'Germany', 'the Prince of Monte Carlo'. Can it be that he is speaking about the countries and the politicians who have failed to recognise Seborga's independence so far?

The patrons listen to him with their mouths agape.

By now, both Mitya and I are bored. 'Wasn't it you who said that a writer must suffer?' my son whispers sadistically. 'No. It was Leo Tolstoy actually,' I retort.

The Prince remembers us after course number ten – ravioli.

'Why aren't you eating or drinking?' he asks. 'Try this salami, imported from Italy! Ha-ha!'

He is very pleased with his joke.

'Look at these people in the restaurant. They all love me. Because I *am* the people! I have nothing to do with nobility, just trying to restore the tradition. I am not a dictator like the Prince of Monaco. I am a democrat! I am a historical reality that has to be accepted!'

The only person in the restaurant who doesn't seem to accept the 'historical reality' is the owner. He keeps throwing angry looks at His Serene Highness, especially when the latter orders more and more food and booze.

'I eat like this every day,' the Prince confesses with a burp. I suspect he doesn't pay for his meals, and this explains the owner's irritation.

The puffing Francesco reappears, bringing his own personal camera for me to use. The camera turns out to be without a film. The monarch is furious: he nearly throws his poor Minister out of the restaurant.

Suddenly, the Prince bursts into a song. Having cut it short, he addresses me in German. I tell him I don't speak German.

'And I do!' the Prince assures me. 'My parents were simple peasants, the flower farmers. But I am an educated man. I have two university degrees – in medicine and law. I studied in Genova, Padova and Torino . . .'

For some reason, he starts calling me 'Sir'. I have the feeling that he has forgotten who we are. I also doubt he remembers who he is.

Course number twenty, twenty-one, twenty-two – wild boar, grilled beef, rabbit with corn (or rather with scorn – on the owner's face). By now, the Prince is the only one in the restaurant who is still eating. Soon all the customers leave and we are on our own.

After an unsuccesful attempt to force a lemon cake down our throats, the potentate asks for more wine. At this point, the owner explodes. He screams something in Italian, his every other word being 'denaro' – money. It is plain he wants Giorgio I to cough up.

The Prince stumbles to his feet. I expect him to start fulminating, beating himself on the chest and shouting: 'What do you take me for? I am the Prince, and princes are exempt from paying their restaurant bills!' But, instead, he brushes the owner off with his princely hand and quietly tiptoes to the door. Without paying his bill, of course. It is easy to imagine this scene replayed every single day.

He takes us back to the Il Principe. There are only two restaurants in the whole of Seborga, and the Prince seems to be in the habit of commuting between them. Thrown out of one, he heads for the other – like a sewing machine shuttle.

The short walk to the Il Principe sobers him up a little.

'I am now going to make an important declaration and tell you something that I haven't told anybody else,' he says, sipping a cognac in the empty restaurant. The time is approaching five p.m., and I am frightened by the prospect of our hearty lunch growing into a no-less-hearty dinner. 'I've got a bomb up my sleeve. A bomb not just for Europe, but for the whole world!'

'Here it starts,' I think with awe, ready to grab Mitya at the first sign of danger and mentally drafting a beeline to the door. But the Prince seems to have lost much of his oomph and aggression. There is even a tinkle of sadness in his brown eyes under the bushy eyebrows.

'The bomb is that many other unrecognised small nations might imitate Seborga,' continues the Prince. 'I stand for full sovereignity – nothing less than that, and Italy or any other country can't do anything to stop me, since their own constitutions proclaim freedom of choice and other democratic liberties. I've got complete constitutional legitimacy in Seborga, so what can they do? Crush me with tanks? I know they don't like me, but they are helpless. Of course, we are afraid of a provocation, in which case we shall defend ourselves: I am planning to expand my army to twenty-two soldiers in the near future. You will see that soon many small nations of the world will follow our example.'

Maybe the Prince is not that mad, after all? I think suddenly. He is right: theoretically Seborga's strive for independence is as legitimate as that of San Marino and Monaco. Or of Sardinia. Or of Valle d'Aosta. Or of Friuli. Or of Bavaria. Or of Mecklenburg. Or of Turingia. Or . . .

Any mini-nation that used to enjoy sovereignity some time in the past has an undisputed right to claim it back, if its people so decide.

It is here that the nightmare scenario starts, and the much-publicised 'common European home' collapses like a house of cards, bringing about chaos and possible bloodshed. This was what Giorgio Carbone, an ambitious flower farmer from Seborga, meant by saying he had a bomb up his sleeve. 'Seborga syndrome' might easily prove infectious.

Remembering the tragic results of the hasty fragmentation of Yugoslavia and the former Soviet empire, a European union, no matter how fragile, is certainly preferrable to a chaotic and potentially bloody disunion. On the other hand, how can a natural human drive for independence be curbed by democratic means? A good question which, I think, explains the protracted silence of the Italian government in Rome with regards to Seborga. They are obviously at a loss as to what to do with it. Who wouldn't be?

* * *

With the brand-new Seborgan passports weighing down our pockets, we get into the car to go back to Monaco. The self-appointed Prince with the hands of a peasant is waving goodbye to us from the steps of the Il Principe. We wave back. As his massive bearded figure recedes in the distance, I suddenly understand that despite his boorish manners bordering on madness, despite his lofty rhetoric and decrees, psychologically he remains but an enterprising flower farmer trying to cultivate a rare and capricious bloom of sovereignty and freedom in the small garden of Seborga. I also realise that he is terribly *lonely*.

We are driven back not by Francesco (the Prince has probably deprived him of his ministerial portfolio for failing to provide me with a film) but by another young man, who introduces himself as Seborga's Minister of Public Labour. He travels with his girlfriend, almost a teenager, who turns out to be Seborga's Secretary of State (Giorgio I must be indeed a democrat, having nominated a female to such an important post). They are hoping to visit a discotheque in Monte Carlo.

'There is neither a disco nor a cinema in Seborga — just a church and a primary school,' the Secretary of State complains. 'But there is the Minister of Education,' the Minister of Public Labour adds sarcastically.

They sound as if they don't take their Prince (and their independence) seriously.

'How did Giorgio I manage to get such a good education?' I ask them.

'Good education?' The Secretary of State wrinkles her pretty little nose. 'He did study law and medicine, but has never completed either course. He hasn't got a university degree . . .'

Soon we arrive in Monte Carlo. We head for our hotel, and Seborga's Minister of Public Labour, having put his hand round the wasp waist of the Secretary of State, steers her to the nearest disco — to dance the night away.

25 April, Monaco–London (Gatwick)

It rains in Monte Carlo in the morning. We are packing our bags for the last leg of our Gibanmamorga journey. The bulky volume of Andorra's medieval laws is abandoned in our room. Its place in the suitcase is taken by the helicopter pad-size menu of Alain Ducasse's restaurant. The suitcase is as heavy as before.

Trains are rattling behind our hotel room window as we briefly sit down 'for the road', in accordance with an old Russian custom.

Rain is a good omen for a trip.

Our life-long journey continues.

26 April, London (Heathrow)

I am saying goodbye to my son. He is flying back to Australia, where he now lives with his mother. He is wearing his new black trousers that we finally bought at the Gatwick airport shopping arcade yesterday.

As a child under fourteen, he qualifies as a 'young flyer' to be looked after, and a Sunsuna-type hostess, tall and broad-shouldered, accompanies him to the passport control. Next to her, he looks as tiny and helpless as he did when I left him for the first time at a Moscow day nursery ten years ago.

This morning Mitya wrote me 'A Little Poem about Life'. Here it is:

Life is a funny old trigger,
Sometimes it is smaller, sometimes it is bigger,
For when you are sad and full of doubt,
Life can be bad and chuck you about.

The idiot box we call TV
Is eating us up, especially me.
The junk food is rubbish, it's poison for birds –
Old Mr McDonald is recycling his turds.

The law is crap, no one listens to it,
Our rulers do nothing but swim in birds' shit.
Our pollution is high on every scale,
But no one is noticing that we are all pale.

Little is the Light

Sex is important to most of us now,
You can sleep with your wife or you can sleep with a cow.
The choice is all yours when it comes to sex —
Some desperate ones want to sleep with T-Rex.

The seas are polluted with junk and our shit,
Yet as long as they flow, no one notices it.

But when you are laughing full mouth, galore,
Life can be good for a minute or more!

I stand at the Departures area turnstile, the saddest border in my entire life, separating me from my son. I watch him getting farther and farther away from me.

My little boy. A citizen of Australia. A citizen of Gibanmamorga. A citizen of the free world.

I hope that, unlike his father, he will grow up to be a traveller, not a vagabond.

Appendix

A Phrase or Two on Phrase Books

The old dog-eared volume that I bought in a second-hand book shop in Cecil Court was nothing like a normal modern traveller's phrase book with such handy expressions as: 'Have you seen my uncle's Porsche?' (very useful in Malta), and so on. I once saw a Russian-English phrase book, published in America, which included the entries: 'Maria Alexandrovna, don't you think that this gentleman is more kind than that one and that he will give us more alms?' and: 'It was so cold in the street that an invalid had his crutch frozen.'

The phrase book in question was *The Traveller's Companion* by a certain Madame de Gentils, published in London in 1817. It was full of practical advice and left no stone unturned.

One of the book's sections was called 'In Prison'. (Let's face it: even now the unwary traveller may occasionally end up behind bars which, as we already know, is not a big tragedy, provided it is Liechtenstein's only prison, where they give you gourmet food, or Andorra's only prison, where they let you out for a cup of coffee.) It contained relevant expressions in six European languages:

'You give me seldom clean sheets'

'The mice prevent me from sleeping – pray let me have a mousetrap'

'This trap is good for nothing'

'This room is full of fleas and bugs'

And to crown it all:

'Pray give me some flowers, they will cheer up my life in the cell'

And although the modern traveller doesn't, as a rule, have to endure this sort of hardship, the above-quoted phrases might still prove quite useful in some of the cheaper French or Italian hotels.

The average modern traveller's interests lie beyond both Porches and prisons.

Love Talk in Five Languages: The Essential Phrase Book for the Romantic Traveller, compiled by Jay de Leon and published in London in 1993, makes an attempt to fill the gap by providing today's peripatetic bimbo and gigolo with a blueprint for a quick and painless love affair in English, French, German, Spanish and Italian. It has six sections: 1. the chat-up; 2. the refusal; 3. accepting and dating; 4. romantic talk; 5. intimate talk; and 6. parting (of course).

An average modern European love affair, according to Jay de Leon, can be reduced to ninety-four numbered set phrases such as:

Hello (*Bonjour, Hallo, Hola, Ciao*)

I like your a) smile b) eyes c) hair d) body

Would you like to come to my a) hotel b) apartment?

No, I am a) homosexual b) lesbian c) not homosexual d) not lesbian e) HIV positive

Go away or I will call the police! Variants: a) Get Lost! b) Rape! c) Do you snore?

You are a fantastic kisser! Variants: a) I cannot control myself b) Have you got a condom? c) Please don't stop!

More! (*Encore!, Weiter!, Mas!, Ancora!*)

Will you write to me?

Goodbye, my darling (*Au revoir mon chéri/ma chérie; Auf Wiedersehen, mein Liebling; Adios, amor; Addoi, tesoro mio*)

I think it is very important for Euro-lovers to hang on to this phrase book, especially when saying 'More!'. It is essential to have it open on the relevant page, though: you can't be caught leafing through when you 'cannot control yourself', can you?

Nearly forgot; there was one short entry at the end of this useful phrase book that could easily go unnoticed – number seventy-four which reads simply: 'I love you (*Je t'aime; Ich liebe Dich; Te amo; Ti amo*)'.

Another innovative phrase book came out in London in 1993. This flimsy paperback, compiled by Kelvin Birdseye (probably a *nom de plume*), operates with one word only. But what a word! The book's title speaks for itself – *How to Say F*** Off in fifty languages*. Kelvin Birdseye thinks that the f-word is quite enought to get by in Australia, Bangladesh, Taiwan, Russia (he got it right in Russian, I can assure you!) and forty-five other countries of the globe. Let's take his idea a bit further. Let's try and visualise some likely verbal exchanges the moment you step onto a foreign soil armed with this capacious word.

Customs officer: Have you got anything to declare?

Traveller: F*** off!

Immigration officer: Can I have a look at your passport?

Traveller: F*** off!

And so on.

This peculiar phrase book can prove a great money-saver: after your very first contacts with the locals, you will either be sent back to where you came from or spend the rest of your trip in a public institution with barred windows and all expenses covered by the taxpayers of the country you wanted to visit.

I decided to contribute my mite to the ancient genre of phrase book writing (move over, Mr Berlitz) and came up with:

Ber-Blitz Phrase Book
for Travellers in Mini-States of Europe

Little is the Light

Passport control:

I am sorry, your seal is too big for my passport. Could you stamp my phrase book instead?

Customs:

I have nothing to declare, to say, or to do.

Directions:

How long does it take to walk to the nearest border?
When can I say hello to the President (the Prince, the King, the Captain Regent, the Sindic)?
Is this man sitting at the bar the Sindic?
Is this Sindic sitting at the bar a man?
How far is the nearest hotel (prison)?
How far is the nearest prison (hotel)?

Sightseeing:

Sorry, can you remind me again what this country is called?

Complaining:

What an outrage! I've been here for almost two days already, and the President (the Prince, the King, the Captain Regent, the Sindic) hasn't popped in to say hello yet!
What do you mean I can't play golf because the ball keeps flying across the state border and can be mistaken for a mortar shell by the neighbouring country?
Yourself a Sindic!

332

Making friends:

Nice to meet you, Mr – ! You are the last person in this country to whom I haven't been introduced yet.

No, I am not a cabinet minister, I am an armchair traveller.

No, I am not a cabinet minister: I have only been in this country for a couple of days.

I think I've seen your face before. Weren't you the person walking along the main street at ten a.m. on Sunday morning?

Relaxing and going out:

Where do you think I can have a nice afternoon sleep in this country?

It is only eleven a.m. Where on earth are you bound for at this ungodly hour?

Why don't we go out for a nap before going to bed this evening?

Why don't we go to bed before going out for a nap this evening?

Do they serve decent slumber in this hotel (prison)?

Do they serve decent slumber at this prison (hotel)?

Please, leave me alone: I am resting after my beauty sleep.

Please, leave me alone: I am sleeping after my beauty rest.

Moving around:

Be careful when crossing the road. Always wait for the green light to appear in an hour or so.

Never cross the road without a valid passport in your pocket: you might be crossing the state frontier.

Always give way to landing planes.

Shopping:

I don't have a duty to do any shopping in this country, because shopping here is duty-free.

Little is the Light

Leaving the country:

I have something to declare. I declare: 'Something!'